George Burns
Television Productions

George Burns Television Productions

The Series and Pilots, 1950–1981

RICHARD IRVIN

McFarland & Company, Inc., Publishers

Jefferson, North Carolina

Unless indicated otherwise, photographs are from the author's collection.

LIBRARY OF CONGRESS CATALOGUING-IN-PUBLICATION DATA

Irvin, Richard, 1948–
    George Burns television productions : the series and pilots,
1950–1981 / Richard Irvin.
        p.   cm.
    Includes bibliographical references and index.

    ISBN 978-0-7864-9486-6 (softcover : acid free paper) ∞
    ISBN 978-1-4766-1621-6 (ebook)

    1. Burns, George, 1896–1996.   2. Television producers and
directors—United States—Biography.   3. Motion picture producers
and directors—United States—Biography.   I. Title.
    PN1992.4.B895I88 2014
    791.4502'32092—dc23
    [B]   2014015907

BRITISH LIBRARY CATALOGUING DATA ARE AVAILABLE

Front cover image: George Burns circa 1950 (Photofest)

Printed in the United States of America

McFarland & Company, Inc., Publishers
  Box 611, Jefferson, North Carolina 28640
  www.mcfarlandpub.com

Contents

Acknowledgments

The author would like to thank the following for their assistance with this book: Ned Comstock with the Cinematic Arts Library at the University of Southern California for assisting with access to the Burns and Allen Collection; the staff at the Thousand Oaks Library for details on various scripts related to George Burns–produced pilots; the Wisconsin Historical Society for files from the William Spier and June Havoc papers (1931–1963); staff at the Dolph Briscoe Center for American History at the University of Texas at Austin and William Wellman, Jr. for information about the Filmways pilot *War Birds*; the staff at the Howard Gotlieb Archival Research Center at Boston University for access to the Max Shulman Collection; and Josie Walters-Johnson, Rosemary Hanes, Zoran Sinobad, and Dorinda Hartmann at the Library of Congress Motion Picture Reading Room. The author greatly appreciates the cooperation of Sherry Alberoni, Olive Sturgess Anderson, Ann B. Davis, Yvonne Lime Fedderson, Dean Jones, Denny Miller, Elliot Shoenman, and Diane Stilwell for their recollections on working with George Burns and the assistance of Rachel Wilson in reviewing scripts in the UCLA TV script collection and videos in the UCLA Film and Television Archives related to shows produced by Burns. Finally, I wish to thank my best friend Garry Settimi for helping me in the completion of this work.

Preface

I remember first seeing *The George Burns and Gracie Allen Show* as a youngster growing up in the 1950s. At the time, I preferred the physical comedy of *I Love Lucy* to the verbal comedy of Burns and Allen. Not until I began viewing reruns of *The Burns and Allen Show* on Antenna TV did I come to fully appreciate the type of comedy performed by the couple.

Always intrigued by the credits at the end of TV shows, I saw that *The Burns and Allen Show* was produced by McCadden Productions and learned that Burns himself headed McCadden, which, during the fifties, was one of the major TV production companies in Hollywood. In addition to his own series, Burns co-produced two other successful sitcoms in the 1950s, *The Bob Cummings Show* (aka *Love that Bob*) and *The People's Choice,* as well as the dramatic anthology *Panic!* Although the series he produced may not be considered groundbreaking by today's standards, his input in creating archetypical characters, his idea of using an established series to spin off potential new series, his use of cross-promotion, and his breaking the "fourth wall" and speaking directly to the audience are still being practiced today.

Less well known than the series Burns brought to the television screen are the many pilots and other TV projects that he attempted to develop. Other than the archives of the show business newspaper *Variety,* the only other primary source for information about these projects is found in the Burns and Allen Collection at the University of Southern California. Although the documentation in this collection is often not dated, the files do contain memoranda, proposals, and scripts concerning several of the television projects which McCadden Productions was unable, for various reasons, to make into a TV series.

After *The Burns and Allen Show* ended with Gracie Allen's retirement from show business, Burns continued his producing career on his own and in association with companies such as Filmways, Warner Brothers, and

1

United Artists. The series he helped to produce during this second phase of his career lasted for only a single season: *The George Burns Show, Flight, Wendy and Me, No Time for Sergeants,* and *Mona McCluskey.* One exception was *Mister Ed,* which began as a McCadden pilot, was later made into a series by Burns and Filmways, and enjoyed a six-year run in first-run syndication and then on CBS in the 1960s. Working with Filmways and other production companies, Burns continued to be involved with many TV pilots during the sixties and with a final project in 1981 when he was eighty-five years old.

After an overview of Burns' producing career, the next four chapters of this book profile the longest running sitcoms which he helped to produce. Chapter 6 describes all of the comedy pilots and other projects with which his first production company was involved, and Chapter 7 looks at the dramas he produced. Chapters 8 through 12 cover Burns' producing career after *The Burns and Allen Show* left the air.

1

George Burns, Executive Producer

In response to a publisher requesting that he write his autobiography, George Burns signed the letter, "Cordially, George Burns, singer, dancer, roller skater, straight man, actor, writer, director, producer—author."[1] To many generations, Burns was best known as "America's grandfather"—the silver-haired actor with a cigar and horn-rimmed glasses who played God in the movies and won an Oscar for his performance in *The Sunshine Boys*. To an older generation, with his ever-present cigar, he was known as the straight man for his ditzy wife Gracie Allen in radio and on television. Many saw Burns sing and dance on his TV specials in the seventies and eighties. He probably would like to be best remembered for his singing. Burns had the same love for singing that Jack Benny had for playing the violin.

Born Nathan Birnbaum on January 20, 1896, on New York City's Lower East Side to parents Louis Phillip and Hadassah Bluth, George was their ninth child. He had eight other siblings: Morris, Annie, Isadore, Esther, Sarah, Sadie, Mamie, and Goldie. After his birth, his mother had two more boys, Sammy and Willy, and one more girl, Theresa. His father died from influenza when Burns was seven years old. To help support the family, George left school before the fifth grade and took jobs selling newspapers and shining shoes. He had his first brush with show business when he became part of a singing group of young boys called the Pee Wee Quartet.

Functionally illiterate, Burns would later hire tutors to teach him how to read and write. Once he had become a producer, he remarked to *Look* magazine, "If I could only read and write, I'd be the biggest producer in this town."[2] After the Pee Wee Quartet, Burns became half of a dance act with Abie Kaplan. Although the last name Burns could be considered a shortened version of "Birnbaum," according to George, he and Abie Kaplan would steal pieces of coal from the Burns Brothers Coal Yard, putting them in their knickers to take home to heat the stoves in their mothers' apartments. The two thus became known as the "Burns Brothers." He adopted George as his first name because it was the nickname of his older brother Isadore, whom he admired.[3]

George Burns and Gracie Allen made their first appearance together as a vaudeville team in 1922. Four years later, on January 7, 1926, they married in Cleveland. At first, Gracie played the straight role and George had the funny lines. After a few months, with Gracie receiving most of the laughs, the roles reversed, and George became the straight man and Gracie, his dizzy partner.

Burns developed much of his comedy act with Gracie, first in vaudeville and then in short films. He really gained experience in writing, producing, and directing when he and Gracie made a series of two-reel shorts for Warner Brothers and Paramount in the 1930s. George put the films together by himself, without any writers. Once he could afford to hire writers for the team's radio and television shows, he always worked with them providing input on each script.[4]

In 1932 the team appeared on CBS Radio's Guy Lombardo program, and subsequently starred in their own thirty-minute radio program. Initially, *The Burns and Allen Show* had a vaudeville-style variety format but later, in the early 1940s, it developed into a situation comedy. On October 12, 1950, after eighteen years on radio, *The Burns and Allen Show* made the transition to television.

This book looks at a relatively neglected part of George's career—that of TV producer of comedies, dramas, and pilots, and profiles the various shows he helped to produce. Actually, Burns' behind-the-scenes career is better described as an "executive producer" in the sense that he both supervised the creative content of most of his shows as well as the financial aspects of production. With regard to the creative content of his comedy series and pilots, Burns was involved in developing the premise for many series and working with the writers on scripts as well as in casting and staging issues and in marketing his different series and pilots. Furthermore, as detailed in this work, Burns was not only a producer behind the scenes but also, both implicitly and explicitly, he played the role of producer in the different series in which he starred.

Veteran comedy writer Charles Isaacs said that Burns as editor of his TV scripts knew "the travail a writer suffers turning out material week after week" and understood "the comic's need for surrounding himself with cre-

4

ative men."[5] In working with a group of writers in the office on developing scripts, Burns commented,

> I knew exactly which way we were going and I steered the writers in that direction. They would write it here—three or four writers—at the type-writer. When writers take work home ... let's say you have a scene you want to write. They bring in the scene, and you've got four writers and you have to re-write the scene. Sometimes there is a little resentment because you are taking out a joke that is his favorite—that I don't think is in character or something. You've got discontent. When you sit down from scratch with four writers, nobody knows who said this or that. I found out that's the best way for me ... for what I'm doing.[6]

Sid Dorfman, one of the writers on *The Burns and Allen Show*, remarked, "George was there every morning when we started. He was there from the opening bell, and that's one reason it was so pleasant to work on the show, because by 3:00 he had had enough and we all went home."[7] The time with his writers was spent mostly arguing over improvements to the script for an episode of his comedy show with Gracie. After the writers ended their work, Burns would approve publicity releases, review other scripts, meet with executives of his production corporation, and go over budgets for the rest of the day.

Best known for producing situation comedies, Burns' sitcoms—both series and pilots—contained certain common traits. As he explained about the types of comedies he thought viewers would like, "Television was still so new that nobody really knew what kind of shows the audience would watch, but I figured that people would like the same things on television that they liked in vaudeville, so we did shows with pretty girls and animals."[8] This is something of an oversimplification of the kinds of comedies he produced. All of his comedy series and pilots were character-based vehicles with major characters who had their own unique perspective on life and the world. These character types, developed in the initial sitcoms he produced, would be repeated in virtually all of the other comedy projects with which he was involved.

The most famous character type with which Burns was associated was Gracie's "dumb Dora"—a quirky female with her own unique way of thinking. Gracie (the character) was not really dumb but rather childlike in her lack of understanding of figurative expressions, and she had a simple-minded approach to subjects like science and math. This character type is similar to the "dumb blonde" character that Marie Wilson played in the pilot Burns produced for her. The dumb Dora character also appeared in the Burns-produced *Wendy and Me* and the pilot *I Love Her Anyway*.

Somewhat related to the dumb Dora character but not as simple-minded is the "naïve newcomer" character as exemplified by Sock Miller in *The People's Choice*, Wilbur Post in *Mister Ed*, and Will Stockdale in *No Time for Sergeants*. These characters got into situations because of their naiveté about certain aspects of the world—Sock Miller by his inexperience with politics and assertive females, Wilbur Post by his newness to the world of talking animals, and Stockdale by his inexperience with military life.

Another character type in Burns' comedies was the "manipulative charmer," illustrated best by Bob Collins in *The Bob Cummings Show*. Cummings portrayed a handsome bachelor commercial photographer taking pictures of beautiful models by day and dating a different model each night. If a woman he was attracted to was not attracted to him, he would manipulate the situation to attempt to seduce the woman. He would do the same to discourage a female that wanted him if he was not attracted to her. Hermione Gingold's Theodora Ashley persuaded people to give her free stuff in the pilot Burns produced for her, and Mona McCluskey charmed her husband and others for what she perceived as their own good; they could also be categorized as manipulative charmers.

The final character type most associated with Burns' comedies is the wisecracker, one who makes snide comments about other characters and situations, as best exemplified by himself in *The Burns and Allen Show*, *The George Burns Show*, and *Wendy and Me*. This character trait was also found in the basset hound Cleo from *The People's Choice* and in the famous talking horse Mister Ed from the series of the same name. George seemed to love shows with animals taking on human qualities. While Cleo, the dog, only expressed her thoughts directly to the audience, Mister Ed actually did move his lips and speak directly to his owner Wilbur Post. Burns even extended this character type to talking aliens in a pilot he helped produce, *Moko and Tatti in Outer Space*.

In addition to the common character types found on his television shows, probably Burns' most famous innovation was that of "breaking the fourth wall" or having a character from a fictional work talk directly to the audience. Fictional characters who break the fourth wall exist in parallel worlds. On the one hand, they're characters in a story interacting with other fictional characters; on the other hand, they acknowledge that an audience is viewing the fictional work and address the audience either directly or indirectly about what is going on or what may happen. About "breaking the fourth wall," Burns wrote, "It was a very innovative concept. Nothing like that had ever been done on television before. Of course, television was so new that if an actor burped, everyone agreed it was an innovative concept and nothing like it had ever been done on television before."[9] This concept was used extensively on *The Burns and Allen Show* as well as on *The People's Choice, The George Burns Show,* and *Wendy and Me,* and to a limited extent on *The Bob Cummings Show* and *Mister Ed.*

The combination of the different character types and "breaking the fourth wall" led to a certain fanciful style of many of the sitcoms produced by Burns. In many respects he could be said to be the father of the "golden age of fantasy sitcoms" of the 1960s if this expression is not an oxymoron. *Mister Ed* was the first of many sixties fantasy comedies (*Bewitched, My Favorite Martian, I Dream of Jeannie,* etc.).

Another common characteristic of many of the series Burns produced was the use of his writers' names and the names of other production staff for characters as well as using the names of his different production companies. For example, Bob Cummings' friend on his self-titled show was named "Harvey Helm" after a writer on *The Burns and Allen Show;* Bob's nephew Chuck had a girlfriend named "Carol Henning" (Paul Henning, the producer-creator-writer of the Cummings series, had a daughter named

George Burns (right) and director Fred De Cordova review a *Burns and Allen* script. In addition to television shows, De Cordova directed movies starring Elvis Presley, Ronald Reagan, and Bob Hope.

Carol). In some episodes of *The Burns and Allen Show*, the names Al Simon, Herbert Browar, and Dick Fisher would pop up—all names of production staff members. Likewise, in *The George Burns Show*, an episode referred to a record company as "Laurmac," the real name of Burns' producing partnership with Bob Cummings. In *Wendy and Me*, a character was named William Norman Packard, the names of the writers on the series. The use of such names could be considered an inside joke by the writers, but apparently there was another motive for this. The writers liked to use "safe" names to prevent lawsuits by someone who might be offended if their own name was coincidentally used for a character.

As described in subsequent chapters, Burns had several writers for the series and pilots he produced. As director Fred De Cordova wrote, George "knows exactly how his written material should appear on the air and he has always had enormous faith in his head writer—George Burns."[10] His knowledge of what was funny stemmed primarily from all of his years of experience in vaudeville. Many episodes of the comedy series he became associated with, particularly *The Burns and Allen Show*, were like extended vaudeville routines.

The writer who stayed with George the longest was his youngest brother William, nicknamed "Willy."[11] As George said, "Willy wasn't the kind of writer who put a piece of paper in a typewriter and knocked out a scene, but he was great in a room where everybody would sit around and pitch funny lines."[12] In addition to being a writer and acting as script consultant on Burns' various projects, Willy also handled George's business affairs, checked contracts, and set up interviews for his older brother.

George was not the easiest producer for writers to work with. As Burns himself stated, whenever he would get mad at one of the writers, he would scream at Willy. Paul Henning, who wrote for Burns and Allen before creating *The Bob Cummings Show* and *The Beverly Hillbillies*, relayed the following story:

> I never will forget one of the first days I was in George's office, he was just furious about something—it didn't concern me—he was giving Willy hell. And Willy says, "Listen George, I don't have to take this. I can go back to Brooklyn and do what I was doing when you asked me to come out here." George says, "And what was that?" Willy says, "I was sitting on my ass and you were sending me $25 a week."[13]

Willy worked with his brother on virtually every series he produced right up until his (Willy's) death at age sixty-three in 1966. Reports at the time indicated that Willy died of pneumonia, but according to Lawrence J. Epstein in his book *George Burns: An American Life,* Willy drank too much at George's son Ronnie's wedding reception in early 1966. When Willy returned home, he took too many sleeping pills and passed away on January 20—George's 70th birthday.[14]

As a producer and also as head of his own production company, Burns was extremely cost-conscious. Sponsors would pay a specific license fee for each episode of a series (about $35,000 to $45,000 in the early days of television), and George made sure that production costs, including salaries for the cast and crew and for the sets and wardrobe, never exceeded the license fee. In order to keep costs low, big guest stars did not appear on his series. Director Ralph Levy recalls that Burns was persistent in calling him about budget matters once phoning him at lunch to ask why he was having a set built with three-inch nails when two-inch nails would suffice.[15]

One exception to George's cost-consciousness related to Gracie's wardrobe. During the run of *The Burns and Allen Show,* Gracie never wore the same outfit twice. She frequently wore as many as three different dresses in a single show, and considering that about forty shows were produced each season, one could see how the wardrobe costs would be substantial.[16]

In their book about *The Burns and Allen Show,* Cheryl Blythe and Susan Sackett point out that Burns "was instrumental in developing the concept of pre-production meetings. At these he and his staff would go over upcoming scripts and estimate the costs involved. He realized the sooner scripts were finished, the more time they would have for double-checking production expenses, building new sets, arranging for special wardrobe—whatever might be needed."[17]

George's friend Carol Channing summed up his producing talent: "He always told his writers exactly what subject matter to write about and gave them a taste of what made the idea funny.... He gave them the matrix of his plot, the set design to the set designer, the style of music to Morty Jacobs (his pianist), and so on. That was his talent—directing, writing, producing, and overseeing everything, including finances."[18]

McCadden Productions

Over the course of his producing career, Burns formed many companies—almost a new corporation for each pilot or series with which he was involved. However, the one name that is associated with most of his series is "McCadden." Willy Burns lived on McCadden Place in Hollywood. Burns thought that McCadden had a nice ring to it so he chose the name for his first production company, which was formed in 1952. The company's logo at the end of each episode was an animated "clapboard" opening and closing with "A McCadden Production" or "Filmed by McCadden" displayed on the board.

At the recommendation of MCA, his talent agency, McCadden Productions, jointly owned by George and Gracie with Willy Burns having a small share, was initially established to film *The Burns and Allen Show.* MCA had previously suggested a similar venture for Jack Benny, George's best friend, for production of his TV show. The first two seasons of *The Burns and Allen Show* had been produced live by CBS. Because of a trend in early television to switch from live production, which resulted in poor quality kinescopes (the videotape of the day), to better quality film which could be rerun, Burns formed the McCadden Corporation to produce the third and subsequent seasons of his series with Gracie.

To set up a multiple-camera system for *The Burns and Allen Show*, Burns hired Al Simon, who had been an associate producer for *I Love Lucy* and for the Joan Davis comedy *I Married Joan,* and Herb Browar, who had worked on both series with Simon. Simon and Browar first met when they enlisted in the Air Force, which may be one reason that that branch of the service was often mentioned on many of the series Burns produced. Simon, who eventually became vice-president of production, had developed the multi-camera filming technique used on *I Love Lucy* and later on *The Burns and Allen Show.*[19] Burns also hired Maurice Morton as vice-president of business affairs. Burns' production philosophy was, "I just get good people together and let them do the job."[20]

By 1953, McCadden Corporation was among the top ten production companies in Hollywood with $1.25 million ($10.6 million in today's dollars) in business. The company grossed $6.5 million by 1958 ($51 million in today's dollars).

Most of the series McCadden Productions made were done through partnership deals which, for Burns, helped spread the risk of new productions around. *The Bob Cummings Show* was a partnership among Burns, Cummings, and Paul Henning. *The People's Choice* was a partnership among Irving Brecher who created the series, Jackie Cooper who starred on it, and Burns. For the dramatic series *Panic!*, he partnered with Al Simon and NBC. Burns was not involved to the same extent in all the series he produced. For example, as described later in the book, he was more involved in the day-to-day production of his own series with Gracie and *The Bob Cummings Show* than he was in the dramatic series he helped to produce.

McCadden also used its facilities to film shows for other producers. The company filmed several episodes of *The Jack Benny Program* and the sitcoms *Life with Father* and *That's My Boy* for CBS as well as the pilot for the comedy *Professional Father*. McCadden's commercial division made TV spots for companies such as Carnation, B.F. Goodrich, Winston Cigarettes, Borden, Betty Crocker, Colgate-Palmolive, Dentyne, U.S. Steel, and Chevrolet. Carnation and B.F. Goodrich were the primary sponsors of *The George Burns and Gracie Allen Show*. McCadden, as well, made public service spots for Easter Seals, Multiple Sclerosis, and the Arthritis Foundation.

During the run of *The Burns and Allen Show*, Burns became interested in producing films. *Variety* reported in February 1954 that he and writer-director Eddie Buzzell were in negotiations to finance Buzzell's movie *Third Girl from the Right*. However, the following month, *Variety* indicated that negotiations had collapsed. The film about the head of a conglomerate falling for a nightclub entertainer who is not as refined as his upper-class friends was subsequently made by Buzzell at Universal. Called *Ain't Misbehavin','* it starred Rory Calhoun and Piper Laurie.

Later in 1954, Burns and his long-time friend Jack Benny explored financing a movie starring Jackie Gleason, *The Jack of Spades*. A comedy about spies with Burns and Benny owning one-third of the picture and Gleason and screenwriter Norman Krasna owning the remaining two-thirds, it was never made. Burns backed out of financing the movie apparently based on a phone call from Martin Leeds of Desilu to Maurice Morton. Leeds indicated that Desi Arnaz had considered producing the Gleason movie but gave up the project when a writer threatened suit, claiming he gave Krasna the idea for the film.

In 1955, Burns bought Rodney Rosen's screenplay *Native Lullaby* which was to be made in Jamaica with an all-native cast. This project, like many of Burns' television efforts, also never got off the ground.

This book focuses on the TV series and pilots George Burns produced during the 1950s and 1960s and not on his involvement with making TV commercials or feature films.

Filmways, Warner Brothers and United Artists

After the dissolution of McCadden Productions with Gracie Allen's retirement and the end of *The Burns and Allen Show,* Burns continued his producing career, often in association with established production companies. Most of the series he later produced echoed characteristics of his initial successes.

For Filmways, he participated in the production of *Mister Ed*, about a talking horse that seemed to imitate, in many aspects, the dog who thought out loud from *The People's Choice*. In his association with Warner Brothers, he produced *Wendy and Me* with the Wendy character playing a ditzy housewife like Gracie Allen. He also produced *No Time for Sergeants* where the lead character had a certain naiveté about the Air Force similar to Gracie's naiveté about the world in general. While at United Artists, George produced *Mona McCluskey*, about a movie star married to an Air Force sergeant and over-committed to her marriage—the exact opposite of the Bob Collins character on *The Bob Cummings Show*.

George Burns came full circle with his final production effort in 1981: *I Love Her Anyway*, a reboot of *The Burns and Allen Show*.

2

George and Gracie—
The Live TV Shows

Gracie Allen's character had what Burns called "illogical logic": She just interpreted things differently from everyone else. In his autobiography, George Burns illustrates how his routines with Gracie evolved.

During their vaudeville days, the team's jokes began as silly puns[1]:

GEORGE: I'm a pauper.
GRACIE: Congratulations. Boy or girl?

Their routines then evolved into "illogical logic":

GRACIE: My sister had a baby.
GEORGE: Boy or girl?
GRACIE: I don't know, and I can't wait to find out if I'm an aunt or uncle.

From there, the routines became true absurdist humor:

GRACIE: My brother has a suit like that. It's just the same.
GEORGE: Is that so?
GRACIE: Yes, only his hasn't any stripes. His is brown. It's more like a blue black, sort of yellow.
GEORGE: More like white.
GRACIE: That's it. A white suit, only yours is double-breasted and his is single-breasted and has no pockets, and a bow on the side.
GEORGE: A bow on the side?
GRACIE: My sister wore it to a dance last night.
GEORGE: Your sister wore your brother's suit to a dance?
GRACIE: I haven't got a brother.
GEORGE: You haven't got a brother but your sister has one?
GRACIE: It's a long story—pull up a chair. You see, when my sister and I were children, we were left orphans, and he was one of them.

Like their vaudeville act, George and Gracie's television series also evolved, starting with simple storylines in the first few seasons and advancing to more complicated plots in the latter seasons. Their characters also evolved with George's character changing more than Gracie's.

To decide on a format for the TV series, Burns had a luncheon meeting at a Hollywood restaurant with Bill Paley, the president of CBS; Harry Ackerman, vice-president of the network; and representatives from Burns' talent agency MCA. As Burns described the meeting:

> [I]t was Paley who gave us the hook that we decided to hang the show on. He said, "George, I understand you make a lot of speeches at stag dinners. Why couldn't you do a little monologue on the show?" I said, "I could. And what do you think of the idea of a domestic comedy, with us living in Beverly Hills, where we do, with a dividing line between the actors and the audience, so I can talk to the audience—sort of step over the line and let them in?"[2]

To flesh out the concept, George took his announcer Bill Goodwin and his writers (including his brother Willy) to Palm Springs for a week where it

Burns and his wife Gracie Allen were married for over thirty-eight years.

was decided that he and Gracie would play TV performers but the show would focus on their domestic life, not the TV show in which they appeared.[3]

On their television series, George and Gracie portrayed the same married characters they had played on radio. Gracie was the dumb Dora character, whose literal interpretation of the English language led to confusion and misunderstandings. For instance, George once told Gracie, who was planning to visit a neighbor who was in the hospital, to take her flowers. When Gracie returned from seeing the neighbor with a bunch of flowers, George asked her where she got them. Gracie responded that she did what George told her: When the neighbor wasn't looking, she took her flowers. This bit was used in their first TV show, and one hears the audience laughter build after Gracie's response as many in the audience had to think about the literal meaning of "take her flowers" for a moment before finding it funny.

Gracie's character also had unique understandings of the postal service, science, and math which demonstrated her own "illogic logic." For example, she would shorten the electric cords on all their lamps in order to save electricity. When told by her postman Mr. Beasley (Rolfe Sedan) that she needed another stamp on a letter because of its weight, she removed the letter from the envelope and just sent the empty envelope instead of adding postage. Mr. Vanderlip (Grandon Rhodes), the Burnses' banker, would always be stopping by to figure out Gracie's intent with checks she wrote. She would, for instance, tear a check into pieces in case the recipient needed change. Also illustrating her "illogic logic," Gracie devised her own unique solutions to preparing meals. She would freeze boiling water thinking that, when it thawed, the water would be hot again and so available at any time. When baking, she would bake a small cake and a large cake together so, when the small cake burned, she would know the large cake was done. While preparing peas and carrots for George, she would put toothpicks in each pea and carrot so George could easily pick out the peas he didn't like.

Gracie Allen played a character on radio and television who was extremely naïve about many aspects of life. Her unique world view would often lead to misunderstandings about situations. She would then attempt to come up with a not-too-well-thought-out plan to solve a problem that didn't really exist, with things usually working out in the end in spite of her. However, Gracie would always think she was successful at what she did. As she remarked in one episode, "A lot of people come to me with their problems and I know I must solve them because they never come back again."

In describing Gracie's character, George said, "She is completely earnest about what she is doing and saying, and I think it is the fact that she is so kind to the rest of the world for its lack of understanding of what is perfectly clear to her makes people love her. She is right and everybody else is wrong, but she doesn't blame them—she just gently tries to explain to them, patiently, and puts up with everybody."[4]

Being oblivious to her effect on people, Gracie would sometimes talk to George about her day and mention she was in line for something or with a group of people. When she would volunteer her own unique advice to each person, the person would respond by going to the back of the line or otherwise try to get away from her. Finally, Gracie was the only one left at the front of the line and wondered why everyone was behind her. When she went to find out what the people at the back of the line were talking about, they would say, "There's a crazy lady in line." Gracie was relieved when she heard this since she didn't want to run into that person.

Gracie's character was very methodical about some things. She labeled hats left by men who departed the Burnses' house quickly after becoming very confused speaking with her. She would take a card and write the name of the owner of the hat and place the hat on shelves in her living room closet so that she could eventually return it to the owner. Vanderlip, the Burnses' banker, once left with seven hats of his that Gracie had accumulated.

Gracie's relatives, although never seen, had thought patterns very similar to hers; apparently it was her upbringing in this fictional family that made her the way she was. Gracie's relatives were often the subject of comedy routines between her and George. She had an almost unlimited number of aunts and uncles engaged in various endeavors, like Uncle Otis, the explorer; Uncle Otto, the farmer; Aunt Bridget, the artist; Uncle Harvey, the repairman; and Uncle Waldo in the Foreign Legion.

George's character on the show, in addition to being a straight man to Gracie, was the narrator and monologist, speaking directly to the viewing audience about each week's story. He was the link between the "sensible" world and Gracie's world of nonsense. Only George, and sometimes Jack Benny, knew that he inhabited this world of talking directly to the audience separate from the ongoing storyline of an episode. Although always patient with Gracie, his remarks to the audience would often be sarcastic about other characters. In later episodes George would play the role of a mischievous producer by complicating the plot to extend the story and by deciding how and when a story should end. In several of the storylines, his character was one of naysayer, telling Gracie he didn't want to go somewhere or do something she wanted.

However, Burns' character was not immune to his own brand of nonsense. One of the running gags concerned George's singing talent or lack thereof. Everyone had really extreme reactions to his singing. On the one hand, Gracie loved it, calling him "sugar throat." She would compliment George by saying, "When you sing, it sounds like a songbird built a nest in your throat." On the other hand, others thought his singing was atro-

16

cious. Burns loved to sing obscure songs such as "Augusta J. McCann Is a Henpecked Married Man," "In the Heart of a Cherry" and "I'm Tying the Leaves So They Won't Fall Down, So Daddy Won't Go Away."

In the series, George and Gracie's best friends and neighbors were Blanche and Harry Morton. Blanche (Bea Benaderet) took for granted Gracie's way of thinking and usually entered her world of nonsense by supporting her in her escapades. Blanche's husband Harry, something of a sourpuss, disliked Blanche's cooking, didn't want to be around Gracie, and got into arguments with George. Harry was played by four different actors during

Gracie is labeling a hat left by someone who quickly departed the Burnses' residence after becoming very confused conversing with her.

the course of the series. First Hal March was the handsome Harry Morton who had been on the Burns and Allen radio show and who sold insurance. When he left the series, John Brown became the bespectacled Harry Morton. Brown was replaced by Fred Clark, the bald-headed Harry with a hearty appetite, who was in the real estate business. This all happened during the first two seasons of the sitcom. When Clark departed, Larry Keating became the erudite Harry Morton, a CPA and not a realtor like the previous Harry Morton.

Burns was very honest with the viewers about the changes in actors playing the Harry Morton role. In the middle of the eighth live show, George introduces John Brown as the new Harry Morton, telling the audience that Hal March had gone on to do his own show with his partner Bob Sweeney. He did the same when John Brown left the series and Fred Clark took over the role as well as when Clark left and Larry Keating became Harry Morton.

Bill Goodwin, the show's first announcer, mainly did commercials for Carnation evaporated milk (the show's sponsor) that were incorporated into each week's storyline. Goodwin, who started with George and Gracie on radio, left after the first season to star on his own daytime show on NBC, and Harry Von Zell replaced him. Von Zell became more active in each week's plot, often being talked into helping Gracie with one of her schemes and then being fired by George.

The Burns and Allen Show centered on the domestic life of a married show biz couple who were the stars of a television show viewers rarely saw. In addition to Gracie playing a ditzy wife and George her naysayer husband, the two also had a fictional comedy-variety show on which they played various characters. Viewers only got snippets of this other Burns and Allen TV show on which George and Gracie starred apart from the televised exploits of their married life. In the early seasons of *The Burns and Allen Show,* there were various references to this other show—for example, Gracie playing Cleopatra in one skit; George and Gracie playing Romeo and Juliet in another; and, in still another, reenacting the landing of the Pilgrims. However, as with their characters and the storylines on the series, references to this "other" show also evolved over the years.

And so, viewers of *The Burns and Allen Show* saw the fictional home life of a mostly sensible husband and a nonsensical wife who starred in a comedy-variety show and also saw one of the leads of the domestic comedy step out of his characterization from time to time to whimsically comment on the plot of each episode as well as do a comedy monologue. On top of this, several of the storylines were based on incidents that happened in George and Gracie's real life as a celebrity couple, such as being honored by the Friars Club, being interviewed by *TV Guide,* and, for George, dealing with production issues related to his series. As David Grote states in *The End of Comedy,*

> Probably the most complex and sophisticated of all the comedy series in the fifties was *The Burns and Allen Show.* Not only did George Burns and Gracie Allen use the curtains as [Jack] Benny did, with monologues and routines and direct audience address, but they also built a complex series of overlapping layers within each episode, which has rarely been matched even in the most complex feature films or avant-garde novels.[5]

Most *Burns and Allen* episodes focused on Gracie as either a solver of problems that existed only in her mind or a do-gooder who really, truly thought she was helping someone, leading to a series of misunderstandings, mistaken identities, and plans that went awry. The writers also liked to occasionally place Gracie in a situation most people would find perilous but not Gracie who never felt the situation was dangerous due to her naiveté. In addition, given her way of thinking, Gracie would take any advice from a fortune teller as gospel and act on it as if it were the truth.

Other episodes of the series centered on George, who would try to "teach Gracie a lesson" about misplacing things or overspending, often to his regret. Several situations grew out of the simple comings and goings of the Burnses. Many times, George would say no when Gracie wanted to attend an event that he didn't like such as a movie or party or when Gracie wanted to go on a trip somewhere, and then complications would ensue.

In addition to mixing the real with the unreal, George and his writers would mix the familiar with the unfamiliar. Many of the episodes during the series' first two seasons contained plots and situations that would be repeated during the shows other six seasons.

1950–51 TV Season: Bits and Pieces

First-season *Burns and Allen* episodes were directed by Ralph Levy and written by Paul Henning, Sid Dorfman, Harvey Helm, and Willy Burns. The comedy alternated on CBS with the anthology series *Starlight Theatre.*

Levy, who had directed the original pilot for *I Love Lucy,* produced and directed *The Burns and Allen Show* while simultaneously directing *The Jack Benny Program.* Henning had started working with George and Gracie in 1942 on their radio show. He usually came up with the central idea for each episode. Dorfman and Helm developed Gracie's unique way of interpreting language. Dorfman had also worked with Burns and Allen on their radio show. Helm, who wrote for George and Gracie for twenty years, initially sold jokes to Burns in vaudeville before writing for the radio and television shows. Thumbing through issues of *Popular Mechanics* and looking at different pictures sparked Helm's imagination for much of Gracie's dialogue. Seeing a picture of a glassblower, for example, he wrote the following for Gracie: "My brother Willy got into trouble on account of his new job. He's a glassblower, and yesterday he got the hiccups and blew himself into a bottle."[6]

For the first two seasons, the show was produced by CBS and performed live every other week from the Mansfield Theater in New York City and then from the CBS studios in Los Angeles. Burns began producing the series on film beginning with its third season. The live episodes done on kinescope have never been syndicated. As George once remarked, "The shows were loosely structured. We usually had more plot than a variety show but less than a wrestling match. The real importance of our plots was that it was cheaper to have them than to hire a guest star."[7]

During its initial season, *The Burns and Allen Show* relied mostly on routines from their vaudeville and radio days. Early episodes seemed like two one-act plays with a musical number or dance routine between them.

The first live show aired on October 12, 1950. The set looked like that of a stage play with the Burnses' living room open to the audience. While George could step over the couple layers of fake bricks separating the living room from the rest of the stage (separating the fictional world from the real world), all of the other actors had to use the living room's front door to enter or exit a scene. Burns would do his monologues standing by the right proscenium arch. Although Gracie would never speak directly to the audience, she did nod to the audience, acknowledging their applause when she first entered a scene. In the premiere episode, speaking to the audience, George defines what being a straight man is, describing how he has refined the art of pausing after his partner says a funny line and how he repeats everything his partner says. Gracie appears through a window in the front of the set and uses George's electric razor to trim shrubs in a window box. George then introduces the Mortons and Bill Goodwin.

In the first act, a book salesman (Henry Jones) comes by the house to try to sell Gracie a set of encyclopedias but has no luck. George then joins the singing group The Skylarks for the song "April Showers." The main sketch is about Gracie and Blanche wanting to see a Gregory Peck film, while George and Harry Morton want to go to the fights. Bill Goodwin stops by and does a Carnation evaporated milk commercial in the middle of the sketch. When the Mortons come over to go to the movies, George tells Blanche and Gracie that they have all been invited to Goodwin's place to play a card game called Kleebob. Since this is a made-up game, George thinks that the women won't understand it and will decide to go to the movies themselves, leaving Harry and him to attend the fights. But Gracie and Blanche want to learn Kleebob, and so George proceeds to make up rules that he thinks will drive them crazy. He and Harry play the game with nonsense rules with Blanche keeping score and Gracie observing. However, Gracie catches on to the game and advises George on how to play it. She says the game is just like Mogul, a card game George taught her last week when he wanted to go to a baseball game. In the end, they all go to the movies.

The fifth episode of the first season included several routines that are Burns and Allen classics. Banker Vanderlip stops by to go over Gracie's checking account. Gracie is using checks to send recipes and song lyrics to others, and he wants her to close the account. George brings Gracie flowers to put her in a good mood before telling her that he has to close her checking account. This leads to "the flower vase routine" where Gracie takes bouquets out of one vase to put them in another and another and so on until she ends up back where she began and has George discard the new flowers he brought her.

After the first six episodes done live from New York, the show moved to Hollywood where it remained for the rest of its run. The eighth live show centered on Gracie having circled a date on the calendar but not remembering why. She throws a party to celebrate the date, but none of the guests knows the reason for the celebration until Jack Benny arrives. The date on the calendar was circled to remind the Burnses that Jack was having a party on that date. In the eighth live show, John Brown took over the role of Harry Morton from Hal March. Brown would play that role for ten episodes.

Episode twelve of the first season included another classic routine. Hadley, the tax man, is spending a frustrating day questioning Gracie about her tax deductions. During the episode, George explains to Gracie California's community property law. When Gracie asks George why she receives only one-fourth of what they earn, George pulls out four cigars and says that under community property, Gracie earns half of what he makes, and he gives her two cigars. He then says that he earns half of what she makes and takes back one of the cigars, leaving her with only one cigar (one-fourth of what he started with).

Actor Fred Clark became the new Harry Morton in the series' eighteenth episode that aired on May 24, 1951. John Brown's name had been published in *Red Channels,* an anti–Communist publication, as a Communist sympathizer apparently because of his work in establishing the American Federation of Television and Radio Artists. In the fifties, almost anyone associated with union organizing was deemed a Communist. Brown was blacklisted. He died of a heart attack at age fifty-three in 1957.

Some first-season episodes dealt with situations that would be repeated in later seasons. For example, in the ninth episode, George and Harry Morton want to go duck hunting, while Gracie and Blanche want to take a trip to Palm Springs. Many times, the writers would mine comedy from the Burnses' and Mortons' comings and goings with the men wanting to do one thing and the women another, which would lead to a series of misunderstandings.

Putting Gracie in potentially perilous situations where her naiveté kept her from being fearful was another type of situation the writers would use in future episodes. In episode fourteen, Gracie witnesses an auto accident involving gangster Johnny Velvet. Velvet and his attorney threaten Gracie to persuade her to testify in Velvet's favor, but she doesn't understand the threats and testifies truthfully with Velvet being sentenced to spend one day with Gracie.

The last live episode of the first season concerned Gracie doing an extremely good deed for a woman she hardly knew, in return for a small favor the woman did for Gracie. In the episode, Gracie holds a wedding for Mrs. Nelson's daughter Carol. Midway through the episode, George stops the show to say that their announcer Bill Goodwin went to New York to host a show of his own and that Harry Von Zell is Goodwin's replacement. After spending thousands of dollars for the wedding, George finds out that the favor Mrs. Nelson did for Gracie was to push Gracie's car when it stalled. This same script was later remade as a fall 1954 episode with the only change being that George and Gracie's son Ronnie played the groom on that episode.

1951–52 TV Season: Worth Redoing

Like the final shows of the first season, the scripts for the second season of live shows were more complex. Writing new episodes based on a stock situation was done a lot by the Burnses' writers. But George, in mixing the familiar with the unfamiliar, went one step further and adapted scripts from previous episodes and filmed them again for later seasons. Many of the scripts were recycled from the second season of live shows which Burns probably assumed would never be seen again, but the reuse of scripts was no doubt also due to George's famous frugality and the difficulty of coming up with thirty-nine or forty new scripts a season. The re-use of scripts and plots from earlier seasons was a counterpoint to the evolving nature of the cast, characters, and technology used to produce the series.

Throughout the second season, the series alternated with *The Garry Moore Show* every other week during the fall and with *Star of the Family* during the spring. It was on opposite *Stop the Music* on ABC and *You Bet Your Life* on NBC.

The script for the first live episode of the season involved one of the favorite ideas of the writers—having a psychiatrist examine Gracie. In the episode, Blanche is having bad dreams but is afraid to see a psychiatrist, and so do-gooder Gracie takes Blanche's appointment, leaving the doctor under the impression that Gracie is Blanche. Harry Morton hears that "Blanche" has seen a shrink and, thinking that she must be crazy, he starts treating her better. Gracie then attempts to convince George that she is crazy so he will be extra nice to her, but she ends up acting normal. The same script was used for a March 8, 1954, episode about Gracie going to a psychiatric appointment for Blanche, who was having bad dreams about being on a sinking ship and Harry not saving her from drowning. In that episode, Sandra Burns, George and Gracie's adopted daughter, played the psychiatrist's receptionist. Sandra would appear periodically in small roles on her parents' series usually as a secretary, a telephone operator, or a waitress.

While the examples above are episodes that were essentially remade in later seasons using the same script, some shows during the second season had basic situations that would be reused in later episodes. For example, in a March 1952 show, Gracie loses her engagement ring. George finds it but doesn't tell her in order to teach Gracie a lesson. This situation became the basis of an October 1953 installment when George thinks Gracie is careless for leaving her watch on the kitchen sink while doing dishes. He hides the watch to teach Gracie not to be careless.

Another plot that was later reworked dealt with George's eyesight. In an August 28, 1952, episode, Gracie takes it literally when George says he ran into George Jessel at the Friars Club—an example of her literal-mindedness creating a problem that didn't really exist. She asks a doctor to come to the house to examine George, but the doctor has worse eyesight than George has. This same idea was the storyline of the premiere episode for the 1953 season described in the next chapter, about an iron deer that Harry Morton purchases for his yard.

As noted before, George very rarely had guest stars on the show. However, one celebrity that did appear from time to time was Jack Benny, reflecting their real-life friendship. In a classic episode, George and Gracie are on a train returning from San Francisco where they had appeared at a benefit with Jack Benny, who stole George's opening joke. When Jack, who is also on the train, comes to their compartment, George won't speak to him and leaves. During the episode, while George speaks to the audience on the right side of the proscenium, Jack, holding a cigar, speaks to the audience on the left side and both use their monologues to insult each other with George ridiculing Jack's violin-playing and Jack insulting George's singing. Once home in Los Angeles, Mr. Ackerman from CBS (a reference to Harry Ackerman, the network vice-president) stops by to talk with George about the quarrel with Jack. Ackerman wants George to apologize to Jack. Off camera, Gracie says she talked with Jack's wife Mary Livingstone, who wants her husband to be nice to George. When Jack comes by, he hugs George and apologizes. To show that they are still friends, Jack says that George can ask him for anything. George asks for $100, but Jack gives him $500 which George returns. During the 1952–53 season, Benny again guest starred and once again talked directly to the audience. He was the only one other than George himself to do this on *The Burns and Allen Show*. Also, during this second season episode, the Burnses receive a script to review for their "other" comedy-variety show where Gracie will be playing Cleopatra in a skit.

For its second season, *The Burns and Allen Show* was nominated for its first Emmy as Best Comedy Series but it lost to *Red Skelton*.

3

George and Gracie— The Filmed Shows

Beginning with the third season, *The Burns and Allen Show* was filmed instead of being done live and became a weekly broadcast. The filmed shows were produced at General Service Studios on Las Palmas Avenue in Hollywood. Other sitcoms (*I Love Lucy* for its first two seasons, *I Married Joan,* and *The Adventures of Ozzie and Harriet*) were also filmed there, as were two other series George Burns produced, *The Bob Cummings Show* and *The People's Choice.*

In describing Burns' involvement with the filmed shows, director Fred De Cordova stated:

> George was tremendously involved in every bit of the show, from the writing to the performing to the very careful manner in which Gracie's portion of the show was organized. And even though I was at that time an experienced director, George was meticulous in mapping out a day or two in advance how the show was to be shot.
>
> I would meet with him on Sundays at their home, and we would really plot—as a production supervisor would now—exactly how we were going to shoot the show.[1]

(De Cordova came onto the *Burns and Allen* scene during the 1953–54 season.) Each filmed episode was shot in a single day. As Burns described in his autobiography,

> The method by which we get the show on film in one day is by rehearsing in continuity on Tuesday, line by line just as it is in the script, so everybody knows exits and entrances and attitudes, then Wednesday we shoot, not in continuity, but according to the way our sets are lined up, which is like an assembly line. The sets are always lit, so all we have to do is move in a few key lights, turn on the switch, and the actors are cooking.[2]

The live *Burns and Allen* shows were performed in front of a studio audience; when the sitcom went to film, every other Thursday, Burns would screen two new episodes in front of an invited audience and record their laughter. According to George, "We only sweetened the laughter when a joke went flat and there was no way of eliminating it from the film."[3] Two cameras were used to film the show. As Burns explained the technique,

> Say Gracie is telling me a joke. I react to that joke; she takes a vase of flowers and walks out of the frame, or the range of the first camera. The first camera stays on my reaction; the second follows her to a table where she places the vase. When we show the film [to the invited audience], it is only from the first camera, which is my reaction to Gracie's joke. If we have bad luck and the joke doesn't get a laugh, we use the film from the second camera—Gracie with the vase of flowers—to fill in where the laugh should be, so we don't have to use a phony [laugh] unless it's absolutely necessary.[4]

Burns also remarked, "If there is one thing I do have talent for, it is knowing where the laughs will come, so our timing when shooting the picture is geared to wait for them."[5] Actor Robert Easton, who appeared on *The Burns and Allen Show* as well as *The Bob Cummings Show*, described how Burns had a knack for timing the laughter: "George would say to me, 'Bob, when Gracie says that line, I want you to count one-two-three; I want you to look at me and count one-two; then look back at Gracie and count one-two-three-four; *then* you say your line.' If you did exactly as he told you, he was right every time."[6]

Burns would give his film editors notes on each episode, once after it was previewed before a live audience and again after the episode had aired.[7]

For his monologues and other asides to the viewers at the beginning of the series' third season, Burns continued to use the right proscenium arch on the stage. A curtain was still raised at the opening of an episode showing the cutout of the Burns living room, kitchen, or backyard as if the show was being done live before an audience. However, for Gracie, filming meant that she no longer had to memorize lengthy "illogical" dialogue but could now rely on reading cue cards that contained some of her more difficult lines.

1952–53 TV Season: The "Other" Burns and Allen Show

Head writer Paul Henning left the series when he received an offer to produce *The Dennis Day Show,* a situation comedy starring the singer from

The Jack Benny Program. Nate Monaster and Jesse Goldstein were brought in to work with Dorfman, Helm, and Willy Burns on the *Burns and Allen* scripts, and Helm became the head writer. Monaster and Goldstein wrote for only one season. Monaster had previously worked on the radio version of *Burns and Allen* as well as on *Duffy's Tavern.* After leaving *The Burns and Allen Show,* he did scripts for *Bachelor Father* and *The Donna Reed Show* as well as screenplays for movies such as *That Touch of Mink* and *Call Me Bwana.* Goldstein had been a writer for Eddie Cantor and was one of the creators of the sitcom *I Married Joan.* He later worked for several years on *The Red Skelton Show* before dying of cancer when he was only forty-three.

Most of the storylines during the season continued to deal with Gracie literally interpreting what someone told her or misunderstanding what she saw or heard and so identifying a problem that really didn't exist. Other episodes dealt with behind-the-scenes issues involving George and Gracie's "other" TV show—the one that viewers rarely saw.

In the season premiere, Jane (Elvia Allman), Gracie's wardrobe mistress for their rarely seen "other" show, wins a trip to Hawaii for two. In the opening scene, George asks Gracie if she has looked at her script for the "other" show, and Gracie says that all George worries about is the TV show, illustrating that George's real role as producer is beginning to be worked more into the storylines. Not realizing that Jane is married, Gracie attempts to find a husband for her so she is not alone on the Hawaii trip. George confides to the audience that he is not going to tell his wife that Jane is married since he thinks the situation will make a good storyline for their fictional TV show, and he takes notes on what is happening. After unsuccessfully trying to convince Von Zell to marry Jane, Gracie contacts Mr. Rockford (Hal March, the original Harry Morton), a marriage broker, to find Jane a husband. When Jane's husband Frank (James Flavin) stops by to pick up his wife, Gracie thinks that he was sent by the matrimonial bureau and that they will make the perfect couple.

In the third episode of the season, Hal March returned, this time playing Dick Fisher (the name of the real-life production manager for McCadden Productions). Fisher delivers a script to Burns for the comedy-variety show that requires George to rehearse sneezing. In the script, George and Gracie are to go on a picnic where George catches a cold. When he gives George the script, George remarks that he hopes that Fisher kept the production costs down for this future episode, reflecting Burns' actual concern over expenses. Hearing George sneeze, Gracie assumes that he needs a doctor. But not wanting George to know about the doctor, she has herself examined and does her best to imitate George's symptoms. The doctor suggests she see a psychiatrist, which she takes to mean that George should see a psychiatrist since Gracie was trying to mimic George's symptoms. After George explains to Gracie that the script was the reason he was sneezing, she burns all the copies.

Generally, George's role in speaking directly to the audience, in addition to delivering his comedy monologues, was to remind viewers that the situation they were seeing was only a play—a fiction. However, in one episode about Von Zell mistakenly dating a married woman and Gracie and Blanche wrongly thinking that their husbands were also carrying on with the woman, George announces to the audience that if they saw this happening on TV, they would never believe it but "here it is happening in real life." Burns and his writers loved to have him tease the audience with statements like this and with novel endings (as described later).

In another episode that not only briefly mentioned Burns and Allen's "other" television show but also was a classic example of a comedy of errors, Gracie's Aunt Clara's first husband Frank Clyde wants to stay with the Burnses. Clyde performs an act where he tears papers into different shapes. He wants to get back into show business and appear on the "other" Burns and Allen comedy show. Neither George nor Gracie have never met Clyde, and George objects to Clyde staying at their house. Blanche suggests to Gracie that she pretend to rent her spare room to someone other than Clyde, but really rent it to Clyde. Harry Morton informs George of the scheme and says he will send a friend, Tom Fitzpatrick (Charles Lane), to rent the room first. When Fitzpatrick arrives with his suitcase, Gracie assumes he is her Uncle Frank Clyde. George finds Fitzpatrick's suitcase full of newspapers and also assumes that Fitzpatrick is Uncle Clyde. He kicks Fitzpatrick out of the room and, when the real Uncle Clyde (Howard McNear) stops by, George gives him the room. Both George and Gracie realize the man is Gracie's uncle when he demonstrates his paper-tearing act.

When this episode was rerun, Sandra and Ronnie Burns, George and Gracie's daughter and son, made their first appearance setting up a motion picture projector to view one of the Burns and Allen episodes. Knowing that his filmed shows would be rerun, George thought that if he made new introductions and called the shows "encores," people would be more likely to watch them.

Viewers actually got a look at George and Gracie's fictional comedy-variety show during a February 1953 episode about Gracie deciding to hold a "swamp party" to help Harry Morton sell a piece of swamp land. At the end of this episode, Blanche and Harry are sick in bed with colds. George and Gracie decide to take them some food from the party. They turn on the television in the Mortons' bedroom, and there are George and Gracie doing a dance number on their "other" show.

In a March 26, 1953, episode, viewers got another rare look behind the scenes of George and Gracie's fictional show. As the episode opens, Gracie is in her dressing room getting ready to play Juliet in a *Romeo and Juliet* skit with George. George comes in dressed in tights and says that his

George and Gracie and actress Isabel Jewell are in costume preparing for a *Romeo and Juliet* sketch on the "other" *Burns and Allen Show.*

makeup man whistled in his dressing room. George thinks this will bring him three days of bad luck. After the *Romeo and Juliet* skit, as if to prove that the superstition is true, Gracie says that George fell off the ladder while doing the *Romeo and Juliet* balcony scene. George plans to go to Palm Springs to meet with his writers, but Gracie doesn't want him to travel so nothing else bad will happen to him. She has Von Zell take George's car which George then thinks was stolen. When Harry volunteers to take George to Palm Springs, Blanche gives Gracie her husband's keys for Von Zell to put the Mortons' car in his garage beside George's car. After George rents a car to go to Palm Springs, Gracie tells Detective Sawyer that George stole his own car to collect the insurance so George will have to spend three days in jail.

Beginning with episodes aired in spring 1953, George began doing his monologues and observations from the different sets used on the show and no longer from the proscenium arch. Also, the raising of the curtain at the beginning of each episode was eliminated.

As in season two, many of the scripts for episodes aired in the spring and summer of 1953 were used again in other seasons. In addition to being a problem-solver, Gracie's character was also a do-gooder. Even when Gracie didn't misinterpret a situation and simply wanted to perform a good deed for someone, her plans were not the most logical. The March 30, 1953, episode is a good illustration of this. Ronnie Gilbert, a college student who did yard work for the Burnses, told his girlfriend Sandy that he lived in the Burns house in order to impress her; Gracie agreed to pretend to be his mother so he could invite Sandy over for tea. Gracie wants George to pretend to be Ronnie's dad, but he refuses. Blanche subsequently asks Harry to be the father. However, Von Zell stops by while Sandy and her parents are there, and Gracie introduces him as Ronnie's dad. When Ronnie and Sandy are out by the pool, George walks by and Ronnie thinks that he is pretending to be the father. Needless to say, confusion ensues when George, Von Zell, and Harry Morton are all introduced as Ronnie's father. This same storyline was used in a January 1958 episode during the series' final season. Note that the two young people in this episode had the same first names as George and Gracie's real-life adopted children, Ronnie and Sandra.

In another episode whose script was later recycled, Harry Morton, who always comes home for lunch, misses his noontime repast. Blanche mentions to Gracie that Harry "must be kidnapped or something." Gracie takes this literally and goes to the Missing Persons Bureau to see if they can help find Harry. When the bureau calls Blanche about Harry being missing, she panics and thinks that he really is kidnapped. She goes to his office to find him playing cards with his real estate partner Casey. Harry takes Blanche to lunch at the Brown Derby. Meanwhile, Gracie learns from Von Zell where Harry has his life insurance and wants to collect it on behalf of Blanche. When the insurance agent stops by, Gracie pretends she is Blanche. Later, the insurance agent phones Gracie thinking she is Blanche and informs her that their investigator saw Harry at the Brown Derby with another woman. To spare Blanche's feelings, when Gracie sees Blanche and Harry at home, she says that she was the one with Harry at the Brown Derby. With some slight variations, this script was used again for a March 1, 1954, episode about Harry Morton gone missing.

As mentioned before, Burns' writers loved to develop complications for the couple out of the simple act of going out at night or coming home. In one episode, Gracie and George get locked out of their house after a late night out. A locksmith arrives to open the door; even though he charges $2 an hour and was there for only three hours, Gracie misinterprets when he says he has been on the job for ten years. Thinking she owes him millions of dollars for a decade's worth of work, she makes a check out for $300 because that is all she has in her checking account. Later, Gracie leaves her empty house and locks the door behind her without having her key and with the locksmith's tools inside. This basic situation was repeated in "Locked Out," a June 2, 1958, episode.

There was also the time when Gracie got her shoe caught in a hole in the carpet at a department store, causing her to fall and ruin a pair of nylons. The store wants to assess their liability and suggests $25 to Gracie to settle any possible claim. Gracie misunderstands and thinks that the store wants $25 from her, and so she asks Blanche to loan her the money. Representatives from the store visit Gracie, who responds by saying that she will have to wait for Blanche for the $25. Thinking that Blanche was Gracie's lawyer, the store offers $300 and then $500. When Gracie refuses, the store wants to send their doctor to examine her. After his evaluation, the doctor advises the store that he thinks Gracie fell on her head, and they should settle no matter *what* the cost. The department store informs Gracie that they want to increase the settlement to $10,000. Store representatives visit again, explain to George what has happened, and give him the check for $10,000 which he tears up when they say their doctor will make Gracie normal. This episode, airing on August 17, 1953, was recycled for an episode titled "A Hole in the Carpet" during the series' eighth season and was also used for an episode of the George Burns–produced *Wendy and Me*.

Sometimes, Gracie would be placed in a situation that would frighten most ordinary people, but her naiveté actually helped her. Gracie receives a summons to testify in court after witnessing Johnny Velvet (Sheldon Leonard, who later became producer of *The Danny Thomas Show, The Andy Griffith Show,* and *The Dick Van Dyke Show*) this time hold up a bank. To keep her from testifying, Gracie is kidnapped by Velvet and his cohort Lefty. Velvet talks with Gracie for awhile, finds she makes him crazy and releases her. He decides to kidnap George to keep Gracie from testifying, which leads to an escalating series of mistaken identities. Velvet sends Lefty to the Burns house to kidnap Burns, but every time Gracie says she will get George, someone else comes into the room and Lefty thinks that person is George. Lefty ends up kidnapping Von Zell, a detective, and Ronald Reagan thinking each is Burns. (Reagan made a cameo appearance in this episode at a time when George was to sing at a Friars Club benefit in his honor.) Velvet finally goes himself to kidnap George, only to be mistaken for Burns by a mobster brought in from San Francisco to accomplish the task.

Rarely, but it did happen, George and not Gracie was the one who jumped to conclusions, such as when the Mortons and Burnses come home late one night. While George and Gracie are in their kitchen, Harry goes out to turn off the lights in his car. George, looking out the window, thinks Harry is a prowler. When Burns goes to investigate, Blanche dimly sees him and assumes that *he* is a prowler. Summoned by Gracie, Detective Sawyer arrives and searches the yard; Blanche thinks *he* is a burglar. Burns goes out to investigate one more time, and Harry shoots the frying pan with which George intends to bean the burglar. By morning, both the Mortons and Burnses realize what happened.

In June 1953, Ralph Levy announced he was leaving as producer and director of the series due to "nervousness and ill health."[8] The show was again nominated for an Emmy for Best Comedy but lost to *I Love Lucy*.

1953–54 TV Season: George's New Den

Beginning with this season, *The Burns and Allen Show* moved to Mondays at 8:00 p.m. opposite *Sky King* on ABC and *Name That Tune* on NBC. Fred De Cordova took over as director and Keith Fowler joined Sid Dorfman, Harvey Helm, and Willy Burns on the writing team. Fowler had worked with Paul Henning on the Burns and Allen radio show and had written for the radio series *Fibber McGee and Molly*.

In the first episode of the season, Harry Morton has purchased an iron deer statue for his front yard. Blanche dislikes it immensely. When Gracie informs George that Harry paid $200 for the iron deer, he responds, "I can't see it," referring to the amount paid, but Gracie thinks that George cannot see the statue and needs to have his eyes examined. Von Zell suggests to Gracie that she get accident insurance for her husband since his eyes are so bad. The insurance company sends a doctor to examine George's eyes, but the doctor is as blind as a bat just as the doctor had been in a similar August 1952 installment.

In this episode, Larry Keating took over the role of Harry Morton. When Blanche hears Harry's car drive up, she gets the catalogue from which Harry had ordered the deer statue to hit him over the head with it. As Blanche holds the catalogue over her head waiting for her husband to enter, Burns stops the scene and announces that Fred Clark, who had previously played Harry, went to New York City to appear in a Broadway show (*The Teahouse of the August Moon*). Then from stage right Larry Keating enters, and George introduces him to the audience as well as to Bea Benaderet, who breaks character to meet him. After Larry and Bea compliment each other on their work, George ends the conversation. Larry goes off to make another entrance as Harry Morton; Burns leaves the scene, and Blanche, resuming her position with the catalogue, hits Harry over the head. Blanche later mentions that Harry is a CPA (the former Harry was a realtor).

Apparently, the real reason Clark had left the series was because he wanted more money, and parsimonious George would not agree to Clark's salary demands. As Burns put it, "Fred Clark was getting $1,000 a week as Harry Morton, and after two seasons I offered him $1,200 a week but he wanted $1,500. Good God, I wasn't making $1,500 a week. So he quit, and we hired Larry Keating for the part."[9] In referring to his own salary in this quote, Burns did conveniently leave out the fact that his company produced the series from which he profited very nicely.

Also, in this season, George has a new den built over the garage where he conducts business such as reviewing scripts and meeting with his "production manager" Al Simon (played by Lyle Talbot). The real Al Simon's title on the series' credits was associate producer. Talbot was also featured on the Burns-produced series *The Bob Cummings Show* as Bob's friend Paul Fonda. The Al Simon character appeared in four episodes during the season and Burns' role as producer in real life became more a part of his character's identity on screen.

In the episodes, Al Simon would meet with George to go over production expenses. As in his real-life role as executive producer, Burns would question several of the items like the high price of raw film and paying $5 for a dozen of brown eggs since they film better than white eggs. Talbot's first appearance as Simon was in a February 1, 1954, episode where Simon is meeting with George in his den when a fire inspector comes by and tells Gracie to remove some trash near George's car. The inspector instructs Gracie "to get rid of it by 5:00 p.m. or face possible jail time." Of course, Gracie interprets this to mean that she has to get rid of George's car. "Problem-solver" Gracie contacts a used car dealer to look at the vehicle but, when she says she needs to sell the car or face possible incarceration, the dealer thinks the car was stolen and calls the police. A detective rounds up the Mortons, Von Zell, the dealer, and Al Simon for questioning. George has to explain that the car is not stolen, and the fire inspector comes back to cite the Burnses for not disposing of the trash.

In other episodes featuring the Simon character, Al volunteers to fix a traffic ticket for Gracie even though he has no idea how to do this, and George ends up in jail over Simon's attempt at ticket-fixing. An April episode dealt with Al adding his brother to the McCadden payroll with his brother breaking his leg in a skiing accident the next day. George then is bumped by a door opened by Simon and suffers a black eye. When an insurance investigator comes by, Gracie, not knowing about Al's brother, says that Al must have been injured in a fight with her husband, and the investigator concludes that George has committed insurance fraud. In the final episode with the Al Simon character, Al comes by to work with Burns, but George had previously told him that he was sick because he didn't want to work that night. George confesses that he really wanted to see a movie, and Simon and his wife, the Mortons and Von Zell all get caught up in deciding what film to see.

Burns and his writers liked to mix the familiar with the unfamiliar by repeating storylines and bits from his vaudeville act with Gracie. The best example of this occurred in a January 25 episode where George and Von Zell are discussing a book about vaudeville written by Joe Laurie. The episode begins with George discussing the classic Lamb Chops routine with Von Zell since it was mentioned in the book. Gracie says she doesn't remember the routine, which involved George asking her if she likes boys and she responding that she likes lamb chops. He asks if she could eat six lamb chops alone, and she says no but she should eat them with potatoes. Von Zell tells Gracie that a news article says that one in five men has a secret weakness. After determining that Harry Morton; the mailman, Mr. Beasley; Jane's husband Charlie, and Mr. Vanderlip have no such weakness, Gracie concludes that George must have a secret vice. When predictably George wants to go to the fights instead of to the movies with Gracie and Blanche, he says that the guys are going to stay home and play cards. Gracie believes that card-playing is his secret weakness. The women decide to play cards as well, which prompts George to make up the card game Kleebob which, as in the premiere episode of the series, Gracie figures out, and they all end up going to the movies.

George and his writers started having unusual endings for some episodes using TV technology more or less as a gimmick. In a January 1954 episode, George is reading a play that might be a vehicle for Gracie and him to perform in London. Since Harry is mad at Blanche because she did not fix him breakfast, she moves in with the Burnses. To get the Mortons back together, Von Zell suggests to Gracie that she make Harry jealous by having him think Blanche has a suitor. George informs Harry of the scheme. When Mr. Petrie (Reginald Denny) from London arrives to discuss the play with George, Harry thinks that he is there to romance Blanche. He scares him off with a pistol that is really a cigarette lighter. Harry apologizes to Petrie and, at the end, George says that he has four talented writers but sometimes they come up cold for an ending. Since they couldn't develop a finish for this episode, the screen slowly dissolves to black.

Similarly, in a late February episode, Vanderlip invites the Burnses and Mortons to the opera but, as usual, George doesn't want to go. Mrs. Quigley, a music critic, delivers the tickets to Gracie and attempts to explain the plot of the opera to her. George changes his mind about going once he puts on his formal attire. After the opera, the Vanderlips, the Mortons, and Mrs. Quigley come to the Burnses for a late night snack. Mrs. Quigley mentions the ending from the prior episode where the screen went black and asks George if the writers came up with that finish. This time George says the network devised that ending and then the TV screen goes black from right to left as this episode ends since, as Burns puts it, nothing can stop the sponsor from airing its message. At the very end, George tries to push back the black screen without success.

As noted previously, one of the series' running gags dealt with George's singing to which most characters, except for Gracie, had a strong negative reaction. In a classic February episode, Burns has been kept up all night by a howling dog. The next morning, Von Zell delivers fan letters from the studio, but none of the letters are for George. Gracie decides to do something to cheer him up. She has Blanche write a fan letter to him but sign it Violet McGonigle, a name Blanche randomly found in the phone book. When George receives the letter, he thinks Von Zell is responsible. He calls Violet and sings to her over the phone. Violet's husband overhears, gets jealous, and wants to threaten George with a gun. When McGonigle comes by, he doesn't recognize George and so asks Harry Morton, Von Zell, and George to sing. Before George can sing, McGonigle hears a dog howling. Thinking that is George singing, he leaves to find where the sound is coming from.

An April episode turned the nonsensical world of Gracie on its head. Usually, Gracie would misinterpret something, leading to some misunderstanding, but in this episode, the "truth" (so to speak) becomes stranger than fiction. One of the standard plots used in prior episodes involved Gracie discovering a dent in her car and trying to keep it a secret from George. In this episode, her car fender is smashed by a circus elephant, but everyone thinks it is just one of Gracie's farfetched stories. Blanche is finally convinced of the story when the garage mechanic confirms it. George refuses to believe it. A claims adjuster from the circus comes by to give Gracie a check for damages, but George tears it up thinking Gracie hired an actor to pose as the adjuster. George instructs Gracie not to tell her story about the elephant to their insurance adjuster, and so she describes to the adjuster an accident Von Zell had. When Gracie tells the real story, the adjuster cancels their insurance policy. Finally, George calls everyone together to learn the truth. They confirm Gracie's version of events which means that George owes Gracie a mink coat which he said he would buy her if she told the truth about the accident.

The final episode of the season also dealt with truth versus rumors. Burns attempts to teach Gracie a lesson about spreading rumors like one about his losing at gambling in Las Vegas. Gracie mentions the story to Blanche, and Blanche subsequently informs Clara Bagley that she thinks George won $1,000 gambling but wants to keep it a secret from Gracie. The story spreads to others, and the amount George supposedly won goes from $1,000 to $5,000 and finally to $70,000. Harry advises Gracie that George needs to show some losses to prevent income tax problems and gives her the idea that George should invest in bad stocks. Gracie contacts a stockbroker and informs him that she has to lose $70,000. However, when George comes in and says that everyone now knows that he didn't win or lose any money at gambling, the broker leaves.

Moving to Monday nights, the comedy ended up ranking 20th in the ratings. Nominated for an Emmy for Best Comedy, *The Burns and Allen Show* lost the award again to *I Love Lucy*. Bea Benaderet was nominated for Best Supporting Actress, but Vivian Vance from *I Love Lucy* won the award in this category.

1954–55 TV Season: Demonstrating Burns' Marketing Expertise

Writer Sid Dorfman left *The Burns and Allen Show* near the end of this TV season. He went on to co-create the short-lived sitcom *One Happy Family* in 1961 and later wrote for comedies such as *M*A*S*H* and *Good Times*.

Many episodes during this season showed George's talent for marketing not only *The Burns and Allen Show* but also other projects in which he was involved.

In the season premiere, Gracie is giving a TV party for their first episode. Blanche suggests that, to get an honest opinion of the show, Gracie should invite strangers to their house to view the episode. Meanwhile, Burns wants two TV editors, Jack Hellman from *Variety* and Leo Gill from *The Hollywood Reporter,* to come over to see the episode. Blanche mentions to Von Zell what Gracie is doing, and he tells Gracie "to get in touch with them and tell them not to come." Gracie interprets this to mean she should disinvite the newspapermen—not the strangers. When the two editors call George, he re-invites them and wants to contact the strangers so they don't come, but Gracie has no way to get in touch with them. Burns decides to have the TV editors view the program at the Mortons, but the Mortons invite the strangers to their house. Gracie subsequently asks the strangers to go over to her place where the newspapermen and George now are. Finally, Burns takes the TV editors to a bar to watch their show, that is, their "other" show where George and Gracie dance and perform skits. This was the only episode of the series filmed in color. As an experiment, CBS chose *The Burns and Allen Show* to be their first weekly filmed comedy to be telecast one time in color.

In a November episode showing Burns' talent at marketing projects, a newspaper announces that he is writing his autobiography for Simon and Schuster (which he was in real life). Gracie has an author's wife come by to teach her how a writer's spouse should act. The spouse instructs Gracie to match her husband's moods, and so Gracie imitates everything George does. When the publisher's representative drops by with the contract, he says that his firm will buy the book if it gets laughs. Gracie asks the Mortons and Von Zell to laugh when her husband reads the initial chapters to the representative. Thinking George is reading from his manuscript, the group starts laughing while he is reading aloud the contract.

More references to Burns' autobiography would be made in other episodes during this and the next TV season. For example, in a February 1955 episode, the publishers of George's autobiography need photos of his early years. George looks for the pictures in his old vaudeville trunks. However, he had also mentioned to Gracie that he misplaced $5, and she assumes that he is going through everything looking for a measly $5. Burns overhears Von Zell and the Mortons talking about his obsession in finding the $5. To get his mind off finding the money, Gracie goes to extremes again and says she is divorcing George. George has to explain to everyone that he was looking for his baby pictures, not the $5.

A December 1954 episode showed that Gracie's character was not always a ditz. The Burnses, the Mortons, and Von Zell are going to hear the Antonelli String Quartet. As usual, George doesn't want to go. He obtains a big jigsaw puzzle and thinks he can get everyone interested in putting it together so they won't want to go to the concert. He tries to entice Gracie and Von Zell with no luck. When everyone arrives at the Burnses to go to the concert, George still can't get anyone to help him put the puzzle together until Harry Morton discovers it and then everyone else starts working on it. George says that they can't leave for the concert until the puzzle is finished. Gracie helps them complete the puzzle in record time, and they all go to hear the string quartet.

Continuing with George's talent for marketing, Bob Cummings (the star of another Burns-produced series) appeared on a *Burns and Allen* episode on December 27, 1954. The Cummings show would premiere on NBC the following month (see Chapter 4). On the episode, George has a golf date with Bob. Before playing golf, Bob visits with Burns and Harry Von Zell in George's den and talks about his new comedy series that will be debuting Sunday night. He and George discuss appearing on each other's show, but Bob says he doesn't have time right now to appear on *Burns and Allen*. Was Bob referring to the rarely seen "other" Burns and Allen comedy-variety show, or was he making an ironic comment about his current appearance? During this season, there were fewer and fewer comments about the "other" show and more references to storylines about the actual show. Bob also mentions a play he will be doing concerning a doctor operating on an old man and telling the man that he is in love with his wife. Gracie overhears the last part and concludes that Bob is in love with her and wants to take her away from George. Jane, Gracie's wardrobe mistress, suggests that Gracie should disillusion Bob and pretend that she is after his money. When Cummings returns to pick up a script he left at the Burnses, Gracie says she is not the innocent angel he thinks she is and tries to smoke a cigarette but coughs every time she takes a puff. Bob explains to her that he was simply doing a scene from a play for her husband and Von Zell.

A new recurring character appeared in several episodes during the season: Roger, Blanche's deadbeat brother from Seattle. A manipulative charmer, he first shows up in a February 1955 episode. When Roger visits, Gracie and Blanche are impressed by his politeness and charm and want their husbands to be more like him. Neither Harry nor George like Roger's freeloading and the fact that he is not employed. Gracie thinks that she will get him a job at an aircraft factory that is hiring. But George and Harry don't want Roger to find out that Gracie got him a job, thinking that he will stay longer. They needn't have worried. When Roger hears about the job, he quickly departs for Seattle. Roger was played by King Donovan, who also had a recurring role on *The Bob Cummings Show* as Harvey Helm, Bob's much-married buddy from the Air Force.

In an April 1955 episode, the *Burns and Allen* writers pursued a common story thread of Gracie getting involved with the law. Gracie receives a ticket for parking in a restricted area but doesn't want to pay the fine. Von Zell says he knows a judge who will fix the ticket for her. After George sees the ticket, he gives Von Zell the money to pay it, but Von Zell tells Gracie that he took care of the ticket with the judge. In the meantime, Blanche insults George, thinking he won't pay the ticket but that her husband would if she were in the same situation. To get back at her, George calls Harry Morton and says that Blanche got a ticket. When Gracie hears that Blanche also received a ticket, she goes to the judge to get it fixed. The judge asks Gracie who told her that he fixes tickets, and Gracie names her husband, Von Zell, Blanche, and Harry. They all end up in the DA's office. After Gracie goes back to the judge's chambers to try to explain what happened, the judge lets them all go. This storyline was later revised for an episode of the Burns-produced sitcom *Wendy and Me*.

As indicated above, the writers during this season seemed to cease the fiction of George and Gracie appearing on a comedy series separate from the one TV viewers watched. In an April 1955 installment, George gives Gracie the idea of getting a wall safe so he doesn't have to go to the bank all the time. Gracie ends up putting the combination to the new safe in the vault itself along with some bonds George needs. Von Zell suggests that she get a safe-cracker to open the safe, and Gracie finds an elderly man named Frank in a pool hall who opens it. While showing George how she locked the combination in the safe originally, Gracie locks it in again. George says to the viewing audience that if there is anyone at the pool hall watching the show, tell Frank that "the little lady did it again"—another reference acknowledging that the real *Burns and Allen* show was the one being broadcast.

The May episode "The Uranium Caper" demonstrated how a proposed storyline for a future episode got confused by Gracie with what she thought was happening in her domestic life. Von Zell and Harry are prospecting for uranium. When Willy Burns phones George asking for help on a storyline for the TV show, George suggests doing an episode about him hiring a prospector who finds one of the biggest uranium mines on the West Coast. Gracie and Blanche overhear part of the story idea about discovering the largest uranium mine and that George doesn't want Gracie to know. Gracie thinks that George is keeping secrets from her even though he says he was just describing a storyline to his writers. Blanche mentions to her husband and Von Zell about the supposed discovery and suggests that they tell George they discovered uranium and volunteer part of their find, thinking that he will reciprocate. After they offer George part of their "good fortune," George refuses to do likewise. Meanwhile, Gracie obtains some samples of uranium from a mining engineer and leaves the samples at the Mortons. When Burns visits the Mortons, he finds the samples and thinks that Harry and Von Zell really did discover uranium and offers them a partnership in his fictitious mine, thinking they will reciprocate. In the end, George explains to Gracie, Von Zell, and the Mortons about the storyline for the TV show, and Gracie reveals that the rocks at the Mortons were her samples.

Not only did Burns use episodes during this season to market other projects, he also began taking a more active role in telling viewers the direction he wanted a storyline to take. In a June 1955 episode, Gracie is trying to help Jeanette Duval, whom she met at a party the night before, obtain a visa extension, but the immigration office will not permit it. Von Zell suggests that Jeanette marry an American citizen, and Gracie concludes that Von Zell wants to marry Jeanette. However, Von Zell informs Gracie that he is dating Alice and therefore can't marry Jeanette. He further states that Gracie should tell her to call the whole thing off. While Von Zell was referring to Jeanette in his statement, Gracie, as usual, thought he meant Alice. To Alice, Gracie says that Von Zell is calling off the relationship since he wants to marry Jeanette right away. Alice doesn't believe Gracie, but George confirms to Alice what Gracie told her because he wants to keep the storyline going. In the end, George invites everyone together to clarify what is going on and gets Alice's brother (Ronnie Burns) to marry Jeanette so she can stay in the country.

The Burns and Allen Show ranked 26th for the season. Coincidentally, or perhaps not, with fewer comments about George and Gracie's "other" show in each episode, near the completion of the 1954–55 season and continuing until the final episode in 1958, the couple began doing "Afterpieces" at the end of each show. Speaking directly to the audience, these four-minute routines by George and Gracie were based on the team's vaudeville act and usually dealt with a member of Gracie's family.

The series, along with Gracie and Bea, were all nominated for Emmys for the season but each lost to *Make Room for Daddy,* Loretta Young, and Audrey Meadows, respectively.

1955–56 TV Season: The *Lucy* Influence

In the biggest change for the series since it premiered, Burns decided to move the setting from Beverly Hills to New York City. He thought humor could be mined from having Gracie and him live in a hotel relying on bellhops, room service waiters, and elevator operators.[10] Interestingly, the cast of the other big CBS comedy on Monday nights, *I Love Lucy,* had gone to Hollywood during its 1954–55 season. George told *Variety,* "As long as Lucy comes to the Coast, we're going to New York."[11] *The Burns and Allen Show* was trying to imitate the success of *I Love Lucy* in changing the setting for the series as well as having Gracie become more "Lucy-like" in many of her exploits. And like *I Love Lucy,* Burns and Allen added a son to their cast. However, whereas Lucy Ricardo gave birth to a baby boy, in the Burnses' case, Ronnie Burns, their full-grown son, became a series regular. George decided to add Ronnie to *The Burns and Allen Show* when he saw the great effect that a teenage Ricky Nelson had on the ratings for *The Adventures of Ozzie and Harriet.* Singer Ricky Nelson attracted a younger audience for his mother and father's comedy, and so Burns thought Ronnie would do the same for his series.[12]

This season's episodes were directed by Fred De Cordova and written by Harvey Helm, Norman Paul, Keith Fowler, and Willy Burns. Burns liked to point out how serious Paul was about his work with his mind constantly on the script. Always looking disheveled, Paul could only work while lying on his back on a couch in the writers' room. George told him one day, "Norman, why don't you stand up for a while? You're pressing all the wrinkles out of your suit."[13]

On the season premiere, Harry Morton landed a big accounting job in New York City, and everyone boarded a train to travel there. Von Zell learns that an important scientist is on the train and suggests to George that Gracie have her picture taken with him. The professor is traveling incognito, and Grace unknowingly befriends him while he is reading *TV Guide* with the Burnses on the cover. Of course, Harry identifies the wrong man as the scientist, but in the end the real professor shows up at the Burnses' St. Moritz Hotel suite. Mixing fact and fiction again on this episode, George and Gracie did actually appear on the cover of the October 8, 1955, edition of *TV Guide.*

In the following week's installment, "Ronnie Arrives," eighteen-year-old Ronnie Burns arrives from California. He wants to study drama at the Actor's Academy and doesn't like doing comedy, much to George's disappointment. After Ronnie performs a scene from the play *Picnic,* Burns agrees that his son should pursue drama.

In prior episodes when a new actor was hired for the Harry Morton character, George would break the fourth wall to introduce the new person. However, in a twist, Ronnie appeared while George was doing his monologue. Burns stopped his monologue to tell the audience that he and Gracie had two children—Sandra who was happily married and Ronnie who was studying acting at the Pasadena Playhouse.

Ronnie had originally studied architecture at USC and then switched to cinematography, working for McCadden Productions during the summer as a film cutter. He later enrolled at Santa Monica Junior College to study modern English literature and dabbled in oil painting before becoming a regular on his parents' series. George decided to make him a regular after seeing him play the role of the tramp in *Picnic* at the Pasadena Playhouse.

With the addition of Ronnie to the cast, several episodes focused on him more than on his mother. In "Ronnie Meets Sabrina," Von Zell meets Sabrina Doyle (Paula Hill) who asks him to help her with her show business career. When he is unable to help, she goes after Ronnie, who wants to date her to prepare for his dramatic role as a character involved with an older woman. However, after his dad points out that Ronnie's character goes for an older married woman, Ronnie practices his lines on Blanche.

Like his mother, Ronnie would also jump to the wrong conclusions about certain situations. In the fourth episode of the season, George is working with Miss Knox to put the finishing touches on his autobiography. Meanwhile, Ronnie decides to change his name to Cobb Cochran to be taken more seriously as a dramatic actor. Gracie has the idea to change her name so Ronnie doesn't have to. She assumes the name of Lola Benedict based on the first name of the hotel restaurant waitress and the last name of the special egg dish on the restaurant's menu. When Ronnie overhears his dad approving credit at a department store for Lola, he thinks his dad is having an affair. Word eventually gets to Gracie that her husband is having an affair, and she assumes it is with Miss Knox. When Gracie confronts George and Miss Knox, Ronnie tries to intervene. Miss Knox states that her first name is not Lola, and Gracie ends up explaining to Ronnie that she is Lola Benedict.

Continuing to use his series to plug his autobiography, George's book (which he had begun in season five) is finally published. In "Harry Morton's Cocktail Party," Harry asks George to give a reception for an important executive whose account Harry wants. Meanwhile, George's autobiography goes on sale, and Gracie and Blanche, while at a bookstore, begin selling the book *I Love Her, That's Why*. At the store, Blanche assaults a man whom she thinks is a masher. It turns out he is the important executive. At the reception, Gracie pretends to be Blanche so Blanche isn't exposed as the woman who hit the man. In the end, Blanche reveals herself and explains everything.

In the following week's episode, "The Musical Version," George's book may be made into a musical, and he thinks he should play the lead. He holds a reception for potential investors including the Mortons and Von Zell. Songwriter Mac Gordon is to compose the songs for the musical. Everyone invests their money until they find that Burns wants to be the lead singer, and then they back out. George and Gracie perform "I Love Her, That's Why," an original song composed by Gordon, who had also provided the lyrics for such classics as "Chattanooga Choo Choo" and "You'll Never Know."

The January 1956 episode "Appearances Are Deceiving" was unique in many respects, in particular because Burns felt he was left out of the plot and Von Zell, not Gracie, came up with a plan to resolve a problem. In the episode, Ronnie is rehearsing a play with Mary Brewster, whose puritanical father is coming to New York to see her. He doesn't like the fact that she is living alone in the big city. When he arrives and sees Mary kissing Ronnie, he wants to return immediately to Omaha with his daughter. George tells the audience that he might as well have lunch in the hotel's restaurant because he has nothing to do with the plot upstairs. He says he doesn't mind his writers leaving him out of the plot but at least they could let him know what's happening. After Harry comes by to explain to George what is transpiring upstairs, George thanks his writers. Back upstairs, Von Zell devises a plan to teach Mr. Brewster a lesson about jumping to conclusions: He and Gracie want Blanche to spill tea on Mr. Brewster, have him take off his coat and tie, and then catch him in a compromising position with Blanche. While Blanche spills tea on Mr. Brewster, she can't go through with the idea of putting him in a compromising position. Mr. Brewster then shows Blanche how he found his daughter and Ronnie when Harry enters. Brewster admits that he was wrong in jumping to conclusions. At the end, still in the restaurant, George asks the audience how everything turned out.

Unlike Lucy Ricardo, in past seasons when Gracie pretended to be someone else, she normally didn't dress in disguise trying to *be* that other person. However, in "Ronnie Moves to the Village" (an episode in which Ronnie wants to stay with his friend and fellow drama student Jim Boardman who lived in Greenwich Village with his father), Gracie disguises herself as an artist's model in a wig and smoking a cigarette and calls on Mr. Boardman, an artist, to see how Ronnie is doing. Ronnie knows the woman is his mother right away, but Mr. Boardman plays along with her until George arrives with some groceries for Ronnie. Everyone says they knew the woman was Gracie, and Ronnie decides to move back with his parents.

Other episodes that season showed Gracie's character becoming more like Lucy Ricardo. In an episode titled "Politeness Never Pays," Gracie and Blanche want their spouses to be more romantic. Von Zell suggests that Blanche and Gracie should be more exciting and alluring to their husbands, and so Gracie, like Lucy would do, dresses up with false eyelashes and a cigarette holder, but this has no effect on George.

Similar to Lucy and Ethel, Blanche and Gracie in "The Indian Potentate" disguise themselves as women from India in an attempt to see a visiting maharajah staying at the hotel. Also, in *I Love Lucy*, Lucy would often come up with some scheme to try to get a part in a movie. In "The English Playwright," Gracie tries to get Ronnie a part in a play by pretending to be a widow to play upon the sympathies of the play's author. She gets rid of George before the playwright visits her. The playwright comes on to her and invites her to dinner in his room. Gracie says she will bring along the "Widow Morton." When Burns comes back, he introduces himself as "Mr. Johnson," and the playwright invites him to dinner as well for the "Widow Morton." At dinner, the truth comes out.

In another New York–based episode, Gracie and Blanche *a la* Lucy and Ethel become hotel switchboard operators to prevent Harry from receiving a call that could lead to a job change with him traveling around the country, meaning that Blanche would no longer be Gracie's neighbor.

A new semi-regular, wealthy Mrs. Millicent Sohmers (Doris Packer), appeared on several New York shows during the season. Mrs. Sohmers was married to the man who owned Sohmer's Shoes, and Harry wanted to add this company to his list of clients. When Gracie would literally interpret what Mrs. Sohmers was saying, Sohmers would attempt to clarify her remarks for Gracie. However, she would usually give up and become as bewildered as most others who conversed with Gracie.

A special spring episode, "A Night of Vaudeville," was another change of pace for *The Burns and Allen Show*. Since Ronnie's drama school is losing money, Gracie suggests, instead of doing their usual performance of *Othello*, the school should put on a vaudeville show. George directs, and Gracie is mistress of ceremonies. According to a 1956 McCadden press release, this was the most ambitious segment ever filmed for the series. Some of vaudeville's greatest stars were impersonated by students at Ronnie's dramatic school. Jay Wheeler played Eddie Cantor; Judy Clark was Sophie Tucker; and George and Gracie were impersonated by Ronnie and actress Diane Jergens.

Just as the cast of *I Love Lucy* took a trip to Europe during its 1955–56 season, three episodes of *Burns and Allen* had everyone flying to Paris. When Gracie says that she doesn't like a bow on a dress she has, George advises her to take it to the designer to have it removed. He didn't realize the designer, Mr. Broussard, lived in Paris. Besides George and Gracie, the Mortons, Ronnie, and Harry Von Zell all fly to France. While in Paris, Gracie has the idea of opening a dress shop back in New York to sell Broussard designer dresses, and she wants George to finance the endeavor. She tries to keep it a secret from him, but Broussard informs George as the gang departs for New York. Back in New York, George refuses to give Gracie $1,000 to open the dress shop. He wants the twenty-four dresses she brought from Paris to be sent back. Gracie has Von Zell pretend to be a bellboy who picks up the boxes of dresses supposedly to mail them but actually takes them to Blanche's apartment. Not knowing what is going on, George asks the viewers to phone him if something is happening concerning the dresses that he doesn't know about. Harry discovers the dresses in his apartment and returns them to George, but subsequently Ronnie, dressed as a bellboy, retrieves the dresses. Finally, Gracie gets a loan from Mrs. Sohmers for the shop. However, Gracie ends up selling her own dresses because she gave the twenty-four designer gowns to Mrs. Sohmers for security.

In "The Triple Surprise Party," viewers get a rare glimpse of Gracie doing physical comedy. Blanche wants to give Harry a surprise party. George offers to hold the party at his apartment, and he will keep it a secret from Gracie. George makes up a story that he is giving a surprise party for Ronnie, who will soon complete his term at the Actor's Academy. To make sure that Ronnie is there for the party, Gracie says that she is having a surprise party for his dad's birthday. Gracie discovers the birthday gifts intended for Harry, thinks they are not suitable for Ronnie, and exchanges them. Harry is not too pleased with his new gifts—a motor scooter and rock 'n' roll records. Like something Lucy would do, Gracie rides the motor scooter through her hotel suite.

Before the Burnses and Mortons returned to California, the writers based another episode on one of their favorite ideas: Gracie keeping a doctor's appointment for someone else. This time, Mrs. Sohmers is worked into the storyline. In "Mrs. Sohmers Needs a Psychologist," Millicent Sohmers has been visiting a psychologist because of her bewilderment with Gracie's unusual way of thinking. After twenty-one visits in three weeks, Dr. Hendricks (Dabbs Greer) says she no longer needs treatment. But after seeing Gracie again, Mrs. Sohmers goes back to the psychologist. The psychologist wants to meet with Blanche to see if what Mrs. Sohmers is saying about Gracie is true, but Gracie keeps the appointment instead, and the doctor now understands what Millicent has been telling him. Dr. Hendricks' secretary calls Harry in error and says that the doctor wants to talk with him about his wife. When Harry acts nice toward Blanche, she explains that it was Gracie who went to the psychologist, not her. Dr. Hendricks goes to the Burnses' apartment, thinks Von Zell is George, and concludes that the whole family is crazy.

Fred De Cordova left the series after the New York season. He had received an offer from CBS to produce and direct *December Bride* with Spring Byington. He would later direct episodes of *The Jack Benny Program* and *My Three Sons* and produce *The Tonight Show with Johnny Carson.*

For the season, *The Burns and Allen Show* ranked 28th in the ratings.

Nominated for two Emmys, Gracie lost the award to Lucy for Best Actress and to Nanette Fabray for Best Comedienne.

1956–57 TV Season: George's Magic

On their October 1, 1956, episode, the Burnses and the Mortons finally return from New York City to California. Gracie was the instigator of the move: she missed Ronnie who had returned to California three days earlier to enroll at USC. While in New York, Gracie had her California home completely redecorated. The series' new director Rod Amateau, who had directed *The Bob Cummings Show,* decided the *Burns and Allen* sets needed a complete upgrade, hence the reason for the newly decorated homes of both the Burnses and the Mortons. For a brief time, Amateau was also Burns' son-in-law, having married Sandra Burns after her divorce from her first husband and *his* divorce from his second wife, Joan Andre.

In "Return to California," Ronnie has fellow students staying at the Burns home as well as the Morton place and is surprised when his parents and the Mortons arrive earlier than expected. George, Harry, and Von Zell end up spending their first night back in California at a hotel.

With many episodes during this season focusing on Ronnie attending USC and dating different girls, additional characters were featured during this season. Ronnie's best friend was Ralph Granger (Robert Ellis). Ronnie also became acquainted with another college student, Brian McAffee (Robert Easton) from Texas, who had been attending USC for nine years.

Almost like a young Bob Collins from *The Bob Cummings Show,* Ronnie dated a variety of girls including Brian's sister Bonnie Sue (Judi Boutin, who changed her name to Judi Meredith in the series' next season), Kathy (Kathy Marlowe), and a French exchange student, Marie Bardot (Jacqueline Beer). Judi (Boutin) Meredith had been spotted by Burns when she was performing in summer stock. She continued her role of Bonnie Sue on *The George Burns Show* and then got the role of Monique Deveraux on the 1959–60 CBS western series *Hotel de Paree* with Earl Holliman. After *The Burns and Allen Show,* Kathy Marlowe appeared on several 1960s series such as *Mr. Lucky* and *Surfside 6.* Jacqueline Beer, Miss France of 1954, later had a continuing role as switchboard operator Suzanne Fabray on *77*

Sunset Strip. She subsequently married Norwegian adventurer Thor Heyerdahl, best known for his Kon-Tiki expedition.

Like he had done with promoting his autobiography, Burns used episodes of the series to publicize Ronnie's real-life acting career. During the previous season in New York, an episode was devoted to Ronnie's appearance on Jackie Gleason's *The Honeymooners*. This season, Ronnie got a role in the teen movie *Bernardine* starring Pat Boone and Terry Moore.

However, the biggest change during this season was the introduction of George's magic television set on which he could watch the activities of the other characters. A newspaper account at the time indicated that Burns had the TV set, which he called the "27-inch keyhole," installed to make it easier for him to see what Gracie was up to. Since George could watch the events of each episode on the television set, he could figure out ways to foil Gracie's schemes.[14] The television set gave him virtually complete creative control over an episode's storyline in his ability to see what Gracie, Ronnie, the Mortons and Von Zell were doing. None of the characters knew that Burns could view them on his set. Blanche and Harry, in particular, were at his mercy if either would say something negative about him. He would then, for example, call Blanche and repeat what she just said without her having any clue how he found out what she said. As Harry once stated referring to George's omniscience, "I can't imagine how he does it, but he knows everything that goes on in this house." Usually Burns would view everyone's activities on the TV in his den, but sometimes he would use the television in the living room to see what was happening. When Von Zell or another character would enter his den, George either switched off the set or changed it to a channel showing westerns.

The idea for the magic TV set apparently came up in a conversation between Burns and Rod Amateau. As Amateau and Burns were going over a script, the director remarked, "Too bad you can't have one of those television sets on the show like they have in the department store—where they watch for shoplifters." To which George replied, "Why not?"[15] For Burns, the magic TV was the technological equivalent of Gracie's illogical logic. His ability to see what was going on during an episode was particularly magical since his television seemingly did not rely on closed circuit cameras. Whether scenes relating to the story took place in his home, the Morton residence, or somewhere else, Burns, and only he, was privy to them through his magical box. He would use the magic television to not only determine what was transpiring in an episode but also many times to add complications to a situation.

The magical TV was first introduced in the November episode "The Missing Stamp" where Gracie goes to the Mortons' to borrow a stamp for a letter she wrote to her sister Hazel but takes a valuable stamp from Harry's collection. Gracie gives the letter to Harry to mail. He doesn't look at the envelope and forgets to mail it. Harry then gives the letter to George to mail. George sees the valuable stamp but keeps quiet about it since, as he says, if he tells Harry, "the show will be fifteen minutes short." George advises Harry to report the missing stamp to the police and puts the letter in his desk drawer. He turns on the TV set in the living room to see Von Zell and Ronnie discussing the missing stamp and finds out that they discovered that Gracie mistakenly put the stamp on her letter. Gracie finds her letter in George's desk and gives it to Blanche's brother Roger to mail. Roger identifies the valuable stamp, but before he gives the letter to Harry, he offers a $5 reward for the return of the stamp. He says he wants to clear his "good name" since Harry accused Roger of taking the stamp. George, thinking the letter is still in his desk, ups the reward to $100. Harry and Von Zell also add more money to the pot. When the reward totals $300, Roger hands over the letter, collects the reward, and leaves for Seattle.

In the following week's episode, the magic television also played a crucial role showing that George could view what was happening all over town through his set. Gracie wants to mail George's gray suit to Blanche's brother Roger, but she doesn't say anything to her husband because it is one of his favorites. George switches on his magic TV and sees his suit being sent by the post office to Roger. He calls the post office, instructs them not to send it, and goes to retrieve the package. In the meantime, Gracie comes up with a story that a burglar broke into their house and stole the suit and three of her dresses. When the Mortons hear the story, Harry phones the police to request an additional patrol for the neighborhood. Gracie explains to George that they were robbed, and the police come to investigate. George wears his gray suit while the police are there, as Gracie describes it to a tee. Harry comes in and says he found Gracie's missing dresses in Blanche's closet. In one of his bizarre twist endings, George tells the police that his writers came up with the idea for a story about a missing gray suit but couldn't come up with an ending, and so they never did the story.

Several other very unusual episodes also aired during the season. In an episode titled "The Ugly Duckling," George conjures up his own genie. Mildred McCoy, Ronnie's plain-looking tutor, doesn't have a date to the class prom. Ronnie and Ralph each want to date beautiful Joyce Collins with Joyce finally choosing to go with Ronnie. Upset, Mildred confesses to Gracie that she isn't attractive enough for the opposite sex. Gracie decides to help Mildred get a new dress and hair style. When Joyce decides to go to the prom with someone other than Ronnie, his dad gives him $35 to go out with Mildred. George says to the viewers that he is a "fairy godmother" having given his son money and then, to prove his magical powers, he conjures up a genie in his den. He asks the genie for the $35 that he gave Ronnie, and the genie answers "Are you kidding?" and disappears. Subsequently, Joyce comes in to say she was stood up by the guy she thought was taking her to the prom, and then Mildred stops by to show Gracie how attractive she looks and reveals she is going to the prom with the guy who stood up Joyce. Ronnie takes Joyce to the prom, and everyone leaves except George. George summons the genie again to spend the rest of the evening with him.

In another episode that relied on gimmicks for laughs, Gracie wants to have her bedroom redone without George knowing. A decorator arrives at night and Gracie introduces him as a famous explorer who is going to lecture at her club. But George sees the real story on his magic television. After watching Gracie and the decorator discuss redoing the bedroom, Burns walks to the balcony of his den and asks the crew to bump up the lights for his monologue. After completing his monologue, he tells the crew to make it night again. Gracie needs to get George out of the house for two days in order to redecorate the bedroom. Ronnie and Ralph rig the living room to make it appear that the Burnses have termites so that his dad will take Gracie to Palm Springs while the house is being fumigated. Chairs, lamps, and pictures on the wall move up and down to show termites running through them, but George pays no attention. In the end, Burns says they can go to Palm Springs and the "explorer" can redo the bedroom.

Additional episodes showed the magical, mischievous side of Burns the producer. In an episode where the Burnses are staying in a Houston hotel, a crowd of noisy people end up in George and Gracie's room. George tells the audience that he likes a quiet finish and asks the sound man to cut the sound so the noise can't be heard. In another episode, while viewing his special TV, Jack Benny appears. Apparently Jack is the only other person to know that George has a magical TV just like he was the only person other than Burns to speak directly to the audience on some earlier episodes.

Near the end of the season, viewers got to see Blanche's mother in "Blanche's Mother Arrives" with Bea Benaderet playing both roles. Ronnie is dating French exchange student Marie Bardot. Meanwhile, Blanche thinks Harry is going out of town, and so invites her mother Natalie Baker for a visit. Harry's trip is canceled, but Blanche doesn't want to let him know right away about her mother coming from Seattle. She has Gracie pick Natalie up at the airport and wants to keep her mother's visit a secret from George as well. Gracie introduces Blanche's mother to George as the French exchange student Ronnie is dating, but Burns knows who she really is. While George tries to fix Natalie up with Von Zell, Blanche forces Harry to ask her mother to stay with them. At the end, Burns announces that "Blanche" will be receiving two checks this week—one for playing herself and one for playing her mother. For this episode, director Rod Amateau used the same split-screen technique he had used on *The Bob Cummings Show* when Cummings portrayed both himself and his grandfather.

A season wouldn't be complete without Burns satirizing his writers. Gracie is concerned that when Ronnie turns twenty-one, he might marry someone that she doesn't like and so wants to find the right wife for him. Meanwhile, George phones his writers about a script that he thinks needs more jokes and says they need to get on the ball. They ask if he can wait until Sunday night for a new script because they want to watch *The Jack Benny Program* and get some jokes from him. When Gracie describes the problem she perceives about Ronnie, George says that might make a good script. He suggests that Gracie go to a matrimonial agency to find Ronnie a wife. To complicate the story, he decides to have Gracie take Von Zell's picture and tell the agency it is Ronnie. Misinterpreting the agency's instructions, Gracie takes a photo of George. George turns on his TV to view the matrimonial agency interviewing a prospective wife that he thinks is for Von Zell, not realizing that Gracie took his photo to the agency. He calls Von Zell to come over. Burns answers the door when the prospective wife arrives and realizes, after the woman kisses him, that his picture was the one seen at the agency. When Von Zell informs Gracie of what happened, she calls the agency to have them send over a possible husband for her. George then introduces Gracie's prospective husband to his prospective wife, and the two decide to marry. In the end, Burns decides to fire his writers since he developed the storyline for the script.

One other item of note happened during the 1956–57 season: Burns decided to bring in a new character to serve as the basis for a possible spinoff series. Cusperd Jantzen, a plumber played by Howard McNear, was introduced in four spring 1957 episodes. McNear, later known as Floyd Lawson the barber on *The Andy Griffith Show* for several years, played Jantzen as somewhat befuddled and absent-minded much like he portrayed Floyd. Jantzen was first featured in an episode titled "The Ring" where Gracie gives her engagement ring to Ronnie so he can give it to Kathy with whom he wants to go steady. Gracie has Blanche make up a story that Gracie lost the ring down her kitchen sink drain, and Burns calls Jantzen to retrieve it. Jantzen is a widower with four daughters who is looking for a new wife. In the following week's episode, he asks Gracie, upon whom he relied for "sage advice," to watch his daughters, while he goes to San Diego to meet a possible marriage prospect. His daughters, all models, are Jean (Jody Warner), Joy (Yvonne Lime), June (Darlene Albert), and Joan (Mary Ellen Kaye). In a third episode, Gracie places an ad in the newspaper for a wife for Jantzen. The ad claims he is thirty-five. Gracie receives a reply from a woman who is thirty, but the lady, upon seeing that Jantzen is really in his fifties, declines to pursue a relationship. In another episode featuring the Jantzen character, Gracie again volunteers to find a wife for him. Jantzen's daughters are in a photo shoot with Bob Collins (Bob Cummings from the McCadden-produced *The Bob Cummings Show*) as the photographer. Gracie thinks that Miss Emerson (Jean Willes), the advertising account executive at the photo shoot, would be a good prospect for Jantzen. However, when Miss Emerson comes to the Burns residence, she thinks Von Zell is the marriage prospect.

In May 1957, George said that he planned to spin off the Jantzen character into his own series tentatively titled *The Plumber and His Daughters*.[16] As Yvonne Lime (Joy Jantzen) recalls, "I do remember playing one of the daughters of the widowed plumber. We had a lot of fun working together and I know George Burns truly thought *The Plumber and His Daughters* could be an interesting series. Unfortunately it didn't work out."[17] One can speculate that if *The Plumber and His Daughters* had become a series, the storylines would have continued to focus on Jantzen's efforts to marry and his daughters' modeling and dating activities. The Jantzen character did re-appear in some episodes during the final *Burns and Allen* season.

The Burns and Allen Show ranked 28th for the year. Norman Paul, Harvey Helm, Keith Fowler, and Willy Burns continued as writers. Gracie received another Emmy nomination but lost to Nanette Fabray for Best Actress in a Comedy.

1957–58 TV Season: The Final "Good Night"

After the beginning of the 1957–58 season, perhaps in response to the competition his series was receiving from a show on NBC, Burns wrote a letter to Bill Paley, the head of CBS, complaining that his show should be on at a later time. He began the letter with his dry sense of humor: "I don't know if you ever watch CBS but you ought to watch the network some night ... they have some pretty good shows."[18]

The episodes during the series' final season satirized TV westerns and Italian actresses, inverted some of the classic plots of prior shows, remade some episodes from earlier seasons, and continued to have some unique finishes.

In "The General," the first episode of the season, Ronnie's friend Bill Masterson just married his girlfriend Kay, and Bill's father, who is in the Army and got him an appointment to West Point, is coming to visit before Bill goes on his honeymoon. After Bill explains to Gracie that he doesn't want to be a soldier, do-gooder Gracie says she will handle everything. When Bill's father General Masterson arrives, he informs Gracie that he doesn't want his son to be married, and so Gracie introduces Kay as Ronnie's wife. Gracie explains to her husband that Bill needs to go for his physical for West Point, and George suggests that she get someone to take his place who is not physically fit. Gracie recruits Von Zell, who fails the exam. After George explains to the general that Bill and Kay are married, the general decides that maybe his grandson will be the one to go to West Point.

In his opening monologue, Burns, dressed as a cowboy, says that if you want to stay on TV, you need to go western and that he really planned a western-themed episode for their season debut. On his magic TV, George shows a clip of the western they were planning to do. He talks about the different trends on television over the years, from cop shows to private eyes to quiz shows, and says that he rented a ranch and hired actors to play cowboys and Indians for their premiere. Von Zell also appears in western garb, which he would continue to do for the next three shows. In the "Afterpiece," Gracie, dressed as a cowgirl, talks about her uncle who was a Pony Express rider.

To satirize westerns, George and Gracie also appeared on the cover of the September 28, 1957, issue of *TV Guide* with Burns wearing a cowboy hat. In an article about the trend toward westerns on TV, George wrote that he was looking forward to playing a cowboy on their first show. He went on to say, "I know this: The only comedians not coming back this fall apparently made a terrible error. They were funny. That's a mistake I never made in my whole career, and I won't make it as a cowboy, either ... " [19]

This season *The Burns and Allen Show* was up against *Restless Gun* on NBC. Burns' satirical comments about TV westerns may have been the first time a sitcom made fun of its competition. *Restless Gun* ended up beating *Burns and Allen* in the ratings, ranking eighth overall for the season, and bumped George and Gracie out of the top thirty shows. All during the season, Burns, when viewing his television, would often flip to the other channel to watch a western, sometimes even directing the Indians as to which way the cowboys went.

An October episode was a satire of Italian movie actresses. Ronnie wants his mother to help Bonnie Sue McAfee get a movie role. Since Italian actresses are all the rage, Gracie makes over Bonnie Sue as Tina Cacciatore and tries to get her to speak Italian. Ronnie also asks his dad to help Bonnie Sue's career. George gets her a role that requires a Texas accent. When Bonnie Sue tries to audition for the director as Tina Cacciatore, the director recognizes her Texas accent right away and gives her the part.

In February 1958, gossip columnist Louella Parsons announced that Gracie Allen was retiring from acting. She quoted Burns as saying, "Gracie has had it. She has been in show business since she was five. We have been married 32 years and we have made motion pictures, appeared in vaudeville, nightclubs, and worked hard in every phase of entertainment all our married life." [20]

With the announcement of her retirement, the writers saw the opportunity to do one of their greatest inversions and make Gracie's character brilliant. On an episode titled "Hypnotizing Gracie," Gracie, again wanting to have a dress designer fix a bow on a gown she bought, goes to the wrong hotel room, which is occupied by English hypnotist Professor Spencer Clifford. The news people in the room, recognizing she is Gracie Allen, challenge the professor to hypnotize her to be the opposite of what she is. After George agrees that it would be great publicity, Clifford hypnotizes Gracie and tells her she's the smartest woman in the world. The news people ask Gracie history and science questions which she answers correctly. The hypnotism does generate a lot of publicity. When George wants the professor to snap Gracie out of the spell, he finds that Clifford has flown back to London.

In this episode, the writers really didn't address Gracie's literal-mindedness and have her become adept at understanding figurative expressions. Instead, they opted to have Gracie's character gain knowledge about math and science in particular. They probably decided to go that way since having Gracie begin understanding figurative speech, identifying a real problem that needed solving, and coming up with a rational plan to resolve the problem really would not have been that funny. In the "Afterpiece," Gracie doesn't want to discuss her relatives. Instead, she wants to talk about nuclear fission. George has to get Ronnie to do the routine about Cousin Noah, a zookeeper.

In the following week's episode, "Gracie Is Brilliant," with her new-found intelligence, Gracie appears on a big-money quiz show and wins $50,000. She agrees to come back the following week to answer the $100,000 question. George is concerned that he no longer has an act and wants to get Clifford to return to the States and undo the spell. George is cooking meals, while Gracie is tutoring Ronnie, meeting with geophysicists, and finding Blanche somewhat shallow. She has lost all interest in show business. George says he just doesn't understand the new Gracie and further remarks that he "didn't understand the old Gracie either but at least he made some money with it." Burns phones Clifford, who says he can undo the hypnotism by talking to Gracie over the phone. While George goes to find Gracie, Blanche picks up the phone. Thinking she is Gracie, Clifford makes Blanche think like the ditzy Gracie. Burns realizes what happened, saying that now there are two Gracies and he "has the wrong one under contract." George finally has Clifford return to the United States, get the old Gracie back, and make Blanche her normal self. When Gracie returns to the quiz show to answer the $100,000 question, the emcee realizes she is the old Gracie and gives her an easy question: "Who is buried in Grant's tomb?" She answers incorrectly, "John Keats." Gracie had been told about

Newly intelligent Gracie brushes up on Einstein's theory, while George serves breakfast.

Keats previously by a girl Ronnie brought home to be tutored by the new Gracie about English literature.

Other final-season episodes centered on Burns as producer and on his fondness for unique finishes. A March episode, "Frozen Passion," focused on George's producing career. As noted in the first chapter, McCadden Productions flirted with the idea of doing movies but never did. In the episode, producer-director Jack Bradley (Raymond Bailey) is meeting with Burns to discuss the possibility of McCadden Productions making a feature film. Gracie suggests Ronnie, Bonnie Sue, Von Zell, and Blanche could all have parts in the movie. She wants to find out what the script is about. In his den, George mentions to Bradley a bad script he got called *Frozen Passion* about a Canadian Mountie and his sweetheart. When Gracie asks Bradley about the different roles in the picture, he decides to describe the characters from *Frozen Passion*. Gracie enlists Ronnie to be the Mountie and Bonnie Sue his love interest. She also recruits Blanche for one of the two dance hall girls and Von Zell for an Eskimo. Gracie decides to portray the other dance hall girl herself. After dinner with Bradley, they all audition for him and George. Gracie even has a special effects guy make it snow in their living room. Burns loses the deal to make the movie.

In an April episode, Gracie is on a jury for a trial about a counterfeiter. When the district attorney passes around a counterfeit bill to the jury, she gets it mixed up with her own money and gives it to Blanche who, in turn, gives it to Von Zell. Von Zell is later caught trying to pass the bogus bill. Through his magic TV, George sees what is happening in the courtroom and phones the judge to explain that Gracie mistakenly switched the counterfeit money with her own money. He informs the judge that if Von Zell is found guilty, the actor playing the judge will never appear on *The Burns and Allen Show* again.

In a May episode about Ronnie joining the Army to gain sympathy from Bonnie Sue, Ronnie says he is being sent to Alaska. When Gracie finds this out, she goes to see the general to get him transferred to a warmer place. His dad calls the general to inform him that Ronnie has another year of college and can't go in the Army now. The general asks how Ronnie's name got on the list of recruits in the first place, and George says the storyline was just conceived by his writers for this episode and, if they hadn't come up with it, the actor playing the general (Ned Wever) wouldn't be appearing on the show. The actor responds by saying that he enjoyed playing the part and compliments all the actors on the show but doesn't mention George. Burns replies that next week he needs an actor to play a doctor and asks Wever if he is working next week. Wever says no, and George responds, "That's right."

Three episodes during this season were remakes of earlier ones, and since Ronnie Burns was now part of the cast, they were all modified to reflect this. The December episode "A Hole in the Carpet" was a variation on a show from August 17, 1953. But in this version, Ronnie is working at the department store during the Christmas holidays where Gracie trips in a hole in the carpet and ruins a pair of stockings. Like the 1953 episode, the store's claims adjuster calls and tries to settle any liability for $100. Since Gracie again thinks she is the one who has to pay the store $100, she asks George and then Blanche for the money. However, unlike the earlier episode, the store promotes Ronnie to the position of claims adjuster, and he suggests calling the whole thing off.

Another January 1958 episode, "Too Many Fathers," was a remake of an episode from the series' 1952–53 season. Ronnie lets Jerry Gilbert, a friend, use the Burnses' pool to meet Sandy, a girl he likes, and now she thinks that Jerry lives at the Burns house. When her parents want to meet Jerry's parents, Gracie pretends to be his mother. As in the original episode, after Von Zell, Harry, and George all say they are Jerry's father, confusion ensues, and George has to explain everything to Sandy's parents. In the original episode, Jerry Gilbert's first name was Ronnie. However, since Ronnie Burns was now part of the cast, the character's name was changed to Jerry.

A June 1958 episode repeated the plot of a 1953 episode about Gracie and George being locked out of their house, needing a locksmith to open their front door, and then Gracie relocking the door with the locksmith's tools inside. In this adaptation, George and Gracie finally get in their house when Ronnie comes home from a date.

With the popularity of Elvis Presley and the success of Ricky Nelson singing on *The Adventures of Ozzie and Harriet,* other young sitcom stars tried to emulate this success. Dwayne Hickman on *The Bob Cummings Show* and Shelley Fabares and Paul Petersen on *The Donna Reed Show* are some examples. Ronnie Burns also tried his hand at recording a hit song in a May 5, 1958, episode, "Ronnie Makes a Record." In the episode, his dad gets Ronnie a recording contract with Verve Records. Gracie thinks that George himself wants a recording contract. When Jack Stanley, a Verve executive, calls Gracie about Ronnie making a record, she is upset thinking that her husband should be the one to record. Mr. Stanley's daughter tells Ronnie about the recording session, but Gracie says that his dad will be broken-hearted. At the studio, Ronnie pretends he has laryngitis until Mr. Stanley explains that George wanted his son to record. Meanwhile, Mr. Granz, the president of Verve Records, phones Gracie and wants to meet Ronnie. Gracie introduces Von Zell as Ronnie so Mr. Granz can see that her son is not as young as he thought, and thus may want to consider her husband for a recording contract. George enters and explains that Ronnie is at the studio rehearsing. The Burnses, the Mortons, and Von Zell all go to see Ronnie sing "She's Kinda Cute." Ronnie did really record "She's Kinda Cute" for Verve Records, whose president was Norman Granz. Lyle Talbot portrayed Granz in this episode.

In "The Exchange Student," the final episode of the series, Ronnie asks Marcel, a French foreign exchange classmate, to stay with his family since Marcel wants to live in a typical American home. George doesn't want Marcel living there for the whole school year and, when Marcel charms Bonnie Sue, Ronnie also changes his mind about Marcel living with the Burnses. Because Gracie wants to ask Marcel to leave in a nice way, she says that Von Zell will be his roommate. When that doesn't work, Gracie tells Marcel that he took Bonnie Sue away from Ronnie. Marcel, however, says that he is not interested in her. He invites his own girlfriend, Collette, over, but when Ronnie charms her, Marcel decides to move out.

In the "Afterpiece," George and Gracie appeared together for the last time. The routine was about Gracie's Uncle Robinson Allen, who was shipwrecked on a desert island:

> GEORGE: Castaway?
> GRACIE: Well, naturally after he came home after thirty years, what could his wife do with him?
> GEORGE: How did he get shipwrecked on this island?
> GRACIE: Well, you see, he rented a rowboat to go fishing and a big storm came up and for ten days it blew him out into the Pacific.
> GEORGE: Well, he was in real trouble.
> GRACE: He certainly was. The boat was costing him 25 cents an hour.
> GEORGE: He was away for thirty years and finally came back?
> GRACIE: Of course, he didn't want the man at the boathouse to think he was dishonest.
> GEORGE: Well, look, on the island, where did he live—in a hut or a cave?
> GRACIE: In a hut. Yes, you see he'd never been on a desert island and so he would not know a cave from a hole in the ground.
> GEORGE: What did he do for clothes?
> GRACIE: Well, there were a lot of goats on the island, and so he killed a mother goat and used the skin to make himself a pair of pants.
> GEORGE: Then his problems were over?
> GRACIE: No, no. When he wore them with the hair on the inside, it tickled him all the time and drove him crazy.

GEORGE: Then why didn't he wear them with the hair on the outside?

GRACIE: That was even worse. The baby goats chased him all over the island. They thought he was their mother.

GEORGE: How did he get along with the other animals?

GRACIE: Well, his favorite companion was a chimpanzee. You see, my uncle even taught him how to play checkers, and they had many games together.

GEORGE: Sounds like a beautiful friendship.

GRACIE: Oh, it was, but one day the chimpanzee got mad and never came back.

GEORGE: Why did he get mad?

GRACIE: Well, Uncle Robinson finally won a game, and the chimp was a sore loser.

GEORGE: Say good night, Gracie.

GRACIE: Good night.

In his book about Gracie, Burns describes what happened after filming their last show on June 4, 1958:

> We didn't even mention the fact that it was our last show together. But there was a tremendous amount of emotion on the set.... It really was her last scene, the last time she ever appeared on a stage.... The crew gave her a standing ovation. Someone popped open a bottle of champagne and paper cups were passed around. Bea gave Gracie a big hug. Gracie took one cup of the champagne, just to be polite, and said, "Okay, that's it." Then she paused for just a second, really no more than that, took a long look around the set, and added, "And thank you very much, everyone."[21]

The September 22, 1958, issue of *Life* magazine covered Gracie's retirement and the filming of the final show. Among the photos is one showing George and Gracie leaving the studio a final time together with both holding bouquets of flowers given to Gracie by the crew.

After the series ended, Gracie Allen never appeared on screen again. She was Emmy-nominated for the 1957–58 season but lost to Dinah Shore for Best Performance by a Comedienne, Singer, Hostess, etc. Since some of the first-run episodes were broadcast in September 1958, Gracie was nominated for the 1958–59 season but lost the award for Best Actress in a Comedy to Jane Wyatt in *Father Knows Best*.

George, Ronnie, Bea Benaderet, Larry Keating, and Harry Von Zell went on to star in NBC's *The George Burns Show*. In a multi-million dollar deal, McCadden Productions sold the rerun rights to *The Burns and Allen Show* to Screen Gems.

4

George and the Charming Bachelor— *The Bob Cummings Show*

The first successful series McCadden Productions made other than *The Burns and Allen Show* was *The Bob Cummings Show*, which premiered on NBC in the middle of the 1954–55 TV season, one of the first series to debut at mid-season. Bob Cummings played charming bachelor Bob Collins, a professional photographer taking pictures of beautiful models during the day and dating a different model almost every evening. The character lived the life of a sophisticated playboy who not only had a job many men would kill for, but also whom most women found irresistible. He was suave and debonair and dressed differently from most men in fifties sitcoms. Hardly ever attired in business suits, he would wear short sleeve shirts open at the collar.

Cummings had previously starred on another situation comedy, *My Hero,* where he played Robert S. Beanblossom, a bumbling realtor. That series lasted only one season. Cummings had also appeared in many movies in the 1930s and 1940s such as *Three Smart Girls Grow Up, The Devil and Miss Jones,* and *Saboteur.* Between the time he filmed the pilot for *The Bob Cummings Show* and the time it was picked up as a series, Cummings had a featured role in the Hitchcock classic *Dial M for Murder.*

On his show, Bob lived with his widowed sister Margaret MacDonald (Rosemary DeCamp) and her son Chuck (Dwayne Hickman). Bob's secretary was Charmaine "Schultzy" Schultz (Ann B. Davis). Other actresses had been in contention for the part of Schultzy. Paul Henning originally conceived the role for former child actress Jane Withers. Davis remembers that Withers "was in the running for the part, "but she, being a 'name,' wanted more money—and I would have done it for scale."[1]

Other characters on the sitcom were Bob's friend from the Air Force Reserves, Paul Fonda (Lyle Talbot); Pamela Livingstone (Nancy Kulp), a

Ann B. Davis, Bob Cummings, Dwayne Hickman, and Rosemary DeCamp from *The Bob Cummings Show.* **The series ran for five seasons.**

bird-watcher, who lusted after Bob; and Josh Collins (Bob Cummings in a dual role), Bob and Margaret's grandfather from Joplin, Missouri. Each episode opened with Bob aiming a camera and saying, "Hold it. I think you're going to like this picture." Cummings' character would infrequently make asides directly to the audience as Burns did on his own series.

63

A middle-aged Casanova (Cummings was forty-seven when the show started) who was always chasing women and never wanted to marry, Bob Collins spent most of his time trying to maintain his worldly lifestyle, which meant fending off any attempts to get him to tie the knot, pursuing attractive women even if they were not that interested in him, and trying to get away from any unattractive woman who found *him* irresistible. Collins' lifestyle made it difficult for him to be the proper role model for his nephew Chuck. Bob wanted his sister Margaret to date men but, of course, not play around with them like he did with women. It was considered a sex comedy at the time, but since it was the 1950s, sexual intercourse was never mentioned. The most risqué the series got was referring to Bob's nighttime adventures on Mulholland Drive. As Davis recalls, "The show was about sex only in that they called him a wolf and he was always looking at women and always making come-on remarks. They were terribly tame and it wouldn't play now because comedy has changed so much."[2]

The Bob Cummings Show was as subversive to marriage as *The Burns and Allen Show* was to logic. Like *The Burns and Allen Show,* certain elements from Cummings' real life were incorporated into some of the episodes. Both Bob Cummings and Bob Collins were from Joplin, both had an elderly grandfather, both were in the Air Force Reserves, and both loved flying. Cummings was actually taught to fly while in high school by his godfather Orville Wright, one of the Wright brothers. However, unlike the character Bob Collins, Bob Cummings was married in real life, and Mary, his wife at the time, was the head of his production company.

According to Cummings, the idea for this series was born during the making of a *My Hero* episode which he wrote.[3] In that episode, Beanblossom gets real-life Hollywood photographer Paul Hesse (playing himself) to photograph a house he is selling. The bill for the photo shoot is $2,356, which is more than the selling price of the house. Beanblossom's boss wants him to meet with Hesse to resolve the bill. As one of Hesse's attractive female photo subjects is leaving in a huff because she doesn't have the right male model to work with her, she sees Robert in the waiting room, is instantly attracted to him, and asks him to pose with her for a soap commercial. Beanblossom works out a deal for Hesse to cancel the bill for the picture of the house in return for him posing with the actress-model.

Paul Henning, who had previously written for *The Burns and Allen Show* and had also been born in Missouri—Independence to be exact—

created *The Bob Cummings Show*. After MCA asked Henning to develop a sitcom for Cummings, he partnered with McCadden Productions and with Cummings' Laurel Productions to produce the series. Like McCadden, Laurel Productions got its name from a street: Laurel Way, where Cummings lived. The NBC series began its Sunday night run on January 2, 1955, at 10:30 p.m. Although the comedy was sold in August 1954, Cummings wanted several episodes filmed before the show premiered so that the scripts and characters could be fine-tuned.

Henning admired Cummings' acting and thought, when developing a series for him, that he would make Cummings' character a commercial artist. However, afraid that not many people would know what a commercial artist did, Henning decided to make Collins a photographer, similar to Paul Hesse. He sought to balance the character's bachelor life with more mundane family responsibilities and with a female assistant who would make sure there wasn't a lot of hanky-panky with the attractive models.[4] While *The Burns and Allen Show* contrasted the nonsensical world of Gracie with the more sensible world of George, *The Bob Cummings Show* contrasted the sophisticated world of Bob Collins with the ordinary world of his sister, nephew, and assistant. Humor was extracted from situations that would attempt to puncture Collins' playboy world such as Bob being threatened with marriage, having a plain-looking woman pursue him, etc. The series also ventured at times into the surreal world of dreams and fantasies.

As a producer, George Burns sat in on the cast auditions for the original pilot along with Henning and Cummings. Once it became a series, Burns attended each run-through of the Cummings show and would suggest changes. As Rod Amateau, the director of *The Bob Cummings Show* during its initial seasons, pointed out, "Everything George suggested was so apropos, so right, and just *tasty*. For instance, he would advise against two jokes in quick succession because one would cancel the other out. The logic of his suggestions was always obvious."[5]

Each episode was filmed in one day with a two-camera set-up like *The Burns and Allen Show*. Bob admitted that Burns would personally come to the rescue when he was looking for a tag to end an episode of his series.[6] According to Rosemary DeCamp, George would often bring Jack Benny to watch the run-throughs. "We would go all-out to make them laugh. George was stingy with his laughs. He was always figuring out some new twist for a scene, and laughed out loud not more than twice a year."[7] In his autobiography, Dwayne Hickman remarked that Burns could look at a scene, quickly identify any problem, and come up with the perfect solution.[8] Like he did on his own show, Burns would also meet with the writers of *The Bob Cummings Show* to provide input on the scripts. Amateau recalled that, while working on the Cummings show, George would "sit in, walk out, take phone calls, have meetings, come back, go out to lunch."[9]

1955 TV Season: Setting the Themes

Most of the episodes in the initial season were directed by Amateau and written by Henning and Bill Manhoff. Manhoff would later author the play and movie *The Owl and the Pussycat.* Laurmac Productions produced the first 148 episodes with Cummings and Burns each owning 37.5 percent of the company and Paul Henning owning the remaining 25 percent. The name Laurmac was a hybrid of Laurel and McCadden.

The first-season episodes pretty much set the themes as they related to Bob's sister Margaret and his nephew Chuck for the remainder of the series run. In the first episode "Calling Dr. Baxter," co-directed by Fred De Cordova, the first scene is of Schultzy dressed as a gorilla for one of Bob's photo shoots. In a surreal moment, Mrs. Anderson, one of Bob's customers, comes to his office to pick up photos, sees Schultzy in the gorilla costume, and comes to believe that Bob's assistant really is a highly trained gorilla who can cook and drive a car. In the meantime, Margaret receives a letter from an old flame, Dr. Tony Baxter (Frank Wilcox). Bob takes glamour photos of Margaret, and Schultzy mails them to Dr. Baxter hoping that he might marry Margaret. Schultzy thinks that if Margaret marries, that would encourage Bob to marry *her.* After Baxter flies to California to visit Margaret, everyone finds that he is already married. Meanwhile, Chuck wants to go steady with Francine Williams (Diane Jergens). Bob advises Chuck to focus on his education and not on girls, basically saying, "Do as I say, not as I do," because at the end of the episode Chuck sees his uncle fawning over his attractive models. The themes of Margaret's love life and Chuck's upbringing with Bob not wanting Margaret to act like him but secretly flattered when Chuck acted like him, were the subjects of many other episodes.

The episode "Bob to the Rescue or Unhand My Sister, You Cad" introduced Paul Fonda (Lyle Talbot), an airline pilot and Bob's friend from the

Air Force. Fonda was like Bob in his pursuit of women. However, much to Bob's dismay, Fonda wanted to pursue Margaret. The real Paul Fonda was a friend of Paul Henning's; they met when both worked on CBS Radio in Kansas City.

To be a role model for Chuck, Bob attempts but doesn't succeed in staying away from women in "Bob Gives Up Girls." Both Bob and Chuck acknowledge they need women in their lives. However, while Bob was promiscuous, he didn't want Chuck to imitate him in this respect.

Other themes during the first season included Bob's platonic relationship with Schultzy, despite her not-so-hidden desire for Bob. In the second episode, their relationship goes south when Bob hires an attractive young woman instead of one with extensive experience to help Schultzy in the office. This episode, "Hiring a Receptionist," introduced another recurring character, plain-looking bird-watcher Pamela Livingstone (Nancy Kulp), a woman with excellent secretarial skills, who pursued Bob even more forcefully than Schultzy did. The original ending had Collins harshly rejecting and insulting Pamela. Burns had the ending rewritten to be more sensitive towards the Livingstone character.[10] In the revised ending, Bob kisses Pamela. She evaluates the kiss and asks for another. After the second kiss, Pamela says, "No thanks," and walks away, showing her snubbing Bob instead of the other way around.

In many episodes, Bob tries to fix Schultzy up with another man to get her mind off having an affair with him. In the last episode of the season, "Bob Glamorizes Schultzy," Collins makes over Schultzy to pique the interest of sailor Frank Krenshaw (Dick Wesson) who has come to find the girl whose legs were shown in a magazine photo Bob took. Wesson's character appeared periodically on the Cummings show as Schultzy's boyfriend. He also co-wrote several episodes and became a regular on *The People's Choice*, another comedy produced by Burns.

In the rather surreal episode "Choosing Miss Coffee Break," Collins tries to teach actor Bob Cummings a lesson. Bob Collins and Charlie Henley (Hal Peary) are judging a beauty contest for secretaries. The prize is a week of dates with actor Robert Cummings, whom Collins dislikes ever since Cummings convinced Bob to be his stunt double in a movie scene with Betty Grable where she pushes Collins off a roof. Bob wants the homeliest secretary to win. He convinces Pamela Livingstone to be a contestant, and he chooses her as the winner. However, Charlie selects a more attractive contestant. Collins receives a phone call from Cummings asking Bob to take his place for the week of dates. Charlie asks Cummings to break the tie vote. Cummings says he respects Collins' opinion about women, and so he casts his vote for Bob's selection. Pamela wins the contest.

Of course, the series' major theme was Bob's bachelor lifestyle and his resistance to conforming to the standards of the time (settling down and getting married). In "It's Later Than You Think," Bob's Air Force buddies Harvey Helm, Sid Dorfman, and Keith Fowler (all named after Burns' comedy writers), who are married, try to convince Bob that he is getting older and needs to settle down. Bob dreams of himself as an old man—a character that would later become Bob's Grandpa Josh Collins. This was the first of many dream sequences worked into the series. In this episode, when Bob finds that Schultzy can do the mundane tasks he needs like cooking and sewing, he decides he doesn't need to marry since Schultzy will take care of him. The idea of Collins "having his cake and eating it too" was also reflected in an episode titled "Bachelor Apartment" where another friend of Bob's thinks he should move into his own apartment, away from Margaret and Chuck, so he can throw parties whenever he wants. While Bob likes being a bachelor, he finds that living alone isn't what it's cracked up to be because of noisy neighbors and having to do his own cooking. In the end, he moves back with his sister and his nephew.

In an episode "The Air Corps versus Marriage," Bob's buddies Harvey Helm and Sid Dorfman again try to convince him to marry. Harvey sends Bob a fake telegram saying that all single reserve officers are being called to active duty to the North Pole. However, Bob learns that the telegram is a fake and tells his friends that he was planning to marry until he read the telegram which he says didn't mention "unmarried" men. Bob then invites them home to see his intended—a stripper who comes on to Harvey and Sid. The character of the much-married and henpecked Harvey Helm played by King Donovan—Roger from the *Burns and Allen* series— appeared in several episodes run as a counterpoint to playboy Bob.

1955–56 TV Season: Introducing Grandpa

The episodes this season continued to be directed by Rod Amateau and written by Paul Henning along with William Cowley, Shirley Gordon,

Bill Manhoff, and Phil Shuken. Cowley would subsequently create the TV version of *Hazel* with Peggy Chandler. Gordon, one of the first female writers hired to work on a TV sitcom, would later pen episodes of *My Three Sons* and *The Courtship of Eddie's Father*. Shuken, a former musician with the Paul Whiteman Band, had previously been a writer for the television series *My Friend Irma* starring Marie Wilson. He went on to help write the pilot for *Mister Ed* as well as several scripts for Paul Henning's *The Beverly Hillbillies*.

The *Bob Cummings Show* producers wanted to move it from 10:30 p.m. to an earlier hour so more teenagers could view it. This prompted a move from NBC to CBS beginning with the July 7, 1955, episode. The sitcom was slotted at 8:00 p.m. Thursdays opposite *Life Is Worth Living* on ABC and *You Bet Your Life* on NBC.

In the season opener "Bob Rescues Mrs. Neemeyer," Mrs. Neemeyer (Marjorie Bennett) is an older woman whom, in this episode, Bob rescues from a guy after her money. She becomes attracted to charming Bob and wants to pose for him in a bathing suit. Showing his sensitivity toward a veteran actress who had begun her career in silent films, normally thrifty Mr. Burns instructed his wardrobe department to have Ms. Bennett make her own choice of oversized swimwear from an expensive Beverly Hills shop.[11]

Several of the 1955–56 episodes involved the character of Kay Michaels (Lola Albright) as a potential love interest for Bob. The character first appeared in "Bob Meets Fonda's Sister," the third episode of the season. She is not really Fonda's sister but an actress that Fonda enlists to play his sister and have Bob date, to show Bob how it feels when the shoe is on the other foot. When Bob finds that Kay is Paul's sister, he becomes very afraid until he learns that it is all a ruse. Bob and Kay plan to get Paul and Margaret married off in "Wedding, Wedding, Who's Having the Wedding," while Paul and Margaret try to do the same for Bob and Kay.

Tab Hunter guest starred on "The Letter," in which Bob receives a letter from Kay who is on location making a movie in Death Valley. Before opening her letter, he decides to write Kay a response including a love poem he copies from a book. When he finally opens Kay's letter, he sees that it simply contains a news article "Man Bites Lizard" along with a short note telling Bob that she will see him soon. Bob tries to get his letter back from the postman but fails. While at his masseur's, he fantasizes about flying to

Death Valley to retrieve his letter with Kay so enamored of him that she turns down a date with Tab Hunter. Chuck later informs his uncle that his letter was returned because of insufficient postage. When Kay returns from Death Valley to see Bob, she says that he promised to write first and produces a lengthy letter that she was writing to him. However, since Bob had Schultzy burn his letter, he has no evidence he was writing to Kay. In the end, Tab Hunter comes to pick up Kay and take her away while reciting the love poem Bob put in his letter.

Bob's pursuit of attractive women sometimes led to a comedy of errors like in a *Burns and Allen* episode. In "Bob Avoids Another Niece," Margaret thinks Bob should hire Mrs. Neemeyer's attractive niece to help Schultzy, but Schultzy wants him to hire Bertha Krause (Kathleen Freeman), a switchboard operator for McCadden Corporation (another inside reference). He gets the two confused and thinks that Bertha is the niece and the woman named Helen is the less-than-attractive switchboard operator. Bob phones Bertha believing she is the model and invites her for an interview. Meanwhile, Mrs. Neemeyer comes by and informs Bob that her niece is shy and afraid of Bob's reputation as a ladies' man. Bob thinks that he can scare the niece away from being interested in the job by coming on to her. When Bertha arrives, Bob thinks she is the niece and flirts with her, but she likes the flirtation and begins kissing Bob passionately. Bob's son Robert Cummings, Jr. had a small role as a newspaper boy.

Episodes were not always about Bob pursuing the other sex or the other sex coming on to him. Cummings' real-life association with the Air Force was acknowledged in many shows such as when Bob encourages Chuck and his friends to join the Air National Guard instead of the Navy in "The Air Force versus the Navy." In "The Boys Join Up," Bob helps a short friend of Chuck's become a pilot. Brigadier Gen. Clarence Shoop and his wife, actress Julie Bishop, appeared in this episode. As a colonel, Shoop had been Cummings' commanding officer in real life when Bob was in the Air Force.[12] Bishop had co-starred with Bob on his previous sitcom *My Hero*.

This season introduced Grandpa Collins, basically an older version of Bob when it came to women but also a little like Gracie Allen in his literal interpretation of things. Grandpa's physical appearance was based on Cummings' real grandfather, who lived to be more than 100. As Grandpa Collins, Cummings appeared with gray hair, glasses, and a moustache and spoke using an old man's voice.

In "Grandpa's Christmas Visit," the old codger's first appearance on the series, he celebrates the holidays with Bob, Margaret, and Chuck and tires everyone out with the pace he keeps. Margaret wants to slow him down, and so Bob fixes him up with elderly Mrs. Taylor for a quiet evening of checkers. When Mrs. Taylor comes by to meet Grandpa, Bob also stops in with his date—an attractive model, of course. Grandpa assumes that Bob's date is for him, and they go out together, leaving Bob with the elderly woman. Later in the season, in an episode that was essentially another advertisement for the Air Force, Grandpa gets in trouble for flying his World War I plane over the Air Force Base in Joplin. Bob wants the old gentleman to stop, but he persists in flying with his girlfriend Dixie (Bea Benaderet) in "Scramble for Grandpa." The Air Force finally is able to stop Grandpa from flying over the base when it convinces Dixie and him to volunteer for the Air Force ground observer corps.

Rosemary DeCamp thought that Bob's character of Grandpa was the most memorable acting in the series. "His makeup took three hours, and when he came on the set he was another person. The voice, the walk, the mannerisms were so far from Cummings, we almost found ourselves complaining to him about working conditions and hours."[13]

Concerning Bob's pursuit of the opposite sex, Bob temporarily gets tired of spending all of his time with beautiful women. In "Too Many Women," he decides to get away from it all at a mountain cabin with Paul Fonda. In the following week's episode, Bob and Fonda become "Snowbound" in the mountain cabin with the Air Force unable to rescue them for a few days. Bob's lack of interest in women doesn't last long. He begins dreaming of being with models, while Fonda dreams of eating food. Meanwhile, Schultzy starts receiving gifts of nylon stockings from different models so that she will call them first when Bob gets back, thinking that he will be desperate to see them. Bob amuses Fonda with stories of him teaching women to fly planes, and one of the models wants to be with Bob so much that she crash lands her plane near the cabin. Fonda, unaware that the injured pilot is a woman, goes for help, but Bob knows the pilot is one of his models. However, before Bob and the model can fool around, the Air Force rescues them.

The Bob Cummings Show was nominated for an Emmy for Best Comedy during the season but lost to *The Phil Silvers Show*. Cummings was nominated for Best Comedy Actor but lost to Silvers. Other nominations went to Ann B. Davis for Best Supporting Actress and to Rod Amateau for best directing; neither won.

1956–57 TV Season: A Spinoff and a Crossover

The episodes produced during this season were directed by Amateau, Norman Tokar, and Bob Cummings. Most episodes were penned by Paul Henning, Shirley Gordon and Phil Shuken with Dick Wesson co-writing a few.

As Rosemary DeCamp wrote about Cummings' directing ability, he "knew exactly what he wanted and could show us how to do it. It may not have been what we wanted, but he was the sole arbiter on the set—by reason of his investment, his leading role, and finally by becoming the only director who could successfully direct himself 26 consecutive weeks a year."[14] Cummings being both the star of the series and its director meant increased income for him.

This season featured one of the first proposed sitcom spinoffs and one of the first crossover episodes with the cast from *The Burns and Allen Show*. Other episodes continued to deal with Bob Collins' rejection of marriage and with his various girl-chasing plans going awry.

The season opener had a big-name guest star—something rare, at the time, for a Burns series. Grandpa Collins informs Bob he is going to marry Dixie, this time played by Lurene Tuttle, after he kneels in front of her to apologize for kissing a beauty contest winner and she thinks he is proposing. He doesn't marry Dixie but as a result of the usual comedy of errors, Bob flies to Joplin while Grandpa comes to Hollywood and meets Zsa Zsa Gabor, whom Bob has been trying to photograph.

In "Bob Tangles with Ruthie," another episode involving fantasy sequences, Bob's influence on Chuck is questioned by Ruthie (Mary Lawrence), Harvey Helm's wife. Ruthie protests when Chuck keeps her niece Carol Henning (Olive Sturgess) out until 2:00 a.m. one night. Bob is taken aback by her opinion of him. In preparing for a photo shoot about Cleopatra, Bob fantasizes that Ruthie is Cleopatra, that he is Caesar, and that Harvey is Marc Antony. While Marc Antony confesses that he is a prisoner of love, Caesar declares that he will never be a slave to Cleopatra. In the fantasy, Bob as Caesar kisses Ruthie, and she becomes his slave. After the dream sequence, Harvey leaves a message at Bob's office to inform Ruthie that he has to fly to Reno to close a furniture deal; Bob sees an opportunity to get back at Ruthie for her opinion of him as a role model. He has Schultzy tell Ruthie only that Harvey is flying to Reno, giving her the impression that he is getting a divorce. Ruthie promises Bob to be a different person if he can get Harvey back, but she subsequently learns the truth.

The character of Carol Henning was introduced as Chuck's new girlfriend when Diane Jergens, who had played his previous love interest, left the series for other projects. Carol Henning was the name of one of Paul Henning's real-life daughters. Olive Sturgess recalls seeing George Burns

Dwayne Hickman with Olive Sturgess. Sturgess' last television appearance was in 1979 on the police series *The Rookies*. Photograph courtesy of Olive Sturgess Anderson.

watching the filming on the Cummings show on occasion and that Cummings ran a "tight ship." She remarked, "You had to know your lines. Be on time and be ready."[15]

Chuck was the subject of many episodes during this season, one of which was a pilot for his own series. In October 1956, Dwayne Hickman as Chuck appeared on an episode of *The Adventures of Ozzie and Harriet*. That series was filmed at General Service Studios as was the Cummings show. In the *Ozzie and Harriet* episode, even though Hickman's character hadn't gone to college yet on *The Bob Cummings Show*, he was seen on campus with David Nelson where they are both members of the Kappa Sigma fraternity.

On the Cummings series, Chuck graduates from high school and begins looking for a college to attend. Bob starts meddling in Chuck's selection of a school in "Bob Picks a College" when Ruthie Helm wants Carol to go to an all-girls school and Chuck decides to go to an all-male college. In the end, after Bob realizes the two colleges are next to one another, both Carol and Chuck go with their original choice.

"Chuck at College," broadcast on February 28, 1957, represented one of the first attempts to spin off a featured character on a television series into a show of his own. The spinoff *Chuck Goes to College* was marketed to all three networks but never sold, and Hickman stayed with *The Bob Cummings Show* for most of its remaining run. In the episode, Chuck starts attending Gridley College for Men with his friend Jimmy (Jeff Silver). His girlfriend Carol is attending Beaumont College, the girls' school next door. Mr. Bassett, the guys' counselor, informs Chuck he will be under close surveillance because of his uncle's well-known reputation with women. Chuck is asked to arrange a date for an upperclassman named Madison (played by Jody McCrea, son of movie actor Joel McCrea). Knowing it is impossible for him to sneak a girl into his dorm room as requested, Chuck decides to have his roommate Jimmy dress in drag as a girl named Gertrude. Madison likes what he sees, but then Mr. Bassett arrives and looks for the girl supposedly in Chuck's room. He finds Jimmy, but not his alter ego Gertrude. Later at the malt shop, Madison asks Chuck to fix him up with Gertrude for an upcoming dance.

In "Bob Handles the College Boys," a college-themed episode aired March 28, 1957, Bob tries to teach Chuck another lesson about dating models. Margaret informs Bob that Chuck has fallen into the wrong crowd at school. But when Chuck brings home one of his new friends, Bob is impressed because Chuck's friend calls Bob "king" based on his reputation with women. After Bob discovers that Chuck is ignoring Carol and wants to date models, Bob arranges a very expensive date for Chuck and his friend knowing that they can't afford it. But after Bob leaves his wallet at home and phones Chuck to bring it to him, Chuck and his friend find the money to go on their date.

In addition to the proposed spinoff involving the Chuck character, the Cummings show also had one of the first crossovers with characters from another series. Before the episode with the characters from *Burns and Allen*, Bob's sister Margaret made some satirical remarks, worthy of George Burns, about his show with Gracie in an episode titled "Bob Clashes with

His Landlady." In that episode, Bob unsuccessfully tries to flatter his new landlady, who wants to raise his office rent. Meanwhile, Chuck's girlfriend Carol and Margaret are doing their nails in a hot pink shade and Carol says that she favors orange sherbet to which Margaret responds *a la* Gracie that she prefers eating it. Margaret says that she has been watching too much *Burns and Allen*. Carol asserts that she can't believe any woman is that dumb, and Margaret answers, "Of course not. It is written by men." One would presume that this exchange was written by Shirley Gordon, the Cummings show's only female writer.

Despite Margaret's reference to *Burns and Allen* as a fictional TV show, lo and behold, Bob Collins meets the Burnses and Mortons in a special episode. In this crossover, Collins has an appointment with accountant Harry Morton to go over his income tax deductions. Harry invites Bob to his home to work on his taxes where Bob meets Blanche. Blanche and Gracie decide to find a wife for Bob. They select Schultzy and arrange a blind date for her and Bob at the Morton home.

After the cast of *Burns and Allen* appeared on his series, Bob returned the favor by playing his character in a June 10, 1957, *Burns and Allen Show,* as noted in Chapter 3. The crossovers continued in the last season of the Cummings show during George Burns' attempt at a successful series on his own. Paul Henning maintained the concept of having casts from one series cross over to other series in the later seasons of the comedies he produced: *The Beverly Hillbillies, Petticoat Junction,* and *Green Acres.*

In other episodes of the Cummings show during this season, a recurring guest star appeared for the first time in "Bob Meets Miss Sweden." Ingrid Goude, Miss Sweden of 1957, starred in a story about Schultzy and her friends wanting Bob to fly them to a secretaries' convention in Reno. To make sure he will take them, they invite the beautiful Ingrid to go along since she is representing European secretaries there. Bob tries to put the moves on Ingrid, but she pretends to understand and speak only Swedish. Actor Gordon Scott is waiting to date her when she arrives, but Bob convinces him that she is ugly. In the end, Ingrid reveals that she can speak English and that Bob doesn't have a chance with her, unlike most women to whom Bob is attracted.

While Goude played herself on the series, another real-life character, Wally Seawell, appeared in a few episodes. Portrayed by Dan Tobin, Seawell, a real photographer in Hollywood, was, along with his mentor Paul Hesse, a technical advisor to Cummings on the series. In a May episode titled "Bob Enters a Photography Contest," Collins says he is too busy to take a photo of Chuck because he is working on his entry for an annual photography contest. Margaret takes Chuck to Seawell, Bob's rival, for the photo, which is entered in the contest. In turn, Bob takes a photo of Wally's wife for the competition. Because of a mix-up, Bob's winning photo is credited to Seawell.

Near the end of the third season, the character of Kay Michaels returned to play a joke on Bob about his marital status. In "Bob Calls Kay's Bluff," Kay tries to convince Bob that he proposed to her before she left for New York City a few years ago. When Bob learns that this is not true, he pretends he wants to marry Kay right away. Bob calls an old Air Force buddy to arrange a fake wedding ceremony, but the friend wants to have a real ceremony to take Bob out of circulation. When the friend discovers that Bob is marrying Kay, his former girlfriend, he stops the ceremony. Realizing he came very close to actually marrying Kay, Bob passes out.

Cummings was again nominated for an Emmy as Best Actor in a Comedy for the season but lost this time to Sid Caesar. Ann B. Davis lost to Pat Carroll for Best Supporting Actress.

1957–58 TV Season: The Birth of the Hillbillies

During the sitcom's fourth season, Bob Cummings directed all the episodes which were written by Paul Henning, Shirley Gordon, and Dick Wesson. Also, the series moved back to NBC on Tuesdays at 9:30 p.m. opposite *Red Skelton* on CBS and *Telephone Time* on ABC.

Many episodes featured Cummings in his dual role as Grandpa Collins. But since Cummings also directed these episodes, the result was that the Bob Collins character and the Grandpa Collins character would often get their wires crossed and end up in different locations so that both characters never appeared in the same scene.

In "Grandpa Attends the Convention," Josh Collins is in Hollywood and finds that Pamela Livingstone's grandmother had wanted to marry him when they were both young. When he sees Pamela, he mistakes her for her grandmother. Grandpa and the elder Mrs. Livingstone (Nancy Kulp in a dual role) never do get together. In a follow-up episode "Grandpa's Old

Buddy," Bob takes Mrs. Livingstone home to meet Grandpa, but the elderly gentleman has left to pick up his old friend Charley (Andy Clyde) to go to Bob's studio to meet models.

Like George Burns did on his comedy with Gracie during its final season, *The Bob Cummings Show* also attempted to satirize TV westerns which were extremely popular at the time. In another fantasy episode titled "Bob, the Gunslinger," Schultzy volunteers to be one of Bob's models and ends up playing Billy the Kid and then dressing in a horse costume for a western photo shoot. She fantasizes about the woman she would like to be: Delores Schultz, a dance hall girl in the Old West. Bob, a gunfighter, tells Delores that she is beautiful, and they kiss passionately. Meanwhile, Chuck is upset that Carol is seeing a football player. When he goes to Bob's office, two models whom Bob is dating at the same time flirt with Chuck to make Bob jealous. Chuck fantasizes about being a gunfighter (Chuck the Kid) and having a showdown with Bob, the gunslinger, over the models. Chuck, the Kid shoots Bob with water pistols to get what he wants. After the fantasy sequence, Chuck announces that he will be dating the two models. They confess that they were just using him to get back at Bob but, at the end, Bob asks Chuck to accompany him on his date with the models.

Margaret tries to teach Bob a lesson about his pursuit of the opposite sex and rejection of marriage because she continues to be concerned that her son will end up just like his uncle. She says that Bob treats women like "paper plates," discarding women after he is finished with them. In the final show of the season, "Bob's Forgotten Fiancée," Margaret tries to teach Bob a lesson about breaking up with women: she has a stewardess, Patricia Plummer (Constance Towers), another wannabe actress, pretend she is a girl from Bob's past who has come back to marry him. It seems that while Bob was in the Air Force Reserves, he would give girls friendship rings and say that if they meet in a few years, he would turn the ring into an engagement ring. When Bob meets Patricia, he can't remember her but nonetheless hurries out of town, boards a flight to Mexico City, and then sees her as the stewardess.

Another new character based on a real-life person joined the series in "Bob Meets Bill Lear." Bob arranges a golf date for Margaret with aviation inventor Bill Lear (John Archer), but Bill brings along another woman whom Bob tries to monopolize so that Bill and Margaret can be together. The other woman turns out to be Bill's business manager. The real Lear, responsible for the automatic pilot and the Lear jet, was a friend of Cummings.

In a January 1958 episode that foreshadowed Paul Henning's *The Beverly Hillbillies,* Chuck dates wealthy debutante Melinda Applegate (Connie Stevens, who would later star with George Burns in *Wendy and Me*). Margaret prepares a special dinner for the couple with Schultzy pretending to be a maid, but Chuck has second thoughts about Melinda seeing where he lives after she says that poor neighborhoods outside of her estate depress her. Chuck disappoints his mother by not bringing Melinda to dinner and continues to put on airs which further upsets his uncle and mother. To teach Chuck a lesson, Schultzy calls to invite Melinda to meet Chuck's family. Bob has everyone dress as hillbillies in "Bob Goes Hillbilly" since he and Margaret came from Joplin, Missouri, near the Ozarks. When Melinda sees the family, she quickly leaves, and Chuck resumes dating Carol.

Some have pointed out similarities between certain characters on *The Bob Cummings Show* and characters on *The Beverly Hillbillies* since both comedies were created by Henning. Grandpa Collins has been likened to Granny; Chuck MacDonald to Jethro Bodine; and Pamela Livingstone to Jane Hathaway. The latter comparison is particularly relevant since both characters were portrayed by Nancy Kulp.[16] Also, Joi Lansing, who appeared as a model on several episodes of the Cummings show, played the wife of musician Lester Flatt on episodes of *The Beverly Hillbillies*. Furthermore, Henning used several actors who had been featured on *The Burns and Allen Show* in various roles on *The Beverly Hillbillies,* the most famous being Bea Benaderet who played cousin Pearl Bodine before getting her own series, *Petticoat Junction,* also created by Henning. Both Raymond Bailey and Frank Wilcox, who had appeared numerous times on *The Burns and Allen Show* in different roles, portrayed banker Milburn Drysdale and oil company representative John Brewster, respectively, on *Hillbillies*.

In its July 24, 1958, issue, *Variety* reported that McCadden was looking for the right format for a spinoff from *The Bob Cummings Show* starring Ann B. Davis. However, according to Davis, this was apparently just a "feeler" to see if there was any interest in such a spinoff and apparently there was not.[17] (Davis later starred as Alice on *The Brady Bunch*.) There was also a report that a spinoff was planned for Rosemary DeCamp, but that never materialized either.[18]

Again, for the season, *The Bob Cummings Show* lost the Emmy for Best Comedy Series to *The Phil Silvers Show,* and Cummings lost the race for Best Actor in a Drama or Comedy to Robert Young from *Father Knows Best.* Ann B. Davis won the award for Best Supporting Actress.

1958–59 TV Season: Guest Stars and a New Regular

LHM (Laurel, Henning, McCadden) Productions made most of the final season's episodes. Cummings' share of LHM was 45 percent, Henning's share 30 percent, and Burns' share shrank to 25 percent. In its final season, Bob continued to direct each episode with Paul Henning and Dick Wesson as the writers. The comedy followed *The George Burns Show,* Burns' sitcom without Gracie. The final season was characterized by many guest star appearances and, near the end of the season, by the introduction of a new regular, which may have changed the direction of the show if it had been renewed.

The premiere episode picked up the story that began in the last season with Schultzy leaving Bob's employ for a job at a missile factory to meet some eligible men. To replace her, Bob hired a diner waitress, Marian Billington (Barbara Nichols), who turned out to be the stereotypical "dumb blonde." Of course, Collins never learned about hiring attractive women with no experience as his assistant. At her new job, Schultzy is harassed by a muscle-bound guy. Since Bob regrets hiring Marian and wants to get Schultzy back, he gets rid of Marian and "Bob and Schultzy Reunite." However, in the following week's episode "Bob and the Dumb Blonde," Margaret has Marian watch the office while Schultzy is preparing a meal for her boyfriend Frank Krenshaw, who is on leave from the Navy. Marian makes a play for Bob while he is trying to romance a new model. Bob wants Margaret to convince the model that Marian's flirtation was just a joke. Margaret says she will do this if Bob convinces Frank to marry Schultzy. Bob makes up a story about being miserable as a single man and missing a chance to marry Marian. The model then sees Marian kissing Bob after Frank told her that Bob wanted to marry her.

Bob Cummings as Grandpa returned in the November episode "Grandpa Clobbers the Air Force." Because the Air Force rejected him as a recruit, Grandpa bombs a base near Joplin with bottles of hard cider. Bob phones Grandpa to order him to stop. In response, Grandpa decides to fly to California and bomb Nelson Field. The general at Nelson Field is up for a promotion and has asked Bob to take pictures when Grandpa arrives at the field and begins bombing. The general forces Bob to go up in a biplane and engage in a dogfight with Grandpa to get him to stop. However, after Bob crash lands, the general surrenders to Grandpa. This episode, written by Paul Henning and Dick Wesson, was nominated for an Emmy for Best Writing for a Comedy Series—the only time the writers of a Burns-produced series were ever so acknowledged. Henning and Wesson lost the award to Jack Benny's writers.

As a follow-up to Grandpa bombing Nelson Field, General Tallman puts "Bob in the Brig" where he ends up digging ditches and cleaning out stalls. Grandpa takes over for Bob at the studio photographing models. When Bob finally has a chance to phone Schultzy to let her know where he is, Grandpa overhears and vows to resume bombing. However, another general confiscates Grandpa's plane which Bob shoots down, thinking Grandpa is in it.

The Bob Cummings Show had several special guest stars during the season. As mentioned before, George Burns' frugality when it came to producing his own series meant that he didn't usually have guest stars on *The Burns and Allen Show*. Apparently, because Burns' share in the final season's episodes was only 25 percent, Bob Cummings, in an effort to boost ratings, brought in a lot of guest stars in the final season. In "Bob Helps Anna Maria," he makes a date with Anna Maria Alberghetti and finds that she is not the "skinny little kid" he once knew. In "Bob Judges a Beauty Contest," an Air Force general asks Bob to get Peter Lawford to judge a contest of females representing fifty-three different Air Force bases. Bob tries to convince the general's wife to let him be the judge instead of Lawford. Lawford made a cameo appearance in this episode in exchange for Cummings' appearance on Lawford's series *The Thin Man*. In "Bob Clashes with Steve Allen," Bob rids himself of a pesky blonde by sending her to New York to appear on *The Steve Allen Show* as a billboard girl. Bob tries to get Art Linkletter to emcee the annual charity dinner at Margaret's women's club so that Bob can be master of ceremonies at a dinner given by the model's guild in "Bob versus Linkletter." In "Bob Meets Mamie Van Doren," the actress asks Schultzy for help in gaining practical experience as a secretary for an upcoming movie role; Mamie is warned that she won't learn a thing if Bob sees her. She deglamorizes herself so he cannot recognize her. In the last episode of the season, "Bob Clashes with Ken," Ken Murray learns that Bob is responsible for the girls in his show keeping late hours.

Crossovers between *The Bob Cummings Show* and *The George Burns Show* (which preceded it on NBC) were common. Harry Von Zell appeared in a two-part story where "Bob Helps Martha" hook up with Von Zell, who really prefers Latin model Rosita (Elena Verdugo). In the second part, George Burns pays a surprise visit to Bob and creates an uproar in "Bob Helps Von Zell." Schultzy has to pinch hit as Rosita to try to save the romance between Von Zell and her friend Martha (Rose Marie).

Several episodes still revolved around the series main theme of pursuing the opposite sex and attacking marriage. In "Bob Restores Male Supremacy," Bob thinks that Harvey and his son are henpecked. He has them spend a weekend with Paul Fonda and him while Margaret is away and makes Harvey commanding officer of the group so his son can see his dad giving orders instead of always taking them from Ruthie. However, Harvey gets carried away with his position of authority. Bob calls Ruthie, giving her the impression that there are a lot of girls at his house so she will come and get her husband and son. In one of the last episodes of the series, "Bob, the Last Bachelor," Collins finds that he is the last of his poker-playing buddies who isn't married.

The rock 'n' roll success of Ricky Nelson on *The Adventures of Ozzie and Harriet* had an impact on *The Bob Cummings Show* as it did with Ronnie Burns on *The Burns and Allen Show*. Chuck auditions as a recording star, but Bob doesn't think he has a good voice. Chuck's friend gets Ozzie Nelson to stop by to hear Chuck sing. To have Bob become interested in Chuck's talent, Ozzie says that Chuck is no Ricky Nelson and that, since his talent is inherited, Bob's family must have no talent. Collins is upset over these comments, and "Bob Becomes a Stage Uncle." Chuck makes a recording, and, after George Burns stops by to ask Bob to photograph Ronnie Burns' royalty check for his son's recording, Bob sees how much money a hit record can make. He decides to get DJ Fred Beck to promote Chuck's recording of "Pretty Baby" in "Bob Butters Beck—Beck Butters Better." In the following week's episode, "Collins the Crooner," everyone except Bob thinks it is great idea if he also makes a record. Schultzy, Martha, and Bertha want to be Bob's back-up singers The Bob O'Links, and Harvey Helm has a merchandising tie-in for the album. Because of Bob's reluctance to record, Harvey says that he got Chuck to replace him, which makes Bob jealous. He decides to record in his car with a model on Mulholland Drive.

This season's episode about Margaret continuing to dislike Bob's influence on her son, titled "Bob Plays Margaret's Game," had Schultzy dressing as a man to date Margaret. In the story, Bob advises his sister that she needs to date more and to stop criticizing him. She pretends to take her brother's advice and dates Pierre, a gigolo who is really Schultzy in disguise. When Chuck subsequently overhears a phone conversation between his mother and Schultzy revealing that Schultzy is Pierre, he informs his uncle in return for some cash. Bob then decides to double date with Margaret and Pierre to call Margaret's bluff. But, in return for more money from his mother, Chuck blabs that Bob knows what Schultzy is doing, and Chuck then pretends to be Pierre to go on the double date with his mother and uncle.

Schultzy continued to try to rope Bob into marriage with her. The opening scene of "Bob's Boyhood Love Image" showed Bob marrying Schultzy, at least in her dreams. Schultzy had read a book that says that men are looking to marry the type of girl with whom they were childhood sweethearts. She asks Margaret for details about Bob's childhood sweethearts so she can assume their traits. While looking through Bob's family photo album, she sees pictures of Bob's childhood girlfriends, a Southern belle and a tomboy. She assumes the persona of each, but Collins is not impressed.

Even if this season hadn't been the final one for *The Bob Cummings Show,* it would have been the last for Dwayne Hickman as Chuck, since Hickman had gotten the lead role in *The Many Loves of Dobie Gillis* which was due to premiere during the 1959–60 TV season. In the last "Chuck-centered" episode, "The King and the Chorus Girl," Chuck falls for Las Vegas chorus girl Beverly Bradford and hopes to marry her. The chorus girl really wants Chuck to introduce her to Bob so he can take publicity photos that she can show to a producer like he had done for actress Jayne Mansfield. Bob sees through her and talks Beverly into using a "special" makeup which causes her to look much older. Having been taught by Bob to only look at surface beauty, Chuck sees Beverly in the makeup and quickly loses interest in her.

The producers decided to reduce Hickman's appearances in the last half of the 1958–59 season, and they introduced a new character, six-year-old Tammy Johnson (Tammy Murihugh), to take his place. In somewhat of a change in character, Bob Collins becomes less of a playboy and more a father figure to Tammy. In "Bob, the Baby Sitter," Margaret and Mrs. Engel (Jean Willes) babysit Tammy while her father is working. When Margaret forgets it is her turn to babysit and goes away for a weekend, Bob has to look after Tammy which ruins his evening plans with a beautiful girl. He finds a babysitter (Sheila James, who later starred with Dwayne Hickman on *Dobie Gillis*) who turns out to be irresponsible. Bob subsequently has one of his models babysit, but when his date arrives and sees the other model, they both want to take care of the girl.

Tammy Murihugh was signed to a five-year contract. When *The Bob Cummings Show* was canceled after this season, there was discussion about a new show starring Murihugh; Paul Henning thought that a dramatic-type series might be a possibility. A new production company with Burns, Cummings, and Henning each owning one-third was proposed, but it appears that no pilot was ever produced. Murihugh failed to avoid the curse of child actors when they mature. As an adult, she became an exotic dancer and was later found guilty of murdering her abusive husband.

Tammy appeared in several episodes during the last half of the 1958–59 season. Bob thinks that Tammy's dad should get married, and so "Bob Seeks a Wife" for him. However, one of his models assumes that it is Bob who is seeking a wife and does her best to demonstrate her domestic skills including preparing a meal for Grandpa Collins. "Bob Buys a Dog" named Hilda for Tammy so that Tammy will play with the dog and not go to Mrs. Engel's. He lets Mrs. Engel think that Hilda is really a little girl from whom Tammy cannot be separated. In "Bob, the Matchmaker," Bob pictures Tammy's dad Fred (Robert Clarke) and Margaret as the ideal couple. But he gets the idea that Fred is dating a woman that Tammy calls Aunt Jenny and so decides to date her himself to advance plans for Margaret's romance. Jenny turns out to be Fred's rotund sister. Bob is embarrassed to be with her as she overeats at a restaurant. In another episode, Bob wants to have western star George Montgomery teach him to be a cowboy to impress Tammy in "Bob Goes Western." "Bob Tangles with Engel" when she keeps Tammy out late with the Bluebirds. Collins thinks Engel is the leader of a girlie act called the Bluebirds, unaware that they are junior Camp Fire girls. When he learns this, he wants to repair his relationship with Mrs. Engel and, since she is interested in sailing, he claims to be an expert seaman even though he suffers from seasickness. Bob begins to date Tammy's pediatrician, Dr. Lisa Beaumont (Anne Jeffreys), in "Bob and the Pediatrician." After he discovers that his main competition for Dr. Beaumont is his own family physician, he tries to interest his doctor in Margaret.

Bob and his show were both nominated for Emmys during the final season but lost to Jack Benny and his program. Ann B. Davis won her second Emmy for Best Supporting Actress in a Comedy.

After the end of the series, reruns were sold to ABC and aired every day of the week for a few years in the early 1960s under the title *Love That Bob*.

Always a health food advocate, Cummings wrote a book titled *Stay Young and Vital* (1960) about his diet and exercise recommendations for positive health. He subsequently starred in two short-lived CBS series, *The New Bob Cummings Show*, a comedy-adventure series, and the sitcom *My Living Doll*. He reprised his role of Bob Collins one final time in an episode of *Here's Lucy*, "Lucy's Punctured Romance." In the February 2, 1972, episode, Kim (Lucie Arnaz) is told by the milkman that Bob Collins always has a lot of girls going in and out of his apartment and suggests that she break up her mother's relationship with him. Kim enlists Uncle Harry's help in convincing Bob, who has been invited to dinner at Lucy's place, that Lucy is a deaf alcoholic who has been married six times. After Bob scurries off, he comes back, and Lucy explains what Kim and Uncle Harry were trying to do. It turns out that Bob Collins is no longer a photographer but is now a representative for a cosmetics company and the girls going in and out of his apartment are employees.

Cummings paid one more visit to *Here's Lucy* during the series' fifth season when he played an antique dealer named Robert Henning in "Lucy and Her Genuine Twinby." The last name Henning was a tribute to the creator of *The Bob Cummings Show*, Paul Henning. Bob Cummings passed away in December 1990 at age eighty.

5

George and the Wisecracking Dog—
The People's Choice

The third successful comedy series Burns helped to produce was *The People's Choice* starring Jackie Cooper as Socrates "Sock" Miller, originally an ornithologist for the government's Bureau of Fish and Wildlife specializing in tracking migratory birds. Because his job entailed a lot of travel, Sock lived in a trailer with his Aunt Augusta "Gus" Bennett (Margaret Irving). Amanda "Mandy" Peoples (Patricia Breslin), Sock's girlfriend, happened to be the daughter of Mayor John Peoples (Paul Maxey) of New City, California, located near Los Angeles. During the course of the series' three-year run, Sock went from being an ornithologist to a lawyer to the manager of a housing development. Sock and Mandy's relationship evolved from dating to marriage to preparing for a baby in the comedy's final season. The one constant on the series was Sock's dog Cleo.

The People's Choice was Cooper's first television series. As a child actor, he had appeared in films in the 1930s and 1940s such as *The Champ* and *Treasure Island*. As an adult, Cooper had parts in Broadway plays before landing the *People's Choice* role.

Sock Miller was probably the most "normal" of all the lead characters in the comedies Burns produced. Miller was somewhat a naïve fellow who seemed to love animals more than people in many cases. He was pursued by Mandy Peoples and inadvertently became involved in the politics of New City. *The People's Choice* would have been a typical romantic comedy exploring the relationship of Sock with Mandy and her father if not for one thing: Sock's pet basset hound Cleo, the wisecracking character on this fantasy series. Cleo appeared in almost every scene. Much like George Burns did on his own series, speaking directly to viewers unbeknownst to the other characters, Cleo inhabited a parallel world and voiced observations about herself and the events of each episode directly to the audience.

The voice of Cleo was provided by actress Mary Jane Croft. In addition to Cleo's breaking of the fourth wall, Cooper would usually speak to viewers before the beginning of an episode, telling them want to expect.

During an episode, Cleo would comment (in a close-up) on such topics as her love life, usually with bad puns: "I just got a telegram from my fiancé—a poodle. He got clipped today and so now everything is off." Cleo was a frustrated single female worried about her weight and looking for a mate. She would advertise: "If there are any bachelor dogs in the audience, I'm an old maid and my father's loaded." And she would try to trap male dogs with a sign reading FREE LUNCH. When a male dog came by and went into a cage holding food, Cleo attempted unsuccessfully to pull the cage door shut, thinking out loud, "Why can't I learn to shut my trap?" She thought of placing an ad in the newspaper for a mate: "Wanted: Handsome boy basset to marry girl basset. Object: Bassinets." When Sock told

Cleo, Sock Miller's pet basset hound, giving a "lecture." The dog's real name was Bernadette.

her to get off the top of the stove in his trailer, Cleo thought out loud in western slang, "Pardon me but every so often I get a hankerin' to ride the range."

Cleo was a little jealous of Mandy, making observations like "I don't like her, her uncle's a dog catcher." When Mandy shows Sock her new swim suit, Cleo observes, "I have a collar that covers more than that." She would also insult Mandy's rotund father, Mayor Peoples. When the mayor says he got carried away, Cleo thought, "Now there's a moving job."

In his autobiography, Cooper professed no real love for *The People's Choice* and acknowledged that Cleo was the series' main attraction. "It was really a gimmick show, and I was the star in name, but really I was supporting the gimmick."[1] However, he did admit that making TV films for Burns' company "was an honest, profit-making business."[2]

Irving Brecher, the creator of *The People's Choice,* had previously written screenplays for two Marx Brothers films, *At the Circus* and *Go West,* as well as for the movie *Meet Me in St. Louis.* He had also created the radio and television comedy *The Life of Riley.* Before *The People's Choice,* Brecher had worked with Burns on the movie *Somebody Loves Me,* about vaudevillians Blossom Seeley and Benny Fields—friends of Burns from his vaudeville days. To help Seeley and Fields financially, Burns got Paramount to produce a film based on their romance and careers, and Brecher wrote and directed it.

While Brecher conceived *The People's Choice,* Burns helped to finance the series. Brecher's agent from the William Morris Agency convinced him that he could not afford to finance the pilot for *The People's Choice* by himself and that he should seek Burns' help in return for 50 percent ownership of the sitcom. Reportedly, Burns invested $45,000 in the series.[3] Following is Brecher's account of how he sold the show to Burns:

> George, this first program opens with a young guy, Jackie Cooper, as Socrates "Sock" Miller. Sock works for the U.S. Bureau of Wildlife and he lives in a trailer.... Sock studies the lives of endangered species, which we see some throughout the series. At this particular moment, as we fade in, he is walking through the woods followed by a dog. You may know the type; it's a basset hound.... Sock Miller reaches a tall tree, followed by that basset hound. Sock takes out his hunting knife, and looking around to make sure no one is watching, he carves a heart in the trunk of the tree. He carves "S Loves M" in the heart. And then the dog says—-

Burns interrupted. "The dog says?"

> Yes. The dog says: "I don't know what he sees in her."
> Burns said: "The dog says?"
> Well, her lips don't move. We hear what she says in her *mind.* She throws the lines like Groucho.
> Burns turned to his brother and said: "Willie [*sic*], give Irv the money."[4]

No doubt the idea of a wisecracking dog reminded George of a novelty act from his days in vaudeville. Burns later confided to Brecher that the

William Morris Agency probably brought him to George to try to entice Burns to leave his current talent agency MCA and return to William Morris, who had represented George and Gracie during their vaudeville and radio days.[5]

Brecher wrote almost all of Cleo's lines. In addition to expressing her thoughts to viewers, Cleo would have to do various tricks during an episode, such as dancing with a stuffed basset hound or standing on her head imitating a yoga position. Frank Inn, the man responsible for other famous animal actors like Benji and *Green Acres'* Arnold the Pig, trained Cleo. Commenting on Cleo in the *TV Guide* article "Cleo Gets in Her Licks," Cooper, who began directing *The People's Choice* in its second season, said, "The only time I get provoked with her is when I'm directing and time is running out. A dog can't concentrate more than a few minutes at a time. Cleo is usually perfect on the first take, but if one of the actors blows a line and we have to do it over again, Cleo gets bored."[6] To help prevent Cleo from getting bored, the producers used a stuffed version of the dog to light the scenes.

Norden Productions produced the comedy. The word "Norden" was derived from Brecher's wife's hometown of Norfolk, Virginia, and Burns' McCadden Productions.

In thanking him for his support of *The People's Choice,* Brecher wrote to Burns stating in part: "I hope that fate, vitamins and mazel will combine to bring all the success to *The People's Choice* that your faith, encouragement and advice justifies. I can only add that I am deeply grateful for your friendship."[7]

While Burns provided financing and production facilities for *The People's Choice,* it does not appear that he would sit in on rehearsals as he did for *The Bob Cummings Show.* For the most part, he seems to have let Brecher run his own series since the pair's instincts about what was funny were about the same. However, Burns apparently did read and critique the *People's Choice* scripts. George related the following about his participation:

> I would read a script ... and know something's wrong. But I don't know how to fix it. So I go out to Hillcrest [Country Club], I wander around the clubhouse until I spot some $250,000 comedy writer. I tell him the story. I say it's great. He looks at me like I've got two heads. To show how smart he is, he points out how it can be fixed. Now I've got $250,000 worth of comedy brains for nothing.[8]

Burns added, "I go back to the office and call Irv Brecher. I tell him how to fix his script, but I don't say where I got my ideas. And everybody tells everybody what a genius I am."[9]

Although this story fits with Burns' frugality when it came to TV production, one is not sure how accurate this account is, keeping in mind that he never let the facts get in the way of a funny story and understanding that he considered himself a good story "doctor." Moreover, it was probably rare in the 1950s to find comedy writers worth $250,000.

The People's Choice was the most fanciful of the sitcoms George Burns produced in the 1950s. In addition to the concept of a dog expressing her thoughts directly to viewers, *The People's Choice* made liberal use of fantasy sequences involving the cast. Unlike *The Burns and Allen Show* and *The Bob Cummings Show,* there were no crossover episodes involving any of the stars of those series and *The People's Choice,* and there were no biographical elements from Jackie Cooper's life worked into the show. However, several of the featured actors from Burns and Allen and the Cummings show appeared on *The People's Choice.*

1955–56 TV Season: Sock—The People's Choice

During the first season, Pierre (Leonid Kinskey), a portrait painter, was Sock's neighbor in the Paradise Trailer Park where Sock and his aunt lived. Kinskey, who had played Sascha the bartender in the film *Casablanca,* replaced actor Damian O'Flynn, who originally had been cast as the neighbor. During the first season, while Mandy wanted to marry Sock, Sock kept using the excuse that he needed to be more financially secure before tying the knot. Supposedly, he wanted to complete his doctoral thesis in biology in order to earn enough money to marry Mandy, although as the series progressed, Sock's career goals kept changing.

While Brecher directed the pilot and the second episode, most of the other episodes during the season were directed by Peter Tewksbury. Describing the directors of the series, Jackie Cooper remarked,

> We did discover one good one—Peter Tewksbury—but *Father Knows Best* had a bigger budget and stole him away from us very quickly. George Burns, our boss, was very conservative in some areas ... Burns would not ... give a sizable guarantee to the writers or directors we had. So the good

ones, like Tewksbury, we lost to companies that would and did give such guarantees.[10]

The teams of Bob Fisher-Alan Lipscott and Frank Gill, Jr.-George Carleton Brown wrote most of the scripts. Lipscott had worked with Brecher on the original television version of *The Life of Riley* starring Jackie Gleason. Fisher and Lipscott had penned the premiere episode of *Make Room for Daddy* (aka *The Danny Thomas Show*) as well as scripts for *The Donna Reed Show, The Ann Sothern Show,* and *Bachelor Father.* After Lipscott's death in 1961, Fisher teamed with Arthur Marx and wrote the Broadway hit *The Impossible Years.* He also partnered with Arthur Alsberg for the series *I Dream of Jeannie* and the George Burns–produced *Mona McCluskey.* Frank Gill, Jr. and George Carleton Brown had done scripts for the Gale Storm comedy *My Little Margie* and later wrote episodes of *McHale's Navy.*

NBC's *The People's Choice* premiered at 8:30 p.m. October 6, 1955, opposite *Climax* on CBS and *Stop the Music* on ABC. The debut episode told the story of how Sock became a councilman for New City.

Similar to how Brecher described the show to Burns, in the opening scene, Sock is in the woods looking for a yellow nut hatch and sees a tree carved with the phrase "Sock Loves Cleo." The viewers, expecting a girl to appear, instead see a basset hound following Sock. The first thoughts Cleo expresses to viewers are, "Who were you expecting, Grace Kelly?" The storylines of most episodes had Cleo as a supporting character and not the focus.

The first episode introduces Roger Crutcher (John Stephenson) who is running unopposed for city council from the 5th district in New City. Pierre suggests that Sock be a write-in candidate since Crutcher wants to get rid of the trailers in his district, like the one where Aunt Gus and Sock live. Crutcher asks Mandy to go on TV and endorse him for city council. Although Mandy is in love with Sock, he doesn't want to marry her since his job requires a lot of travel and he feels he doesn't have the financial resources to support her. Sock has been instructed by the government to leave California for Ohio to view birds in that state. Because Mandy doesn't want him to leave, when she goes on TV, she encourages voters to write in Sock's name for city council. She says that since Sock wouldn't propose to her, the mayor's daughter, this demonstrates that he won't be a rubber stamp for the mayor. Mandy then shows Cleo to the viewers and says that if you find a friendly dog, you'll find a friendly owner. Sock wins as a write-in candidate but, due to Aunt Gus turning his alarm clock back at the behest of Pierre, he sleeps through the election. When he finds out he is a new councilman, Sock says he will resign. However, he changes his mind after Mandy says she was wrong to try to keep him in New City, and Sock agrees to stay. Cleo's thoughts to the viewers are, "What a revoltin' development this is," which was Chester Riley's catchphrase on the Brecher-created *The Life of Riley*. Sock is the people's choice for council and Mandy Peoples' choice for a future husband.

The second episode told "How Sock Met Mandy." Sock is looking for a yellow-necked nut hatch when he comes upon Mandy, whose car has a flat tire. Since she doesn't have a jack, he takes her back to the trailer to call her dad. Sock's boss, Miss Hilda Larson (Elvia Allman, who played the wardrobe mistress in *Burns and Allen*), comes to see him to determine if he is really working. She finds Mandy in Sock's bedroom changing clothes (a naughty neighbor boy turned on the shower while Mandy was looking around the trailer). Larson fires Sock. When Larson's boss, Dr. Sidney Baxter (Richard Deacon), comes to the trailer, he finds Larson in Sock's bedroom changing her clothes since she too got wet in the shower. Since Larson now understands what happened to Mandy, Sock gets his job back. In the end, Mandy spots the yellow nut hatch that Sock had been looking for. But, while climbing the tree to get the trap holding the bird, Sock appears and scares Mandy, and the bird escapes.

Narrated by Cleo, the December 29 episode "An Adventure of Sock" explained how she came to be Sock's pet. Having just gotten out of the Marines, Sock wants to propose to Barbara Andrews (Myrna Hansen), a girl he had corresponded with while in the service and whose father owned a bobby-pin factory. When Sock proposes, she accepts. Sock takes Barbara and her dad to meet Aunt Gus and mentions that the trailer will be home for him and Barbara; she and her dad are less than impressed. Although Barbara's dad wants Sock to work in his factory, Sock says that he is not interested. Sock purchases Cleo, a basset hound puppy, as an engagement gift for Barbara, but she thinks the dog is ugly. Later, when Sock goes to Barbara's home, her dad asks him to sign a prenuptial agreement that includes payments for each child the couple will have. The last straw for Sock is when he finds that Barbara's father has given Cleo to an animal shelter. He breaks up with Barbara and retrieves Cleo.

Other episodes during the series' first season focused on Sock and his nemesis Roger Crutcher, with Crutcher putting Sock in untenable situations and Sock having to come up with ways out of them. In "The Unseating of Councilman Sock," the mayor receives an affidavit indicating that Sock has been a resident of New City for only eighty-nine days instead of the required ninety days. Roger initiated the affidavit, and Sock needs to prove that he has been a resident for the full period of time. He does this by finding a duck he tagged on the day he arrived in New City.

In one episode that did focus more on Cleo, "Sock vs. Crutcher," the dog supposedly bites Roger on the ankle, and Crutcher wants her sent out of state thinking that Sock will go with the dog and Roger will have Mandy all to himself. Pierre finds a witness who says that Roger injured his ankle on a locker door at the health club. While at the health club, Sock takes over for the masseur, giving Crutcher a rubdown. Sock begins giving him a rough massage, and Roger finally admits the truth.

As might be expected, many episodes dealt with Sock and Mandy's relationship: Mandy puts Sock into uncomfortable situations, and he is often stuck in the middle between her wishes and her dad's demands. Reluctantly, "Sock Hires Mandy" to fill in as his secretary but then transfers her to another department since she is the mayor's daughter. He becomes jealous of her working with a new boss and makes up a story about Mandy having a big brute for a boyfriend in order to get her transferred back to his office. At the beginning of this episode, Cleo's remarks, expressed in a monotone, were, "This is New City—people, laughter, heartbreak. I work here. My name is Cleo. I'm a dog." The iconic detective series *Dragnet* followed *The People's Choice* on Thursdays, and Cleo was parodying the opening comments of that series' Sgt. Friday (Jack Webb).

In "The Parting of Sock and Mandy," Mayor Peoples wants to know what Sock's intentions are with regard to Mandy since they have been dating for seven months. Because Sock still doesn't think he can afford marriage, he suggests that Mandy should begin dating others. She recommends that they each get dates for the other for the big dance. Both Mandy and Sock fantasize about the type of date they will get for one another. Mandy imagines a model, a dancer, and then a gas station attendant for Sock, while Sock thinks of a football player, a writer, and a farmer for Mandy. Mandy selects Agnes, the gas station attendant; Sock picks Cyril, the farmer. Neither Mandy nor Sock like the dates they get. When their car gets a flat tire on the way to the dance, Mandy and Sock go off together for help, leaving their dates with each other.

Sock appears on television and says he hasn't found the right girl to marry, which upsets Mandy, in a story titled "Sock Proposes to Mandy." In the episode, Sock also recommends an alternative route for a new freeway, infuriating the mayor. As punishment, the mayor decides to send Sock to France to study the feasibility of breeding cashmere goats to determine if such a business can be brought to New City. Sock accepts the assignment but, unknown to the mayor, Mandy decides to go to Europe also. The mayor talks Sock out of going, but Aunt Gus informs her nephew that Roger will be accompanying Mandy on her overseas trip. While looking at a clothes dummy in the mayor's house, Sock fantasizes Mandy's face on the dummy and how she would act in Europe with Crutcher. He imagines her first in England trying to come on to him as a guard at Buckingham Palace but with Roger taking her away; and then in a French bistro with him as an apache dancer who dances with Mandy but she still falls for Crutcher; and finally in the Casbah where she again ends up with Roger. Sock proposes to the clothes dummy, still fantasizing it is Mandy. She overhears and decides not to go to Europe.

In "Sock and the Movie Offer," Mandy becomes jealous when cowboy movie star Stone Kenyon (Gregory Walcott) and his director want Cleo for a movie and Sock pays too much attention to an attractive Italian movie actress who is rehearsing with Cleo. Mandy stops Sock and Cleo from working with the actress by putting pepper on treats that the dog receives when performing tricks. When he discovers this, Sock takes revenge by pretending to come on to the actress.

In the following week's episode, "Sock vs. Stone Kenyon," much to Sock's dismay, Kenyon asks Mandy to the premiere of his new movie. The next day, when Sock visits Mandy, Stone is there. This leads to another fantasy sequence, this one featuring a showdown between gunfighter "Sock-a-Long" Miller and Kenyon over Mandy. In a saloon where the mayor is the bartender and Mandy the dance hall girl, Sock and Stone demonstrate their sharp-shooting skills and then have a gunfight, missing each other. Sock puts a bullet between his teeth and shoots Kenyon, and then Kenyon shoots Sock. Back in the "real" world, do-gooder Sock wants Stone to speak to the local Boys' Club. He learns from Kenyon's agent that Stone is afraid of horses and tells Kenyon that he will have to ride some spirited horses in an upcoming horse show. When the boys from the club come to Mandy's house to hear Stone's speech, Sock talks Kenyon into buying all their raffle tickets for a new swimming pool by threatening that he will divulge to the kids Stone's fear of horses.

Sometimes Sock attempted to perform other good deeds that ended up backfiring on him. In "Sock's Teenage Trouble," Mandy's fourth cousin, teenage Linda (Olive Sturgess who played Dwayne Hickman's girlfriend on *The Bob Cummings Show*), is visiting. When Sock comes to take Mandy to a concert, he politely asks Linda if she wants to accompany them. She unexpectedly accepts the invitation and develops a crush on Sock. Sock tries to interest Linda in his teenage friend Kip (Norman Ollestad), but Kip actually goes for Mandy. Sock decides to come on to Linda to scare her off. He points out how much older he is compared to her and then says he wants to marry her right away. This leads to another fantasy sequence where Linda imagines being married to a much older and grayer Sock Miller with Cleo wearing glasses and moving slower. This image does scare her away from him, and she hooks up with Kip.

In "Sock and the People's Pageant, " Sock wants to put on a pageant celebrating the 100th anniversary of the land grant from the Spanish for the property on which New City is located. The mayor decides to participate in the pageant since his grandfather, Jed Peoples, obtained the land grant after saving a Spaniard from the Indians. The Spaniard's grandson, Don Pasco, is now a Congressman whom Mayor Peoples thinks can help him politically. However, the historical record shows that the mayor's grandfather actually gave the Indians moonshine and they passed out, thereby sparing the Spaniard's life. The mayor becomes upset at Sock after reading the script for the pageant. While reading the script herself, Mandy fantasizes how the pageant would transpire with her dad playing his grandfather making moonshine; she portraying her grandfather's sexy assistant Lola; the Congressman as his grandfather, the Spaniard; Sock as the Indian chief, Swooping Eagle; and Cleo dressed as an Indian princess. To resolve the issue with the story, Sock decides to give a part in the pageant to Miss Hopkins (Ellen Corby) from the historical society who researched and wrote the script and whose ancestor was Lola. Miss Hopkins promises to fictionalize the story to make it more appealing to the mayor.

Other episodes dealt with the relationship between Sock's Aunt Gus and the mayor. In "Sock and the Mayor's Romance," Mandy is trying to play matchmaker for her dad and Aunt Gus. Aunt Gus has the mayor over for dinner, but after dinner, instead of the mayor and Gus being alone, Sock has invited an attractive woman for an interview as the mayor's new secretary. In a later episode, "Sock and the Lonely Hearts Club," Aunt Gus, tired of Sock and Mandy's matchmaking efforts, plans to teach them a lesson by arriving at the mayor's house dressed as an over-the-top glamour girl. This has an unexpected effect on a visiting bigwig from Washington. However, any marriage proposal from the mayor would wait until the following season.

1956–57 TV Season: Everyone Gets Married

As Bob Cummings had done in the later seasons of his series, Jackie Cooper became the director for *The People's Choice* beginning with the 1956–57 season, when NBC moved the show from 8:30 p.m. to 9:00 p.m. on Thursdays. Most of this season's episodes dealt with marriage—the mayor and Aunt Gus getting hitched and finally Sock and Mandy marrying but keeping it a secret since Sock had promised the mayor that he wouldn't marry Mandy until he was better off financially. Sock also began studying law to become an attorney.

In the second episode of the season, Mayor Peoples proposes to Aunt Gus. Sock's preparations for the wedding do not go as planned over three episodes. First, Sock looks for some fast cash to pay for the wedding. He invests in a barbecue restaurant which turns out to be a front for bookmakers in "The Wedding Plans." Sock decides to hold "The Bachelor Party" for the mayor but keeps it a surprise. In "Sock Gives Gus Away," Sock, who is best man, loses the wedding ring in the hors d'oeuvres right before the ceremony. Sock asks Cleo to show him where the ring is and, with the help of trick photography, Cleo leads him to the ring.

Since Sock is now living alone in the trailer, Mandy thinks he should get a roommate in "Sock Takes a Boarder." Sock resists the idea and decides to disguise himself as a prospective boarder in order to be his own roommate. However, Sock does eventually get a roommate when Sock's Marine buddy Rollo Hexley (writer-actor Dick Wesson from *The Bob Cummings Show*) comes to stay in "Sock and the Hex."

"Sock Takes the Plunge" and finally marries Mandy when they elope to Nevada where they have a run-in with a small town sheriff and spend their honeymoon night in jail. They try to keep their marriage a secret, which leads to plenty of subterfuge on Sock's part. For the benefit of Mandy's visiting sorority sisters, they "pretend" to be married while the mayor is out of town in "Mandy's Male Animal." Several episodes related to Mandy and Sock trying to go on their honeymoon while still keeping their marriage secret. Sock plots to get the mayor and Rollo out of town so he and Mandy can spend the weekend together for their delayed honeymoon in "Sock's Secret Honeymoon." Sock goes to the Marine reserves for two weeks of annual training figuring he'll finally have his honeymoon with Mandy since the commanding officer is known for handing out weekend passes in an episode titled "Sock's Bivouac." In "Sock's Master Plan," he and Mandy go to Palm Springs for their honeymoon. Mandy lets her dad know that she is going away to forget Sock, and Sock confesses to Rollo that he is going away to forget Mandy. Both the mayor and Rollo go to Palm Springs to console Sock and reserve a room right across the hall from the couple.

In "The Sophisticates," Sock thinks he and Mandy should pretend to break up so the mayor doesn't get wise to them. They say they are sophisticates and are allowing themselves to date other people. The mayor sees through the ruse and has Roger Crutcher find a real date (Joi Lansing) for Sock. When Mandy sees the date, she becomes upset and reveals that she and Sock are married, but the mayor thinks they are trying to put another one over on him. At the end of the episode, Cleo calls Sock's friend Rollo at 3:00 a.m., wakes him up, and barks over the phone. This bit of an animal using the phone would be used to a greater effect in the Burns-produced *Mister Ed.*

In a fantasy episode that parodied *The King and I*, Sock says that he is "king" and doesn't need to explain a boys' night out to Mandy. She wants Sock to negotiate a land deal involving a shopping center for J.B. Barker (Addison Richards), a tycoon in this story titled "The Queen and Me." Sock relents on his boys' night out and meets with the landowner who turns out to be an attractive female artist. She asks for more money than Barker told Sock to give her for the property. Sock says he will discuss her request with Barker. When Sock comes home, he trips, is knocked unconscious, and dreams he is the king of Siam and Mandy is the U.S. ambassador who wants him to give his multiple wives equal rights. She changes her mind after seeing how masterful he is and wants to become one of his wives. When Sock regains consciousness, he informs Barker that he must pay the landowner more, and Barker appreciates his assertiveness.

At the end of the series' second season, Irving Brecher stepped down as producer to pursue other projects. Among them was a proposed adventure series titled *Big Time.* The pilot script was written by the team of G. Carleton Brown and Frank Gill from *The People's Choice,* but the pilot never became a series.

Cleo was so popular at the time that she was the subject of a 1957 *Little Golden Book* published by Simon and Schuster. It showed a day in the life of the basset hound going to the TV studio, wearing various costumes, and doing different tricks such as climbing a ladder, walking a tightrope, and rolling on top of a large ball.

1957–58 TV Season: Off to Oklahoma

This season brought two major changes to the series. First, Sock and Mandy moved from New City to 119 Muskogee Drive, Barkersville, Oklahoma, where Sock managed a new housing development financed by J.B. Barker (a character introduced during season two), and second, Mandy became pregnant.

In the episode "The Giveaway," Sock passes his bar exam, and he and Mandy finally decide to reveal their secret marriage to the mayor. Before they can tell him, they learn that he has planned to throw a large wedding for them packed with dignitaries. In another fantasy episode aired early in the season, "The Caveman," Sock is again knocked on the head and dreams of being in the Stone Age arguing with the mayor.

Most episodes dealt with Sock accepting the position as head of housing development in Barkersville, Oklahoma, with 300 houses to sell and having difficulty finding buyers for them. Mandy, Cleo, and Sock leave New City and move into a house in the development. Even Cleo is affected by the move. In an episode focusing on the basset hound, Sock finds a prospective home buyer who hates dogs and hides Cleo. Her pride wounded, Cleo becomes "The Runaway Dog."

In "The Wrong Indians," two more actors from Burns-produced series appear: Howard McNear, who played the plumber on *Burns and Allen,* and King Donovan who appeared on both *Burns and Allen* and *The Bob Cummings Show*. Mr. Quigley (McNear) from Barker Amalgamated instructs Sock to find a company to move a factory to Barkersville to entice prospective home buyers. Quigley contacts a woman who heads a company making products from India, but he thinks that her company produces Native American items. After Quigley makes over Sock's house in Native American motif, Mandy has to get rid of the stuff before the head of the company arrives. Donovan appeared as the brother of the company head on this episode.

In "The Male Ego," still another fantasy episode, Sock fails to sell a house because the wife of a prospective buyer objected to a small detail; now he imagines himself in the year 5000 when women run everything.

In addition to moving to Barkersville, the other big news during the season was Mandy in "the family way." After Sock learns from the doctor that Mandy is pregnant, he excitedly waits to see how she will break the news to him. Mandy's casual manner confuses him since he doesn't realize that *she* doesn't know she is expecting. Learning that Mandy is pregnant, her dad visits and decides that Mandy's doctor is too young and that his office is too far away from Mandy's house. This has Sock imagine Mandy and himself as Oklahoma pioneers in "The Veteran." The mayor also thinks that Cleo will be in the way once the new baby is born. Cleo exhibits her best behavior, but her attempt to behave is mistaken for sickness. She faces the prospect of being shipped to a rest home in "Cleo, the Secret Dog."

In "Little White Lies," another episode centering on Cleo, Sock fails to get an additional member for the Junior Chemists of Oklahoma and resorts to submitting the name of his "daughter" Cleo Miller. This results in Cleo being awarded a college scholarship and the chemists' club arriving with congratulations. In the series final episode "Daisies Won't Tell," Sock's boss J.B. Barker visits and is very interested in Aunt Hattie (Elvia Allman, who had portrayed Sock's boss in the series premiere). Sock and Mandy make plans for another wedding.

While no proposed spinoffs came out of *The People's Choice* like they did for *The Burns and Allen Show* and for *The Bob Cummings Show*, a sitcom that imitated the gimmick of *The People's Choice* was produced by Perry Como's production company as a summer replacement for his variety show. Titled *Happy*, the comedy was about the infant son of a young couple who, like Cleo, commented on the plot of each episode directly to viewers.

98

Happy was created by two *People's Choice* writers, Frank Gill and G. Carleton Brown, and ran for sixteen episodes in 1960 and 1961. The show starred George and Gracie's son Ronnie along with Yvonne Lime, who had played Joy Jantzen and also introduced several of the "Afterpieces" on *The Burns and Allen Show*. Commenting on working with George, Gracie, and Ronnie, Yvonne Lime said that she was blessed to have the good fortune of knowing this talented family and treasures the time she spent with them.[11] Lime later married Don Fedderson, producer of the sitcoms *My Three Sons* and *Family Affair*. She thus became the stepmother-in-law of Linda Kaye Henning, daughter of Paul Henning, after Linda Kaye married Fedderson's son, actor-singer Mike Minor.

Shortly after the demise of *Happy,* Ronnie Burns left show business and got involved with designing and building boats and breeding Arabian horses. He passed away at age seventy-two on November 14, 2007. He was survived by his wife, sister, three sons and six grandchildren.

Following *The People's Choice,* Jackie Cooper starred on another comedy which ran for three seasons: He played Lt. Charles "Chick" Hennesey on *Hennesey*. He later directed TV shows, winning an Emmy for directing an episode of *M*A*S*H*. In the sixties, Pat Breslin became a regular on *Peyton Place* and *General Hospital* before retiring from acting after she married Art Modell, the owner of the Cleveland Browns (which subsequently became the Baltimore Ravens).

6

George and His McCadden Comedy Projects and Pilots

Under George Burns, McCadden Productions pursued many comedy projects from 1954 through 1958. The company acquired rights to various properties and developed several of its own concepts. Burns spent a lot of time considering the various properties as potential series. When he selected one he thought had possibilities, he would consult Maurice Morton about the financial aspects of the project before going any further. According to Morton, "He doesn't shoot pilots promiscuously. He runs the business on conservative lines and never questions any deal. He assumes it was the best we could make."[1]

Some of Burns' projects resulted in a pilot being made; many others did not. In several cases, as described below, the projects were picked up by another production company which did produce a pilot. Following is a year-by-year description of these projects.

1954: Fathers, Sidney Sheldon and *Myrt and Marge*

One of the first projects undertaken by McCadden in addition to producing *The Burns and Allen Show* and making commercials was to use its facilities to film television series produced by CBS. *Life with Father* was one such project filmed by Burns' company. The comedy, based on the novel, play, and movie of the same name, concerned a strict Victorian father, Clarence Day (Leon Ames), his wife Vinnie (Lurene Tuttle), and their four sons, all of whom had red hair. Done live when it debuted in 1953 on Sundays at 7:00 p.m. *Life with Father* did not do well in that time slot. The show moved to Tuesdays at 10:00 p.m. in August 1954 and eventually ended up at 8:00 p.m. on that day in January 1955. The series has the distinction of being the first comedy done live in color for one episode from CBS Television City in Hollywood. It eventually went to film in December 1954 to permit greater flexibility in story content. That is when McCadden began filming the show for its final twenty-six episodes.

Burns' production company also filmed *That's My Boy,* based on the 1951 Dean Martin–Jerry Lewis movie of the same title. It starred Eddie Mayehoff as "Jarring" Jack Jackson, an ex–football hero who wants his quiet, intellectual son Junior Jackson (Gil Stratton, Jr.) to follow in his footsteps and become a jock like dad was. Rochelle Hudson starred as Alice, Jack's wife. Done live from Hollywood, *That's My Boy* premiered in April 1954 on Saturdays at 10:00 p.m. When the series resumed in fall 1954, it went from weekly live broadcasts to being filmed by McCadden for twenty-six episodes. The storylines of episodes that Burns' company filmed dealt mainly with Junior attending Rossmore College, the same school where his father went and became a star football player. The comedy was canceled in November 1954 but didn't leave the air until the beginning of January 1955.

Professional Father, which replaced *That's My Boy,* was a family comedy about Thomas Wilson (Steve Dunne), a child psychologist who attempts to apply his knowledge of children to his own family. Barbara Billingsley, who later was the mother on *Leave It to Beaver,* played his wife Helen. Their children were Thomas "Twig" Wilson, Jr. (Ted Marc), and Kathryn "Kit" Wilson (Beverly Washburn). As with most comedies at the time, the Wilsons had friendly next-door neighbors, the Allens, portrayed by Joseph Kearns (later Mr. Wilson in *Dennis the Menace*) as Fred and Phyllis Coates as Nurse Madge. In the pilot filmed by McCadden in 1954, the Wilson children read the manuscript for a book their dad wrote about child behavior and try to emulate the types of behavior described. The series only lasted for half a season and was replaced in fall 1955 by what would become one of the longest running series in TV history: *Gunsmoke.*

Jack Benny used the McCadden facilities to make several episodes of his program, and the company filmed a Bing Crosby special for General Electric in April 1954. Filming shows on a contractual basis for other production companies was profitable for Burns and did not involve the creative talents of Burns and/or his writers.

In addition to filming shows for other companies, McCadden expressed interest in producing two comedies itself created by Sidney Sheldon who later developed *I Dream of Jeannie. Adventures of a Model* was to star Marilyn Maxwell as a New York model who had to fend off advances from various male suitors. However, Burns' company passed on this project, no doubt because it was not financially beneficial to the company. A pilot was eventually filmed in 1956 by Desilu with Joanne Dru starring as model Marilyn Woods. In the episode, directed by Norman Tokar, Marilyn tries to please a Texas sportswear manufacturer in spite of her dislike of sports. Nancy Kulp, a semi-regular on the McCadden-produced *The Bob Cummings Show,* was the second female lead. Proctor and Gamble picked up the pilot for a series but couldn't find a time slot for it. The pilot aired as an episode of *Colgate Theatre* in August 1958.

The second Sheldon project that McCadden considered was called *My Man Sing.* Originally titled *A Man in the House,* this comedy centered on a career girl in New York publishing who inherited a Chinese houseboy when her rich uncle died. Patricia Crowley played the career girl and Joe Wong was the houseboy. However, talks between Sheldon and McCadden about producing the series cooled. The pilot was subsequently filmed at Hal Roach Studios by Dynasty Productions in 1955 for NBC; it was produced by Matthew Rapf and directed by Elsa Schreiber. When the pilot failed to become a series, the project was taken over by P.J. "Pinky" Wolfson, who had produced *I Married Joan.* In 1956, Wolfson wrote and produced a new pilot with Larry Storch as Sing and Sandy Smith as the career girl. After this effort did not sell, there was discussion of producing a third pilot with Dick Shawn as the houseboy, but that never materialized.

Burns also contemplated bringing the radio soap opera *Myrt and Marge* to television as a comedy starring someone like actress Joan Blondell. The *Myrt and Marge* radio serial ran from 1931 to 1946 and dealt with a seasoned chorus girl, Myrt Spear, and Marge Minter, a young girl new to the chorus. Given the last names of the lead characters, it is not surprising that the series was sponsored by the Wrigley chewing gum company. Advertisements for the radio show described it as "the world of the theater and the world of life, and the story of two women who seek fame in the one and contentment in the other." This project, if it had gone beyond the development stage, would have fit in nicely with other Burns-produced comedies involving characters with different perspectives about the world—a character new to entertainment and a mature veteran.

1955: *Dobie Gillis* and Other Projects

During 1955, George Burns acquired the rights to the Dobie Gillis stories about a young man seeking money, popularity, and beautiful girls, particularly the latter. Originally a college student at the University of Minnesota majoring in various subjects ranging from law to mechanical engineering, the Dobie character was created by Max Shulman in a series of short stories published in magazines such as *Good Housekeeping, Cosmopolitan,* and *The Saturday Evening Post.*

Shulman was to be producer and writer for the television comedy that Burns wanted to make. According to a Shulman memorandum to McCadden Productions, Dick Sargent, Jack Dimond, John Stevens, Martin Milner, Mark Rydell, Jeff Harris, and Dwayne Hickman were all under consideration for the lead. McCadden was to own 67 percent of the series and Shulman 33 percent. Shulman even thought of naming the production company Shulden Productions, taking the first four letters of his last name and the last three letters of McCadden (similar to what Cummings and Burns had done in coming up with Laurmac Productions and what Brecher and Burns did in devising Norden Productions). Burns and Shulman wanted to make a series pilot before February 1956 so the comedy could air in 1957. However, the two could never agree on either casting or a shooting schedule, and a McCadden pilot was never made.

Burns wanted his son Ronnie to play Dobie Gillis, but Shulman strongly disagreed with this casting. In a letter to his agent, Shulman stated his reasons for not pursuing the project with Burns: "It's purely a question of money. I would undertake this back-breaking job only if there was a big pile of loot to be made. With Ronnie Burns, I see nothing ahead except cancellation and the destruction of a valuable property. The kid just has no talent, and I'm not going to carry him on my back."[2] In another letter to his agency, Shulman wrote, "George intended from the very beginning to cast Ronnie in this part, and he knows the kid needs a crutch, which is what I don't intend to be. I have a naïve notion that an actor ought to bring something to a part—not just read lines."[3]

When Burns' option on creating a Dobie Gillis sitcom ran out, the property reverted back to Shulman, who later sold the series to 20th Century–Fox. The comedy starred Dwayne Hickman, who had been featured on *The Bob Cummings Show.* Unlike the short stories on which it was based,

Hickman played Dobie Gillis initially as a high school student and not a college student in order to appeal to a younger audience. *The Many Loves of Dobie Gillis* premiered on CBS in 1959 and ran for four seasons. Rod Amateau, who had directed many episodes of the Cummings show and *The Burns and Allen Show,* produced and directed the Dobie Gillis series in which Dobie would speak directly to the audience, like Burns had done, at the beginning of each episode. Dobie was very much like a young Bob Collins from *The Bob Cummings Show* in seeking the favors of attractive girls and, in turn, his being pursued by Zelda Gilroy (Sheila James), a rather plain-looking high school student. Like *Burns and Allen* and the Cummings show, each episode of *The Many Loves of Dobie Gillis* was filmed with two cameras and produced in two days.

In 1955, McCadden had discussions with producer Ralph Freed, the brother of lyricist and producer Arthur Freed, about a project titled *Room-mates,* focusing on the adventures of two young college girls, one an exchange student from France, the other an American. A pilot was eventually produced, not by McCadden, but by Four Star Productions, which had been formed by Dick Powell along with David Niven and Charles Boyer in 1952. Eventually, Ida Lupino became the fourth star. Written by Katherine and Dale Eunson and directed by Harry Keller, *Roommates* starred Diane DuBois as Gabrielle, the French student, and Sue George as Janet, the American student whose mother (Maureen O'Sullivan) had the idea that all French people were immoral. She changed her mind after becoming acquainted with Gabrielle. The pilot never became a series, but did air as an episode of *Chevron Hall of Stars* on October 19, 1956.

McCadden did film, but did not produce, a pilot for the Ashley-Steiner Agency for Ed Wynn's son Keenan in April 1955. Called *How Now, Brown,* it was based on an idea by Don Quinn and a script by Bill Manhoff. The pilot co-starred Doe Avedon, an actress who had been married to famed photographer Richard Avedon. Don Weis directed the pilot, and Bill Manhoff and Dick Steenberg were the producers for Brown, Inc.

The central character in the proposed series was Kelsey Brown (Keenan Wynn), a blowhard, out-of-work actor, who thought of himself as more successful than he really was. He couldn't afford the apartment he lived in and had to rent his suits. Brown was dating wealthy Andrea Hartford (Doe Avedon). Andrea's young cousin in the pilot was played by Noreen Corcoran, who later starred on *Bachelor Father* with John Forsythe.

In July 1955 McCadden used its facilities to film for CBS another pilot, *Amos 'n' Andy's Music Hall*, a sequel of sorts to the *Amos 'n' Andy Show* which had depicted blacks in a grossly stereotypical manner. The music hall version was to star Freeman Gosden and Charles Correll who had played Amos and Andy on the radio, but they would not be wearing black face make-up. James Mason guest starred on the pilot, which never became a TV series. A radio version ran on CBS until 1960.

1956: *The Delightful Imposter* and Marie Wilson

Burns' main focus in 1956 seemed to be on finding the appropriate vehicle for actress Marie Wilson's return to weekly TV. However, McCadden did engage in talks concerning other projects.

In January 1956, McCadden Productions discussed producing a comedy pilot written by Fred Shevin about a press agent. Starring Jack Carson as Danny Scott, a press agent who decides to take a bigger commission from his client than he should, "The Press Agent" ended up being produced by Meridian Productions as an installment of *Schlitz Playhouse* and aired in September 1956.

Singer-actress Betty Hutton approached Burns' company about doing a comedy series, but nothing came of these discussions. Later in 1956, she was set to star in a NBC comedy created by Jess Oppenheimer, who had developed *I Love Lucy*. The sitcom centered on a widow with three children who became a foster mother to her sister's three children. But Hutton dropped out of this project. She did ultimately star in her own self-titled CBS sitcom as a manicurist who inherits the estate of one of her customers and becomes legal guardian of his three teenagers.

NBC tried to get Burns to produce a *Fibber and Molly* pilot based on the radio series about a bumbling husband and his understanding wife. The comedy would have starred Jim and Marian Jordan, who had originated the characters of Fibber McGee and his wife Molly. Several years earlier, the Jordans had made a TV pilot that didn't sell. However, Burns indicated he did not have time in his busy schedule for this project. One can surmise that NBC asked Burns to produce *Fibber and Molly* because its lead characters were similar to him and Gracie but with Fibber being the nonsensical one and Molly the down-to-earth character. *Fibber McGee and Molly* eventually made it on to the air in 1959 starring Bob Sweeney and Cathy Lewis. The sitcom, produced and directed by William Asher, lasted only twelve episodes.

One comedy that McCadden did try to develop was *The Delightful Imposter*. This proposed series was based on the escapades of John Burnett, a professor of anthropology at a small New England university. Burnett came from a wealthy family and lived at home with his mother and father. He liked to do a lot of "field work" involving various ruses and impersonations to help people in trouble. (He could not bear to see people in difficulty because he had led such an untroubled life.) Burnett had a sidekick initially named Joe Pestle and then Joe Kelly, physically able and very loyal, who helped him do his good deeds. They each liked to act and never took any money for what they did. The Burnett character seems to have been modeled after the Scarlet Pimpernel with Burnett as the hero with the secret identity.

The show was created by Al Simon, and Barbara Merlin wrote the script for this project. In later versions of the pilot script, the lead character's occupation was changed from professor to author, and the character was renamed John Somerset. The plot in the pilot scripts begins with the end of a previous case of helping a woman who had some indiscreet letters, and then segues into the story of Beninno Tartini, a young prodigy and his missing violin. The delightful imposter arranges, through a series of meetings, to have a Stradivarius violin available for the boy, which gives him a better chance of being successful as a virtuoso. In the pilot script, John Somerset took on various guises (a hotel doorman, a passenger agent of a steamship line, an impresario, a violinist, a French collector, a psychiatrist, and the curator of a museum) to help Beninno.

The pilot was scheduled to be made in 1956 and then in 1957, but it never got off the ground. Burns and Simon attempted, without success, to get John Forsythe for the lead. At Filmways in 1961, Simon discussed writing a new script for this project with Bill Manhoff, but the idea was abandoned.

As mentioned earlier, the main project undertaken by Burns and CBS in late 1956 was to develop a vehicle for Marie Wilson of *My Friend Irma* fame, who was under contract with CBS for $100,000 a year. In *My Friend Irma* (CBS, 1952–54), Marie had portrayed a "dumb blonde" character somewhat like the dumb Dora Gracie Allen played—only younger and sexier. Wilson had the role of Irma Peterson a sexy but naïve secretary who worked for an attorney, and shared an apartment with Jane Stacy (Cathy Lewis), a level-headed brunette. There was discussion of doing a sequel to *My Friend Irma* titled *My Wife Irma* where the character portrayed by Wilson marries, but CBS failed to approve it.

Wilson then tried a comeback in a pilot titled *Miss Pepperdine* where she was a receptionist for Pontifer & Company, Ladies Fashions, but her character, Marie Pepperdine really wanted to be a model. It was written by Everett Freeman, Milton Pascal, and Morris Freedman, and the cast of characters included Marie's roommate Lily Baldwin (Hildy Parks), a model at Pontifer's; Gus (Jack Durant) and Hazel Hotchkiss (Mary Beth Hughes), Marie and Lily's neighbors; Simon Pontifer (Harry Clark), owner of Pontifer's; Bentley Pontifer (Peter Adams), Simon's nephew, who also worked at the company; Herbie (Paul Smith), another worker; and Miss Caldwell (Jacqueline deWit), the head dress designer. The pilot was produced by Freeman and Jules Bricken for CBS and was filmed by McCadden.

This 1955 pilot episode, "Marie Meets a Prince," involved a case of mistaken identities. Gus Hotchkiss receives tickets to a movie premiere and informs his wife that she will be escorted there by a Charley Adams. Charley needs a tux, Hazel needs a gown, and Marie volunteers to help them procure both. She knows the owner of a tuxedo rental place and decides to ask Mr. Pontifer to lend a gown to Hazel to promote his fashion line at the movie premiere. Meanwhile, Pontifer wants a Prince Igor to endorse the Pontifer brand. When the prince arrives at the office, Marie mistakes him for Charley Adams and takes him to a tuxedo rental place. Marie eventually realizes she made a mistake and apologizes for the mix-up. Gus then goes to Pontifer's in his doorman's uniform to get a gown for his wife, and Miss Caldwell thinks he is Prince Igor. Lily recognizes Gus, which angers Mr. Pontifer since he also thought Gus was the prince. All works out in the end when Prince Igor refuses to sign the endorsement deal unless Pontifer promises to give Hazel a gown for the premiere.

McCadden's first idea for its own Marie Wilson vehicle was to adapt the *Craig Rice Mysteries* (the company owned the rights) and try to make Wilson a mystery writer who solved crimes. Dick Conway and Roland MacLane were to pen the script for the pilot but were unsure if they could pull off a comedy-drama with Wilson as the lead.

When this project went nowhere, the suggestion was made to have

Marie play a character named Marie Harris who inherits a full partnership in the public relations firm of Handley and Harris after the death of her uncle J.P. Harris. She also inherits a New York City brownstone with a full-time butler and his wife. This concept evolved into a script written by Phil Shuken, who had developed scripts for *My Friend Irma,* which had Marie as president of J.J. Wilson Enterprises—a conglomerate bequeathed to her when her grandfather died. Having no experience running a company, she butts heads with the firm's vice-presidents including Frank Rittenhouse, who really ran the firm; Adam Baker, first vice-president, and Anthony Randall, second vice-president. The premise had Marie wanting to learn the business from the ground up. She begins by working on the production line in the electronics division. When Rittenhouse subsequently discovers that the efficiency in that division has declined by 50 percent in a week,

Marie Wilson always seemed to be typecast as a "dumb blonde." She died of cancer at age fifty-five in 1972.

he wants to fire the workers, unaware that Marie is responsible. She signed the papers for the workers' termination without reading them first. But when she discovers what she has done, she rescinds the order.

The Shuken script was totally re-written by Harvey Helm, Norman Paul, Keith Fowler, and Willy Burns but still had the basic idea of Marie inheriting a company from her grandfather. In this new version titled *The Marie Wilson Show* (aka *It's Me, Marie*), which is believed to have been used for the pilot that was actually filmed in December 1956, Wilson played herself, that is, the "dumb blonde" version of herself. Marie has just gained a controlling interest in the J.J. Wilson Holding Company and has become one of the richest women in the world. She decides to quit show business and devote all of her time to the holding company. However, the board members are very concerned about Marie taking her grandfather's place. The character of Frank L. Rittenhouse is now the chairman of the board whose members include Messrs. Bagby, Cartwright, Tobin, and Randall. Bob Randall, the only bachelor on the board (and a possible love interest for Marie), suggests that she be placed in charge of one of their small companies to keep her occupied. The other members like his idea and agree to put him in charge of Marie. When Marie arrives, she meets the board members and invites Randall to her home for dinner to discuss the board's plans for her.

Marie lives in a brownstone (also inherited from her grandfather) with Mrs. Jeffers, her housekeeper, and Henry, the butler. At dinner, Randall discusses different companies that Marie might be interested in helping. They agree on Berkshire Sportswear Manufacturers. The next day, Marie meets Mr. Howard, the manager of the company, which hasn't been keeping up with the competition. Marie decides that the company should resume making knickers which they originally manufactured. She directs Mr. Howard to hire 1200 employees and get the machines back in working order. Because of the cost involved, Howard calls Rittenhouse who, without hearing the specifics, advises him to do anything Marie wants.

A few weeks later, Howard reports that they have manufactured 60,000 pairs of golf knickers but sold only one (Mr. Howard himself bought a pair). When Mr. Randall discovers what Marie has done, he fears he might lose his job. However, Marie gets the idea from him to have Hollywood stars start wearing knickers to create a fashion trend. She contacts George Burns to ask him to wear a pair the next time he plays golf. She also contacts his friends Jack Benny, Jackie Cooper, and Bob Cummings (the latter two, of course, stars of McCadden-produced comedies).

When the auditors bring to his attention the money that Marie has spent on Berkshire Sportswear, Rittenhouse calls an emergency Saturday board meeting interrupting everyone's golf dates. At the meeting, Marie reveals that the sportswear company made a $500,000 profit selling knickers. The board members sheepishly file out of the meeting, all wearing golf knickers.

In the pilot, directed by Rod Amateau, Burns really tried to make the

Wilson character act a lot like Gracie. Note the following dialogue from the script when Marie is getting ready to have Mr. Randall for dinner: "Henry, will you take these cigarettes and cut the filter tips off and throw the cigarettes away and put the filter tips back in the box.... Mr. Randall, who's coming to dinner, is very nice, but he's a little strange. When I asked him if he smoked, he said, 'Yes, but only filter tips.'"

This pilot failed to sell. Wilson's next attempt at a series was a Desilu pilot called *Ernestine.* Ernestine McDougall worked in a loan office for her father (played by Charlie Ruggles), the president of a small loan company. Charles Lane and Nancy Kulp were also in the cast. Ernestine made bad loans to people whom she considered underdogs, but as with TV sitcoms, things always worked out well in the end. The pilot, written by Don Nelson and Jay Sommers, was directed by Sidney Salkow. Like her other attempts at a comedy after *My Friend Irma,* this pilot never became a series.

A final late 1956 project considered by Burns' production company was titled *Harry Hathaway* about a good-natured guy, with a wife named Agnes, who liked to help people in need. The comedy, written by Joe Connelly and Bob Mosher who developed *Leave It to Beaver,* was based on an idea from director Leo McCarey. Leads considered for the projected series were James Whitmore, Burgess Meredith, Eddie Albert, Karl Malden, Walter Mathau, Leon Ames, Wendell Corey, and even Harry Von Zell. According to gossip columnist Louella Parsons, Buddy Ebsen was supposed to star. However, this appears to have simply been publicity for Ebsen since internal McCadden documents do not list his name.[4] Apparently, McCadden executives were concerned about possible copyright infringement if they pursued the series because the script was very close to the Leo McCarey film *Good Sam. Good Sam* had starred Gary Cooper as Sam Clayton who liked to help people so much that he was often broke and unable to support his own family. Ann Sheridan starred as his wife Lucille.

The year ended with only one real sitcom pilot made by McCadden: *The Marie Wilson Show.*

1957: *Oliver Chantry* and *Maggie*

In addition to the *Plumber and His Daughters* spinoff described in Chapter 3 and the pilot for a spinoff of the Chuck MacDonald character from *The Bob Cummings Show* noted in Chapter 4, George Burns engaged with a variety of individuals about developing comedy series during 1957.

Early in the year, Burns was interested in producing a project titled *Hollywood Hook and Ladder.* Writer Ken Englund had come up with the concept for a comedy-with-music series about firemen manning a Bel Air, California, station and being called upon to serve the Hollywood community. The lead characters included Phil Haverstraw, a rookie firefighter with a kind heart but something of a bungler, and Blair Wallace, Phil's handsome bachelor friend, a singer who was always looking for pretty girls. These two characters sounded something like Socrates Miller from *The People's Choice* paired with Bob Collins from *The Bob Cummings Show.* Other characters were Captain Harker, their superior; Jane Pine, the girl who worked next door to the firehouse and wanted to be an actress; a battalion chief, and Smokey, the station's Dalmatian mascot. Each episode was to have a special guest star involved in some type of emergency situation that Haverstraw and Wallace would try to resolve.

In his proposal, Englund outlined possible storylines for the series. In one adventure, the firemen notice smoke at some distance from their station. They jump on the truck and race to a house in Beverly Hills where they see the second floor of the home ablaze. Actress Lana Turner is sticking her head out of a window screaming for help. The men dash in the house to rescue her. However, it turns out that a crew is shooting a film in the backyard with Phil and Blair ruining Lana's scene with her leading man. The director chews out the two firemen and their captain. Back at the firehouse, Phil is teased by his colleagues and is made to wash the fire truck as punishment, while Blair hopes for a date with Lana Turner.

In the second proposed story, the captain demonstrates a new fire extinguisher. Phil chats with Jane Pine who is reading a script in preparation for an audition. To get to the audition on time, Jane asks Phil to watch Albert, the young boy she is babysitting. He plays with the kid, hiding him in the firehouse when called to attention by the captain. Inside the station, the boy wrecks havoc and gets hold of the fire extinguisher. Outside, Phil and Blair notice foam billowing out from under the door. Phil dashes to open the door, goes inside, and comes out in a sea of foam, proudly holding Albert.

There is no evidence that McCadden ever produced a pilot for *Hollywood Hook and Ladder.*

In March 1957, singer-actress Janis Paige and her husband Artie Stander approached McCadden about a co-production deal for a new series starring Paige, who had starred in her own sitcom *It's Always Jan* during the 1955–56 TV season. However, it appears again that this deal never went beyond the discussion stage.

Burns' company also had talks with Ed Wynn to produce a pilot featuring him as an old-time show business character who wanted to prove himself useful. McCadden passed on the project. Eventually, Wynn starred in a self-titled series produced by Screen Gems about a grandfather raising his two granddaughters in a college town. The comedy premiered on September 25, 1958, but lasted only half a season.

The company also held talks with Jay Dratler about a comedy he created, *The Fabulous Oliver Chantry*. Dratler had written the screenplays for *Call Northside 777* and *Laura* among others. The Chantry project centered on a Broadway columnist and critic described as "arrogant, brilliant, elegant and sometimes impossible."[5] Sally Parker was Chantry's secretary and Martin was his butler.

The Chantry character made his first appearance in a 1953 unsold pilot with British actor Gerald Desmonde playing the lead, Melville Cooper as his butler, and Beverly Garland as the secretary. In this kinescoped pilot, a baby is left with Oliver by famous foreign composer Mr. Bolgvanyi (Franz Roehn) and his wife, who are being deported. Apparently, the parents wanted to leave their son with Oliver, who had given the musician a glowing review, so he could grow up in the United States. Oliver doesn't want to keep the baby but then grows fond of him. Chantry's attorney Mr. Atwater (Charles Halton) tries to make arrangements to stop the deportation of the Bolgvanyis. Chantry and his secretary, both in disguise, visit the couple before they leave the United States. Oliver convinces the immigration officer that Mr. Bolgvanyi would sign anything placed before him because of his ignorance of the English language, and he successfully prevents the deportation.

After this pilot failed to sell, Dratler approached McCadden Productions about doing a new version of *The Fabulous Oliver Chantry*. Dratler wrote a new script, and the characters were recast with George Sanders in the lead role. Sanders had portrayed a character similar to Chantry in the film *All About Eve*. Doris Singleton became Chantry's secretary and Steven Geray, his butler. Dratler, Sanders, and Burns were to each own a third of the production. The Chantry character was another manipulative charmer similar to other such characters in Burns-produced sitcoms. However, McCadden backed out of the proposed series, again presumably over financial issues.

Another Chantry pilot, this one directed by Roy Del Ruth (who began his career as a writer for Mack Sennett), was made in 1958 by Hal Roach Studios, but it never went to series. In the story, Rachel (Ellen Corby), a wardrobe mistress, is upset that her niece Lois (Ann Baker from the *Meet Corliss Archer* TV show) wants to give up acting and marry Bob (Doug McClure, who went on to star in TV's *Checkmate* and *The Virginian*), a farmer she knew from upstate New York. Oliver thinks he has a part lined up for Lois in a play being directed by George Richmond. However, Richmond wants the play to star an acting couple, Alfred (Ian Keith) and Lynn Barry (Cicely Browne), who had previously appeared in the work. Chantry convinces Lois not to give up the stage and throws a party for the Barrys in order to pit the couple against each other. He spreads the rumor that Alfred and Lynn don't intend on acting together any more and, at the party, Alfred talks with Lois about her playing opposite him. Lynn and Alfred argue. She says that she will not be in the play and accuses Alfred of starting the rumors. After Lois gets the female lead in the revival, Chantry learns that she is doing a terrible acting job. He thinks this is because she is still in love with Bob. Lois admits to loving Bob and being distraught over his return home. Bob and Lois reunite, and Chantry goes to see Lynn Barry to convince her to work with Alfred. Lynn reconciles with her husband, and they star in the revival.

The new pilot was billed as "The fabulous Oliver Chantry muddles his way into the affairs of the heart and marital bliss; breaking people up and putting them back together, all while maintaining his absolute fabulousness." This pilot didn't sell either.

Burns also tried to develop a comedy for Carol Channing in 1957. Channing's husband Charles Lowe was the account executive with the advertising agency that handled ads for the Carnation Milk Company, primary sponsor of *The Burns and Allen Show*. The Burnses and Lowes were very close friends, and so it is not surprising that George would attempt to create a series starring Ms. Channing.

Burns thought of adapting the Maisie character played by Ann Sothern in several feature films as a comedy for Channing. McCadden was to own 55 percent of the project, Channing 25 percent, and producer Maurice Duke and financial backer Norman Kramer 20 percent. The pilot was to be scripted by Mary McCall, who had written eight of the nine *Maisie* movies. The character Maisie was a brassy showgirl who went by the stage name Maisie Ravier and got caught up in various misadventures. When this idea did not work out, Burns thought of making Carol the oldest sister in a family of pretty girls—all of whom have innumerable beaus, and none of whom can marry until the oldest sister does.

Finally, the idea of Channing starring in a husband-and-wife comedy with music interspersed was conceived; it sounds something like the original *Burns and Allen* show. George, his brother Willy, and Norman Paul wrote the script. It is not known if the role of the husband was ever cast, but Las Vegas comic Hank Henry reportedly got the role of the couple's butler. Commenting on the proposed series, Channing said, "George was going to have a child in the series. He told me, 'Don't worry about it, she'll only be in briefly.' Finally, one day he showed up and said, 'Forget the child—we killed the kid.'"[6] The pilot was supposed to be filmed in June 1957. However, as with several other McCadden projects, the Channing vehicle was never picked up as a series.

After her success in the Broadway musical *Hello, Dolly!*, Channing did make a 1966 sitcom pilot produced by Desi Arnaz and written by Bob Carroll, Jr. and Madelyn Davis, writers on *I Love Lucy*. In this unsold pilot, Carol played Carol Honeycutt, a woman seeking a show business career in New York City.

In 1957, Burns' company produced a pilot for ABC titled *Maggie*. Originally called *Amy,* this project starred former child actress Margaret O'Brien as a charming seventeen-year-old "manipulator in training" living with her actor parents Mark and Annie Bradley in Connecticut. Maggie wanted to be an actress herself and had an extremely active imagination. After considering Don Porter and his wife Peggy Converse for Maggie's parents, the roles went to Leon Ames and Fay Baker. Jeanne Tatum played the Bradleys' housekeeper Esther.

At the beginning of the pilot, Mark Bradley announces that Maggie is "nothing but trouble." Mark introduces himself as part of an acting team and says he appeared on *Life with Father* in which actor Leon Ames did actually star (Burns again mixing facts from real life with fiction). The Bradley family has just moved to Hunter's Ferry, Connecticut, where their neighbor Miss Caldwell (Jesslyn Fax) has decided to build a wall to separate her property from the Bradleys.' In the opening scene, Maggie's parents are being interviewed by the local paper. While her parents try to paint the family as fairly typical, Maggie dresses as Joan of Arc. After her dad instructs her to act normal, Maggie behaves like a giggly teenager. Her mother advises Maggie that she wasn't being very nice and says she should visit the boy next door, whom Maggie calls "Weird Willy." Willy Foster (Edwin Bruce) is a young science student who seems more interested in examining his animals than in talking with Maggie. Maggie fantasizes that Miss Caldwell and her handyman Whitaker (Charles Cantor) are secretly in love but are afraid to say anything to each other. She attempts to get Miss Caldwell and Whitaker to profess their love for one another by transmitting to each a love letter. When they discover Maggie is behind the letters, Caldwell calls Maggie's dad and threatens to press charges against her. Maggie is writing a book about heroine Regina Carstairs, who fights for the underprivileged. Just like a fantasy sequence from *The Bob Cummings Show* or *The People's Choice*, Maggie imagines that Regina is defending her actions in court. After the fantasy sequence, Maggie makes herself up to look frazzled and informs Miss Caldwell that she is running away, Miss Caldwell feels sorry for her and drops the issue.

The pilot, produced by Maggie Inc. and McCadden, was directed by Rod Amateau and written by Bill Manhoff. ABC initially expressed interest in the series for its Monday night schedule for the 1957 television season, and then NBC considered it. The pilot finally aired on August 30, 1960, on CBS's summer replacement series *The Comedy Spot* that featured unsold pilots.

Maggie may not have been the only concept for a vehicle starring Margaret O'Brien. In the "Maggie Pilot File" that is part of USC's Burns and Allen collection, there is a draft proposal for a series about a young married couple, Connie and Owen Barker, living in a New York City apartment with Connie's older, unmarried sister Julia, who had come for a visit six months earlier but is still living with them. Connie's biggest interest in life is to find a husband for Julia. In the proposal, Connie tries unsuccessfully to interest her husband's boss' nephew in her sister. Julia decides to leave Connie and Owen, but Owen brings her back, saying that if this is what it takes to keep his marriage happy (having a sister-in-law stay with them), then he might as well get used to it. Margaret O'Brien may have been contemplated for the role of Connie.

It appears that only one pilot, *Maggie,* was actually produced by Burns' production company during 1957.

1958: *Theodora, Claudia* and a Talking Horse

One of the first projects undertaken by McCadden in 1958 was filming a pilot, Alcott Productions' *Up on Cloud Nine,* in January. Written by Barbara Hammer Avedon, who would later create the characters of Cagney and Lacey, and directed by Fletcher Markle, it starred Sue Randall as Jo Thomas and Theodora Davitt as Libby Marshall, two newly trained stewardesses for International Airlines who share an apartment.

Libby is trying to get some sleep before her first flight and has been told by her instructor Miss Barker that an airline representative will be on the flight to judge her performance. Jo comes home late after partying for most of the night, and Miss Barker phones to say that Jo will be the other attendant on the flight and not the more experienced stewardess Libby expected. The next morning, a cab driver, waiting to take them to the airport, rings the doorbell waking both women. They have to put their clothes on over their pajamas to make the flight on time. After the plane takes off, Libby receives an order for coffee from a rude passenger. When she goes to the back of the plane complaining about the man, Jo still has the cabin announcement system on. The entire plane hears the two comment on the passengers and speculate who from the airlines is the one checking on their performance. The pilots call the girls to serve them breakfast by saying "belly time." Libby and Jo think that they mean the plane must make a belly landing, and they prepare the cabin for this emergency. The women enter the cockpit only to find out that the pilots really wanted food. Back on the ground, Libby and Jo try to apologize to Miss Barker for their performance. Before Jo can finish her explanation, Miss Barker informs the girls that there was no report on them from the checker, since he missed the flight.

This pilot never became a series. Sue Randall, who played Jo, would later play Miss Landers, Beaver's teacher, on *Leave It to Beaver.* Theodora Davitt had a few small roles on TV shows in the 1950s before leaving acting.

Burns also worked on developing a series around the talents of British

116

actress Hermione Gingold, best known for her role as Madame Alvarez in the film *Gigi*. One proposal submitted to McCadden would seem to have been tailor-made for Gingold. Two writers not known for situation comedies—Christopher Isherwood (author of works that were the basis for *Cabaret* and the movie *A Single Man*) and Gavin Lambert (writer of *Inside Daisy Clover* and *Natalie Wood: A Life in Seven Takes*)—developed a treatment for a situation comedy titled *Emily Ermengarde*. Emily had a magic shop called Emily Ermengarde, Jests and Pranks, but the shop was a front for the more serious business of turning America back over to the British. Dressed in Victorian garb and ably assisted by Mr. Mudd who wore Edwardian business suits, Emily gauged her success by looking at such trends as an increase in crumpet-eating in Texas, the number of Americans who played croquet and cricket, and the frequency of drinking tea at regular hours. Her theory was that once Americans started following Britain on "the little things," the country would start following Britain on larger issues. Emily becomes an assistant at a bank where she foils a bank robbery by mesmerizing the robbers with a demonstration on how to properly make tea. She leaves her mark on the bank which starts closing between 11:00 and 11:15 a.m. every day for morning tea. It is not known if Gingold was ever approached by Burns to star as Emily Ermengarde, and it appears that no pilot based on this concept was ever produced.

In March 1958, McCadden did make *The Hermione Gingold Show* (aka *Theodora*) in which Gingold played Theodora Ashley, a charming Elsa Maxwell–type character "famous for being famous." She lived rent-free in a hotel and endorsed products for a living. The hotel didn't bill her for the accommodations since she attracted celebrities there. The pilot episode "Redecorating Mrs. Lanson's Suite" featured Rose Marie as Jenny, a hotel maid; David Lewis as Nelson Harrison, the hotel manager; Joby Baker as the bellboy, and Richard King as the elevator operator. The pilot script, written by Leo Solomon and Harvey Orkin, was produced and directed by Rod Amateau.

The episode opens with a Mr. Fairchild (Raymond Bailey) asking for Theodora's endorsement of Massinet champagne. She tells Fairchild she wants a sample before endorsing it and orders ten cases. The hotel is being repainted, and Jenny informs Theodora that Mrs. Larson's room hasn't been redecorated for a long time. Theodora is determined to have Mrs. Larson's suite redone because she assumes that Mrs. Larson is too poor to have it done herself. She enlists Maria Sorrentino (Lisa Gaye), an Italian movie star, to entertain hotel manager Harrison and has Mrs. Larson (Charity Grace) visit Mr. Bruce (Claude Stroud), a dress designer, in hopes of getting a new dress for Theodora's Aunt Hilda. For Mrs. Larson's rooms, Theodora takes furniture from the hotel's Tower Suite, while newlyweds Mr. and Mrs. Davis (Ted Jordan and Dorothy Provine) are still in the suite. She also has the hotel's painters, Charlie (Jack Weston) and Leffler (Ned Glass), repaint Mrs. Larson's room. While Mrs. Larson is pleased with the results, she confesses that she really is wealthy. In the end, Theodora offers to sell her the ten cases of champagne.

Apparently, the making of the McCadden pilot was less than memorable for Gingold since she failed to make any mention of it in her autobiography *How to Grow Old Disgracefully,* published in 1989—two years after her death.

As production at McCadden was winding down with the end of *The Burns and Allen Show,* George formed a partnership with author Rose Franken, her husband William Meloney and producer Armand Deutsch to make a pilot based on Franken's *Claudia* book series. *Claudia* had been a Broadway play, two movies, and a television series before becoming a pilot for Burns' company. Its first TV incarnation was in January 1952 as a live drama starring Joan McCracken as Claudia Brown, a young woman who marries an aspiring architect, David Naughton (Hugh Reilly), but is still close to her mother. The series lasted for about six months, first on NBC and then on CBS. In 1956, Franken attempted to bring the show back. Four Star Productions expressed interest, and later there was the possibility that Frank Sinatra would finance a pilot. Screen Gems, Jess Oppenheimer, and NBC subsequently became interested in making a pilot but never did.

Burns loaned Claudia Productions $8,000 for a comedy-drama pilot written by Franken and directed by Richard Kinon. Burns' interest in the pilot appears to have been mainly financial and not creative. The character of Claudia Naughton was not a ditzy woman. She was more innocent about the world than naïve. Anne Francis was to star as Claudia after actress Susan Oliver turned down the role because she thought a television series would endanger her film career. Bob Knapp would be Claudia's husband David, and Doris Kenyon, her mother.

In the pilot "The Special Talent," Claudia, mother of a young son named Bobby, lived on a farm. Her husband's office was in New York City and, while having lunch with him and her mother, Mrs. Brown asks Claudia to clear her stuff out of her apartment closet since she is having the place painted. Claudia finds a foot locker in the closet with **Capt. David Naughton, USMC** stenciled on it. She discovers that her husband had been awarded a Silver Star and a Distinguished Service Cross for heroism in the Korean War. She also reads a love letter he wrote to a nurse who cared for him when he was wounded. Claudia later tells David that she opened his foot locker and saw a part of him she never knew before. She asks him about the letter to the nurse, and he responds that the nurse died in a raid. Claudia remarks that she wished the nurse had lived even though it might have meant the nurse would be David's wife instead of her.

The pilot was apparently re-shot with an actress named Pat Michon replacing Anne Francis in the lead role. As was his way with promoting shows, Burns recorded an introduction to advertisers of scenes from the pilot, saying in part: "I'm one of the backers of *Claudia*. I'm one of the lovers of Claudia. I've always been in love with Claudia. I fell in love with Claudia when she was nothing but a little book and making her way in America." Concerning Rose Franken and her choice of Pat Michon, George said: "Now [Franken] insisted on using an unknown Claudia for this television series. Who am I to argue with her? She's always insisted on an unknown to create the part."[7]

When shown to advertisers in early 1959, the pilot did not sell. McCadden then dropped out of the project. There was a report that Four Star Productions was again dickering for the property. However, by the end of 1960 the project was dead.

The best-known comedy pilot ever made by Burns' production company was *Wilbur Pope and Mister Ed* (aka *The Wonderful World of Wilbur Pope*) which led to the *Mister Ed* sitcom of the early sixties, the first of the fantasy comedies that would be prevalent on TV during the 1960s. The initial pilot was directed by Arthur Lubin and written by Bob O'Brien, Iz Elinson, and Phil Shuken. Scott McKay played Wilbur Pope and Sandra White his wife Carlotta; the Popes have been married for eight years and Pope is a lawyer (not an architect as Wilbur Post was in *Mister Ed*). The pilot starts with the Popes arriving at their new home where their neighbors are helping them unpack. The neighbors invite them to dinner that evening. This initial scene was subsequently deleted from the pilot. The revised pilot simply had the Popes arriving at their new home. While reviewing the property, Carlotta steps on a rake which hits Wilbur on the head; they then meet Mister Ed. Carlotta is inclined to sell the horse, but Wilbur wants to keep him. When Mister Ed plays sick, the sale doesn't go through. Wilbur later discovers that Mister Ed can talk, but everyone thinks he is crazy when he tells them about the horse. Carlotta assumes the rake accident is making her husband believe the horse can talk. When Wilbur tells his neighbor Mr. Bigby about the talking horse, the neighbor withdraws the dinner invitation. Mister Ed advises Wilbur how he can show people he is not crazy. Wilbur goes to the neighbors with fish and meat in his pockets and bird seed in his hair. Wilbur explains that he got hit on the head with a rake handle; this, together with his special rapport with animals, made him think the horse could talk. At that moment, a dog and cat jump in his arms because of the food in his pockets, and a bird sits on his head because of the bird seed. The neighbors think that Wilbur must be a good guy because the animals like him, and they invite the Popes to stay in the neighborhood.

Burns invested $75,000 in the production of the pilot. No doubt influenced by the success of the wisecracking dog on *The People's Choice,* Burns was further drawn to the premise of a sitcom built around a talking horse because of Arthur Lubin's involvement: Lubin had been behind the *Francis the Talking Mule* series of movies. The character Mister Ed was based on a series of short stories by Walter Brooks. In the first story, titled "The Talking Horse," published in *Liberty* magazine on September 18, 1937, Wilbur Pope, an advertising account executive living in Mount Kisco, New York, was married to beautiful Carlotta, part Spanish with a bad temper. As Brooks writes about Carlotta, "[W]hen she was in high spirits she didn't pay attention to her husband and when she was low and cranky she didn't pay attention to any one else."[8] While Carlotta wouldn't let Wilbur have a dog, she did permit him to have a horse, Mister Ed. After Wilbur returns from his Sunday morning ride with Ed, he finds a noisy crowd guzzling cocktails on his porch. Carlotta belittles Wilbur in front of the guests, and he decides to go on another ride. When Wilbur starts singing, Mister Ed turns around and says, "Oh for Pete's sake, Wilb, shut up!"—the first words Ed ever spoke to Wilbur. Ed reveals that animals can talk but they almost never let humans know this because "they'd just get a lot of extra work shoved on them."[9] Ed said he finally spoke to Wilbur because he couldn't stand his singing and because Wilbur made him sick the way he let Carlotta push him around.

After the dissolution of McCadden Productions, Filmways remade the *Mister Ed* pilot, and the series enjoyed a six-year run. See Chapter 9 for more details.

A final project contemplated by Burns involved another untitled pilot with a show business background. It starred entertainer Harry Richman and James Mason's wife Pamela. Nothing came of this proposal.

In discussing the making of TV pilots with Hollywood columnist Army Archerd, Burns summed up his experience thusly: "I think you can make more money in oil—it's less of a gamble. You can have a good show and a good sponsor—but you can't get a time slot."[10]

7

George and His Dramatic Anthologies

While George Burns' forte was producing comedies, his production company did become involved with some dramatic pilots and series. Most of them were of the anthology type popular on television in the fifties and early sixties. Like a "movie of the week," anthology series had no permanent cast members. Each week there was a new episode with different stars, but usually the storylines had a common theme such as suspense, mystery, or romance.

Burns' involvement with dramatic series took two major forms: backing projects associated with a well-known writer or star or developing in-house projects (suggested by Al Simon) that were very much like docudramas or "real-life fiction." Either way, his involvement with dramas was basically financial. As far as can be determined, he did not sit in with the writers of dramatic series like he did with his comedies, and the writers and directors used on his comedies did not normally work on the dramas.

Craig Rice and Other Early Dramatic Projects

McCadden's first attempt at a dramatic series was *Craig Rice Theatre*. In 1952, producers Tony London and Sam Neuman acquired rights to all stories authored by mystery writer Craig Rice (Georgiana Ann Craig) and wanted to produce an anthology series based on them. Thirteen episodes were planned but never filmed. In 1954, Burns' company bought all the story rights from London and Neuman and announced a series of thirty-nine episodes to be produced by the duo. Barbara Stanwyck was rumored to be the host for this mystery anthology series. When it failed to sell, McCadden thought of adapting the Craig Rice mysteries for comic actress Marie Wilson (see Chapter 6). That idea never went anywhere, and a series based on the Craig Rice stories was subsequently abandoned by McCadden presumably because of lack of sponsorship. London and Neuman then shopped the concept to Ziv Television Programs and settled a breach of contract suit against them in 1959 for an undisclosed sum. The series never did get off the ground.

In 1954, Burns also helped to finance a drama pilot titled *Deadline* for APB Productions. Directed by Phil Karlson and written by David Dortort, who later created *Bonanza,* the pilot centered on a sportswriter named Mike Connor (John Payne) who turned crime reporter and investigated the murder of a young boxer. Producer Stephen Ames, Payne, and novelist-screenwriter W.R. Burnett made up APB Productions. The pilot, which was not picked up as a series, did air in 1956 as an episode of the *Heinz Studio 57* anthology series. Payne went on to star in the NBC western *The Restless Gun,*

Author Craig Rice (aka Georgiana Ann Craig) who wrote mystery novels like *The Corpse Steps Out* and *Having a Wonderful Crime* as well as screenplays, among them *The Falcon's Brother* and *The Falcon in Danger.*

which knocked *The Burns and Allen Show* out of the top thirty series during the sitcom's final season.

Variety indicated in 1955 that movie actor Joel McCrea wanted to produce a television project in conjunction with McCadden based on the adventures of a resort hotel owner.[1] McCrea would not appear in the series, to be titled *Las Vegas Gentleman.* Peter Graves, who would later star on *Mission: Impossible,* was considered for the lead. There is no evidence that a pilot was ever produced by Burns' production company.

In April 1955, McCadden did film a pilot titled *The Getter and the Holder* (aka *Giver and Taker*) starring Peter Lorre and Francis L. Sullivan and based on a play by Sam Neuman. Sullivan bore a striking resemblance to Sydney Greenstreet, Lorre's costar in several movies. Falcon Productions, whose shareholders included Lorre, Sullivan, Neuman, Irving Yergen, and M.P. Moss, co-produced the pilot with Burns' company. This whodunit with comedy overtones, written by David Friedkin and Morton Fine (who later produced the TV series *I Spy* together) was set in Algeria.

The storyline for the McCadden pilot involved Mr. Constantine (Sullivan) and Mr. Cleo Kobe (Lorre) owning an antique shop where a man named Robert Stone visits and introduces himself as the former curator of the Indo-China museum in Hanoi. Stone is looking for a man named Nelson who stole a Kwan Yin jade statuette from his museum. Constantine agrees to locate Nelson for $5,000. Stone gives him $2,000 with a promise of the remainder after Nelson and the statuette are found.

Cleo finds Nelson and says he has a buyer for the statuette Nelson possesses. Nelson wants Cleo to bring him the buyer in two hours. Constantine visits Stone, tells him that Nelson has been located, and asks for the balance of the money owed to him. Constantine knows that Stone is an imposter because he used the incorrect gender pronoun in referring to the moon he had been looking at earlier on a Japanese print. He lets Stone follow him and Cleo to Nelson's hideout where Stone strides in with a gun and announces that his real name is Muller. He says the real Stone died in Hanoi but not before telling him about Nelson and the Kwan Yin. Constantine says that the Kwan Yin that Nelson has is a fake. Cleo and Constantine go after a furious Muller, wrestle his gun away from him, and corner him and Nelson. Back at their shop, Constantine advises the police inspector that he knew that only one true Kwan Yin existed in jade, and it is in Bombay. *The Getter and the Holder* never became a series.

Billboard reported on September 3, 1955, that negotiations were underway between Zane Grey TV Productions (which owned the rights to Grey's novels and stories) and McCadden Productions for filming a western series. It was contemplated that two shows would result from any such deal: an anthology series and a regular western series based on one of the characters from the stories, possibly Arizona Ames.[2] However, no deal ever resulted from the negotiations. Four Star did reach a deal with Zane Grey Productions, and *Zane Grey Theatre* ran on CBS for five seasons with Dick Powell as host.

The most success Burns' company had with actually producing a dramatic TV series was due to the creativity of Al Simon, who had been with McCadden Productions from the start. Simon had been an associate producer for *The George Burns and Gracie Allen Show* and for *The Bob Cummings Show* and production supervisor for *The People's Choice* before becoming McCadden's vice-president in charge of production. In the late fifties, he formed his own production company, Al Simon Productions, to create and produce dramas for McCadden and became executive producer of *Panic!* and *Flight*. His dramas were usually done in a documentary style and most of his series concepts were based on real-life stories.

Panic!

McCadden's first successful drama, *Panic!,* was a half-hour anthology that placed an individual or a group in a suspenseful, usually life-threatening situation. Created by Simon, it had several different titles before it premiered: *Impact, Turmoil, Impasse,* and *Crisis.* The pilot was made in July 1955. NBC originally planned to put it up against *I Love Lucy* on Mondays at 9:00 p.m. beginning in September 1956, but then delayed the show until March 1957 when it premiered at 8:30 p.m. Tuesday nights. McCadden initially tried to get legendary newsman Lowell Thomas to be the host and narrator of the series but subsequently hired announcer Westbrook Van Voorhis, who was known for narrating the *March of Time* newsreels shown in movie theaters.

Van Voorhis hosted each episode, which typically began with him announcing, "You are now going to live through a moment of panic in a woman's [or man's] life—an experience so incredible that you may not believe it! Yet its premise is true! This is the woman! All you need to know about her you will know in exactly two minutes and fifty seconds ... and then ... *panic*!"

In an interview, Burns said that *Panic!* was an "accident" for his production company. He further remarked that he only knew comedy, "so comedy shows are the only kind I look for."[3] Willy Burns was listed as script supervisor for *Panic!* and Rod Amateau directed a couple of episodes, but there is no indication that Burns was directly involved in the production.

In the premiere episode "The Priest," written by David Dortort and directed by Amateau, John Oliver (John Harmon) comes to Father Dolan's

(James Whitmore) church late at night asking the priest to hear his confession: Oliver claims that he will kill a man tomorrow at 9:20 a.m. with a bomb. Before the priest can find out where the bomb is planted, Oliver has a heart attack and dies. Dolan attempts to find the bomb: From Oliver's wife, he learns that her husband recently received an upsetting phone call asking for a person named John Allen whom the priest discovers was an escaped prisoner. In the morning newspaper, Dolan sees a story that a man was scheduled to testify in court revealing that Oliver was really Allen. Dolan goes to the courthouse and locates the bomb before it goes off.

Another typical episode during the series' first season was "The Boy," written and directed by Sherman Marks. Billy Gray from *Father Knows Best* starred as Tommy Williams. While trying to retrieve his cat from under the front porch, Tommy hears two men saying they are going to kill his father, who works as a lighthouse keeper. Tommy is afraid to inform the police since the two strangers said his dad was hiding from the law. He hitches a ride to the lighthouse with two men whom he recognizes as the killers from their shoes. Tommy gets away from them and eventually takes a friend's bike to the lighthouse. Although the two men get there ahead of him, he is able to elude them again and warn his father, who turns out to have witnessed a murder but didn't want to inform the police since the murderers had threatened his son's life. The police arrive and capture the two men.

Maury Geraghty directed many of the episodes of *Panic!* and wrote one titled "The Subway." When George Mason (Eduard Franz) gets on the subway at 2:30 a.m. he discovers that a man sitting across from him in between two other men is actually dead. He flees the subway at the next stop and tells his wife (Barbara Billingsley) what he saw. The next day, Mason reads in the newspaper about the murder of a man who was going to testify against the mob. He is initially reluctant to get involved but eventually goes to the police station where he sees that the clerk who will take his eyewitness account is one of the murderers. He decides not to say anything and leaves the police station. The other killer follows him home, but the police show up and capture the killer along with the police station clerk, who had been under surveillance.

In addition to directing episodes of *Panic!* and a subsequent series Burns and Simon produced called *Flight,* Geraghty wrote for such television series as *The Gene Autry Show, Annie Oakley,* and *The Addams Family.*

He also produced the *Falcon* series of movies in the 1940s and directed episodes of TV's *Lassie* and *The Virginian*.

Harold "Bud" Swanton wrote several episodes for *Panic!* such as "Two Martinis." Barney Dutton (Kent Taylor), a stockbroker who had suffered a nervous breakdown, has just been released from a sanitarium after ten weeks and visits his partner Gil Beresford (William Ching). Beresford gives him a martini, but Dutton pours the drink back into the pitcher. Unaware of this, Beresford pours himself a martini, drinks it, and dies. Dutton goes to his wife Kit (Peggy Knudson) and relates what happened, but she doesn't believe that his partner tried to poison him. Dutton learns through friends that his wife was seeing his partner while he was in the sanitarium. He visits his late partner's wife Gretchen (Irene Hervey), who informs him that her husband had embezzled $80,000 from the business, lost it in the stock market, and wanted to make it appear that Dutton had embezzled the money and then committed suicide.

Swanton also wrote the June 11 episode of *Panic!*, "Mayday," about Steve Bridges (Richard Jaeckel), a paraplegic ham radio operator. His neighbor's dog knocks over Bridges' wheelchair and a gas heater. Bridges struggles to get assistance as the room catches on fire. Finally he is able to turn on his ham radio to ask for help, and a rescue squad arrives just in time to save him.

Besides *Panic!*, Swanton scripted many episodes of *Perry Mason, Alfred Hitchcock Presents, Wagon Train,* and *Little House on the Prairie*.

The May 7, 1957, episode "Courage," written by Jack Neuman from a story by Richard Grey, was an unsold pilot for another anthology series conceived by Al Simon. *Courage* was supposed to have been bought by CBS for its early 1957 schedule but the deal fell through. In the pilot, an explosion occurs in a holding tank at a chemical factory. One of the men who was repainting the inside of the tank, John Tunney (Trevor Bardette), is still trapped inside, and Dr. David Nelson (Paul Burke) wants to save him, but Tunney is crazy with pain and doesn't want to be rescued. When the doctor informs the fire captain that Tunney is his father, the captain permits him to attempt the rescue. Nelson gets inside the tank, but Tunney threatens to kill him, thinking that the doctor is his boss who wants to take his job away. The doctor convinces Tunney otherwise and rescues him. More details about *Courage* are found below.

The final episode of the season starred June Havoc, the sister of Gypsy

Rose Lee. Written by her husband William Spier, this installment was originally named "Moth and the Flame" and then retitled "Reincarnated." In her theater dressing room, June Sullivan (Havoc) meets Vincent Hawthorne (Alan Napier), who says he is going to murder her. He believes that June is his former wife whom he killed because she was not faithful. June performs the same kind of act that his late wife did. She pretends to be his wife and performs an extremely sultry song and dance which causes Hawthorne to have a heart attack.

Panic! returned on Sunday, April 6, 1958, at 7:30 p.m. for a final brief season. The title was changed to *No Warning*. In the first episode "Emergency," directed by Fletcher Markle and written by Harold Swanton, a young boy has been injured in a bike accident and has to have an operation, but the doctors need his parents' permission. Charlie Pulaski (Elisha Cook Jr.), a cab driver, sees the story on TV, goes to the hospital, and pretends to be the boy's father to sign the release for the operation. The boy's real parents subsequently show up, and Pulaski explains what he did. The doctor advises the real father that if they had waited to perform the operation, the boy would have bled to death.

The second episode "Hear No Evil" was directed by Fletcher Markle and written by DeWitt Bodeen. After seeing her child killed in an accident, Helen Colby (Mercedes McCambridge) became unable to hear or speak. She has her hearing restored but keeps it a secret from her husband Bart (played by director Markle) and her sister Alice (Whitney Blake). One day she overhears her husband and sister planning to kill her by drugging her and leaving their car on the railroad tracks for a train to hit it. At a bar to celebrate their anniversary, Helen's husband puts a sedative in her drink, but she drops the drink. Her sister puts a sedative in Helen's second glass of wine which she partially drinks. She falls asleep in the car, and her husband stops it on the tracks. However, Helen gets out of the car before the train hits the vehicle and writes a note to the investigating officer about the murder plot.

Frequently seen in shows associated with McCadden, Leon Ames starred on a May episode of *Panic!* titled "Amnesiac," directed by Markle and written by Jack Bennett. Henry Hall (Ames), an antique dealer from Yonkers, New York, is found unconscious in a Chicago hotel room. When he regains consciousness, the hotel manager addresses him as Mr. Thomas. Hall phones his wife who says that he had $50,000 when he went to

Chicago; now he cannot locate the money. He learns that he used it to purchase a valuable goblet at an antique auction and that he apparently married an attractive woman who took the goblet. He finds the hotel where the woman is staying and tells the hotel clerk that he is Mr. Thomas in order to get into her room. He finds the goblet just as Mrs. Thomas (Dorothy Green) returns. Hall pretends he still thinks he is Mr. Thomas until the real Mr. Thomas returns and threatens to kill him. The police arrive, summoned by the hotel desk clerk who knew that Hall was not Mr. Thomas.

In "Double Identity" aka "Mistaken Identity," George Burns' son Ronnie made a rare dramatic appearance along with Robert Vaughn, later to star on *The Man from U.N.C.L.E.* Written by Frederic Louis Fox, the episode finds Frank Elliot (Vaughn) stopping in a small town on his way to a new job and being identified as the "Smiling Killer" from a newspaper sketch. The real killer, Joe Kretcher (Ronnie Burns), plants incriminating evidence in Elliot's car. Kretcher steals the police car with Elliot in it and divulges that he is the real murderer and plans to kill Elliot. Elliot causes the police car to crash, and both he and Kretcher struggle to get free from the wreck. Elliot extricates himself, flags down the police, and shows them where Kretcher is.

A pilot for the series titled *Flight* aired in June. Jumpmaster Lt. George Wilson (Richard Jaeckel) is in charge of paratroopers making their first jump from a C-124 Globemaster. One of the plane's engines goes out, and Wilson is told to expedite the jump. The last man to jump gets one of his parachute lines tangled on the plane. Attempts to pull him up fail. Finally Wilson suggests that as they land, they will cut him loose as a convertible Chrysler Imperial speeds under the plane and two men in the back seat catch the parachutist. The plan works, and the paratrooper survives.

Still another pilot, this one called "Fingerprints," also aired in June. Directed by Maury Geraghty and written by Leonard Heideman, this episode starred Paul Stewart as Paul Chase, the former head of a counter-intelligence agency. Chase is asked by the government to enter a carefully guarded foreign consulate to replace the fingerprint card of one of their spies, who has been killed in a fight, with the fingerprints on an American undercover agent who will soon arrive at the consulate pretending he is their spy. Chase is told that the undercover agent is his son. To help him get into the consulate, Chase has a *Mission: Impossible*–type team consisting of Karen Adams (Lola Albright) and Randy Burke (Brian Kelly). He enters the building through the air conditioning duct and, using an odorless gas, puts the consul (John Wengraf) to sleep. Chase is able to substitute the fingerprints of his son, the undercover agent, right before his son arrives at the consulate. This episode was the pilot for a short-lived series titled *21 Beacon Street* (see Chapter 9).

Commenting on *Panic!,* Al Simon remarked that the scripts followed a formula much like a newspaper article, with the main story points laid out early and the remaining minutes devoted to telling how the situation is resolved. Simon also noted that putting quality production into the series through the use of outdoor locations and guest stars increased the normal budget for a half-hour show by about 20 percent—probably a fact that unnerved frugal George Burns.[4]

Flight

This syndicated dramatic series, produced in cooperation with the U.S. Air Force and the Department of Defense, was hosted by retired General George C. Kenney. Kenney had been commander of the Allied Air Forces in the Southwest Pacific Area during World War II. The creator of *Flight,* Al Simon stressed that the stories would emphasize the people within the Air Force and not the technical equipment. Each episode took a basic instrument of flight such as a jet, airplane, or rocket and tied it to a human being.

The pilot, which aired as an installment of *Panic!,* and subsequent episodes of the series were shot at Norton Air Force Base because of its proximity to Hollywood. Many of the episodes combined footage shot at Norton with stock Air Force film of aircraft on various missions.

Because the series was syndicated, it aired at different times on different stations during the 1958–59 TV season. Produced by Robert Stillman; Herb Browar was the associate producer, and Leonard Heideman was the story editor. Filmed by McCadden Productions, *Flight* was produced by Airborne Productions (owned by George Burns and Al Simon) with Willy Burns having a small share in the company. The series was offered to individual TV stations through syndication by California National Productions, a subsidiary of NBC.

Several episodes of *Flight* dealt with human reactions to flying jet aircraft. In "Experiment Oxygen," written by Heideman and directed by Jean Yarbrough, a young Air Force doctor, Capt. Pete Ewing, attempts to determine why two brothers died in separate jet crashes. He finds that each pilot was apprehensive and breathing oxygen too fast, causing hyperventilation.

Ernie Talesco (Herb Rudley), a flight surgeon, examines pilot Charlie Ott (Mike Road) who seems to be having problems with another Air Force pilot, Mike Benedict (Wesley Lau), in an episode titled "The Dart." The two pilots are practicing on a dart-shaped target. During a practice run, Ott hits Benedict's jet instead of the target, and Benedict has to bail out. Talesco attempts to find the cause of what appears to be a psychological problem with Ott. He learns that both pilots have been dating the same Las Vegas showgirl. However, he later discovers the real problem is that at the time of the incident, Ott was in zero gravity and missed the dart target because of spatial disorientation.

In "Atomic Cloud," Colonel Ernest Pinson (Hayden Rorke) wants to see if a pilot can fly through the cloud from a hydrogen bomb blast and survive. He has the peacetime limit for exposure to radiation raised and recruits a crew to volunteer for the test. Pinson finds that jets can fly through atomic clouds, and Air Force tactics are revised to permit penetration of such clouds under military circumstances.

Some of the *Flight* episodes dealt with World War II and with the Korean conflict. "Bombs in the Belfry," based on a story by John Kneubuhl and Major Paul Webber with a teleplay by Kneubuhl and Heideman, concerned Lt. Jerry Rowe, whose father had been a missionary. Rowe was a new bombardier under Lt. Dave Willis in New Guinea during World War II. He performs his missions well until he is instructed to bomb a church that is supposedly used by the Japanese as a radio center. Rowe feels guilty about bombing native villages and requests a transfer. Lt. Willis takes him to the village where the church was, and we find that the building had been used by the Japanese not only as a radio center but also as an interrogation center. Rowe learns that senior military staff members always make the right decisions (the common wisdom at the time).

In "Chopper Four," written by Jack Laird, Capt. B.L. "Browny" Douglas pilots a R4 Sigorsky helicopter during World War II in the Philippines running errands for the Air Force. Browny wants to do something useful with his helicopter and sees the need to evacuate the wounded more quickly from behind enemy lines. On his first attempt to pick up wounded soldiers, he is fired upon by the enemy and has no means to fire back since the helicopter cannot be loaded down with armaments. He decides to go around enemy lines with an auxiliary fuel tank added to his aircraft, but this means he can evacuate only one wounded serviceman at a time. However, two soldiers need to be flown out immediately. He flies directly over enemy lines and this time drops mortar shells on the enemy to stop them from firing on his helicopter.

Some episodes starred actors who would later become more famous. In "Red China Rescue," Capt. Don Adams (Steve Brodie), a pilot with Air Rescue Services in the Philippines, comes to the aid of a Dutch cargo plane that crashed in a storm off the coast of southern China after being shot up by Chinese MIG fighters. Adams locates the one survivor from the crash and has to rescue him before his raft goes into Chinese territorial waters while, at the same time, being observed by Chinese MIGs. Future Oscar winner Louise Fletcher appeared in this episode as Capt. Adams' sister Carol.

Burt Reynolds played Capt. Jack Hilyard in the World War II story "Eye for Victory." Hilyard, a photo-reconnaissance pilot in the U.S. Air Corps, is assigned to take pictures of Japanese strongholds in the Philippine jungles. He comes up with the idea of capturing a Japanese Zero and using it for reconnaissance. Once a Japanese airfield in the Philippines is captured by American forces, Hilyard, with the help of a Japanese-American recruit, flies over the jungle terrain in a Zero and takes the photos.

Reynolds also appeared in an episode titled "Master Sergeant." In that episode, Master Sgt. Gus Miller (Patrick McVey), a flight engineer, is being reassigned as a line chief, which means he won't be flying any more. His superior, Capt. Sam Allen (Reynolds), is reluctant to tell him about the reassignment, particularly after the Korean conflict begins. Allen's crew goes on a bombing mission over Korea with Gus as the flight engineer, and they come under enemy fire. The aircraft loses an engine, but Gus gets them back to the airfield. Sam then officially informs Gus that he will be reassigned. Gus decides to quit the Air Force when his hitch is up, but then learns that Allen's bomber returning from another mission is on fire. When the plane lands, he rescues the captain and the new flight engineer. After that experience, he decides to accept the reassignment as line chief.

Some stars who appeared in George Burns-produced series and pilots guest starred on episodes of *Flight*. For example, Pat Michon, who starred in the *Claudia* pilot, played a suspected German informant in a World War II episode titled "Havana Run." Robert Ellis, who played Ronnie's friend Ralph on *The Burns and Allen Show,* appeared as a co-pilot blinded by enemy fire in "Window in the Sky."

The ratings for *Flight* were apparently not sufficient for it to be renewed for a second season.

Woman in the Case and Other Al Simon Drama Projects

McCadden Productions was often presented with ideas for dramas which they declined to produce. One such idea, presented by James J. Geller in 1957 to Willy Burns, was an anthology series titled *World Premiere* which would feature original and unpublished stories from famous writers such as Aldous Huxley, Christopher Isherwood, and William Faulkner. Maurice Morton recommended that McCadden pass on this proposal. Another possible series for McCadden in 1958 from Dan Leeds Productions, *Assignment: Rescue,* dealt with case histories of those uprooted by tyranny and war. It would have been done in a semi-documentary style, based on the files of the International Rescue Committee. Morton also rejected this project.

Burns attempted to get actress June Havoc her own series produced by his company. Havoc had previously starred in a one-season comedy, made by Desilu during 1954 and 1955, where she played a lawyer. In 1956, she attempted a comeback for ABC in a vehicle titled *My 70 Sons* about a widowed actress with a teenage daughter who inherits a military academy for boys ages ten to eighteen. It appears that the pilot for *My 70 Sons,* written by Nate Monaster and Arthur Alsberg, was never made due to lack of financing.

As noted above, Havoc starred in an installment of *Panic!,* written by her husband William Spier, and this may have led Burns to consider producing *Woman in the Case,* a suspense-mystery anthology series developed by Spier. McCadden Productions announced in summer 1957 that it was working with Havoc and her husband on a vehicle starring the actress. Spier and Havoc were to own a 25 percent share of the project, and Havoc was to star in and host several of the episodes on a rotating basis with other female stars. Other actresses mentioned as possibilities for hostess duties included Ida Lupino, Anne Baxter, Teresa Wright, Bette Davis, and Lilli Palmer.

Woman in the Case would deal mostly with women involved some way in criminal cases. In his proposal, Spier outlined a few storylines. One centered on Jane Stanton, a librarian at the Glendale Public Library. A library patron returns a book with two pages missing. The patron denies tearing out the pages, complaining that because of the missing pages she was done out of a hot love scene. Jane finds strange razor cuts on the pages on each side of those missing from the book. She then compares the vandalized copy of the book with one from which no pages have been removed. She discovers that certain words have been cut out by the razor blade. Jane makes a list of the words and determines that, when placed in the right order, the words are part of a ransom note.

Another storyline concerned Pat Dodger, an out-of-work actress and a member of the Office of Special Services and Investigation, an undercover unit of the police department. Pat was likely to turn up anywhere there was a murder, missing person case, or a narcotics ring, and she would play a variety of undercover roles such as a lady cellist or a cigarette girl.

Negotiations between Burns' company and the Spiers never resulted in McCadden producing a pilot of *Woman in the Case.* In 1959, the proposal was considered as a possible co-production involving CBS and actress Maureen O'Hara, with O'Hara as the hostess and occasional star. The series concept was then passed around to several producers such as Desi Arnaz and Quinn Martin. In 1960, Paul Monash at MGM attempted to make a pilot deal with NBC for the series, but the network rejected this project in 1961 because of excessive costs.

Al Simon also created several unsold pilots for dramatic series while affiliated with McCadden. These pilots included:

- *Courage*: Simon started production on this semi-documentary series in mid–1956. The proposed series differed from *Panic!* in that its stories were to be less melodramatic and were to be based on true cases of heroism. Originally, character actor Dan Riss served as host-moderator. The pilot never sold; as noted above, it was broadcast as the tenth episode of *Panic!* on May 7, 1957.

- *Experiment*: Also in 1956, Simon came up with an idea for this anthology series, to be produced for NBC. The drama was planned for the 1957 TV season. Stories were to be based on social and scientific experiments presented in dramatic form. The pilot dealt with a secret project conducted in the Los Angeles area.
- *Inspector General*: Based on files of the inspector general's office of the Department of Defense and the Air Force, the pilot for this Al Simon–conceived series was written by Leonard Heideman in 1959. Its lead was a character who would be on assignment around the world, working closely with the police and FBI. The series was to be filmed entirely on location.
- *Women*: Simon created an anthology titled *Women,* filmed in early 1958 and intended for syndication during the 1958–59 TV season. The concept was somewhat similar to *Woman in the Case* in its focus on female characters but, unlike the William Spier project, *Women* would dramatize the emotional and romantic problems of women and not necessarily emphasize mystery themes. The pilot was written by Howard Swanton and directed by Fletcher Markle. Simon wanted the show to present the type of situation any woman could find herself in and which would be suspenseful enough to capture a male audience as well. It was rumored that actor Charles Boyer would host the series.
- *War Birds*: This pilot, a spinoff from *Flight,* centered on World War I flyers. Originally created when Simon was with McCadden, the project was later revamped and marketed by Filmways. See Chapter 9 for more details.

In his book about unsold television pilots, Lee Goldberg mentions two pilots McCadden Productions made circa 1958, *Ghost Squad* and *Central Intelligence.* The former was about undercover Scotland Yard detectives during World War II, and based on a book by John Gosling. It did become an ITC series in 1961 and was offered for syndication to TV stations in the United States, but no evidence of McCadden's involvement in this project could be found beyond the reference in Goldberg's book.[5] *Central Intelligence,* a half-hour series based on CIA files, supposedly had as its lead character a secret agent whose cover was a traveling salesman working for a large import house.[6] No other information about these pilots could be found in the archives of *Variety* or in the Burns and Allen collection at USC.

In February 1959, McCadden laid off several employees because production was at a standstill. Al Simon left McCadden Productions to join Filmways on August 15, 1959.

8

George Without Gracie

The Magic Is Gone—*The George Burns Show*

After Gracie Allen retired, George decided to continue the show with the rest of the regulars from *The Burns and Allen Show*. Burns wanted CBS to put his own show on Mondays at 8:00 p.m. the same time slot as his prior sitcom, but his new comedy ended up on NBC. The show was initially scheduled for Fridays at 9:30 p.m. However, it was moved to Tuesdays at 9:00 p.m. (where it preceded *The Bob Cummings Show*) because *Dotto*, a game show originally scheduled for 9:00 Tuesdays, was abruptly taken off the air as a result of the infamous quiz show scandal. (A contestant waiting to appear on *Dotto* found a notebook belonging to a winning contestant that contained answers to the questions she had been asked, and ultimately the New York attorney general became aware of this information. After *Dotto* was canceled during the summer of 1958, Colgate-Palmolive, which sponsored Burns' solo effort, aired a series of unsold pilots for eight weeks in the timeslot until *The George Burns Show* premiered on October 21.)

In his own comedy, George explicitly played the role of a producer which he had by implication portrayed on his sitcom with Gracie. *The George Burns Show* had Burns leasing an office in the same building where Harry Morton had his accounting business. When he started George Burns Productions, Blanche Morton became his secretary. Harry Von Zell and Ronnie Burns continued to appear as themselves. Judi Meredith played Ronnie's girlfriend, and Charles Bagby was Sid, George's piano player. Gracie Allen never appeared on the series, but she was often referred to and her picture was displayed in George's office on the set. Burns' Banda (Burns and Allen) Productions produced the comedy.

In doing promotion for his series, George sent a letter to Walter Annenberg, owner of *TV Guide*, asking to be on the cover. His letter read in part:

I just want a little advice from you. Who do you know at *TV Guide* that's big enough that I can talk to, to get the cover for our October 21st show? I think it would help me a lot if I could get it because I am coming back with a new show and I'm coming back kind of late. If there's a possibility of getting the cover, maybe you can talk to that certain person. In return, I can give you some old Burns and Allen scripts or orchestrations of some of my hit songs like "Tiger Girl" or "In the Heart of a Cherry" or "I'm Tying the Leaves On So They Don't Fall Down" ... or you can sleep with my sister.[1]

Rod Amateau directed all the filmed episodes of *The George Burns Show*. They were written by Norman Paul, Keith Fowler, Harvey Helm, and, of course, Willy Burns. Some episodes focused on George the producer; others on George the singer; and still others on the show biz careers of his son Ronnie and Judi Meredith. However, George was never able to construct a character for himself with a unique world view apart from

his usual role of being a straight man who liked to sing and perform monologues. Gone were the more surrealistic aspects of the prior sitcoms he helped to produce unless one considers Burns' singing surreal. There were no ditzy characters, no charming manipulators, no snarky animals, no bizarre endings, and no magic television set. The storylines were fairly typical sitcom fare. Probably because he was the central character, George no longer attempted to complicate the plot or foresee plot developments as he had done on *The Burns and Allen Show*.

Burns playing a producer on *The George Burns Show*. Viewers probably never realized that Burns always wore a toupee on TV.

The first episode, "George and the Private Eye," began with Burns saying that he doesn't want to retire like Gracie and thinks he can do his own show. Harry Morton suggests that George can be a producer. Burns has a script that he thinks would be great for a private eye series. Ronnie brings in a musical group to audition for his dad and sings his Verve recording "She's Kinda Cute." Jack Benny appears on a TV interview show and is asked if George can be a success on his own. Benny says that he will be the guest on George's next episode. When Blanche wants to be George's secretary to make sure he is not enticed by any young, attractive secretary, he reluctantly hires her. Jack Albertson brings a seal to Burns' office to be George's new partner. Bob Cummings stops by and says that George's private eye script is the worst script in town. George decides to get out of the deal, but the writer won't tear up the contract. Burns responds that he will use the seal instead of a dog in the proposed private eye series, and the writer then decides to abandon the deal.

The seal act in this episode was a reference to an old vaudeville act called "Flipper and Friend" in which George had second billing to a trained seal. In one of his books, Burns relates the story of working with a seal:

> With a seal you do really nothing. After each trick you just throw the seal a piece of fish. Well, anyway, Flipper and I were playing the Dewey Theater on Fourteenth Street, and that night I had a date with a very pretty girl. Her name was Betty McGrath. I was ashamed to meet her, because after doing four shows a day with your pockets full of fish, you don't smell too good. But when I met her she never even noticed it. In fact, she complimented me on my aftershave lotion. It turned out that she did an act with Fink's Mules.[2]

About the premiere episode, *Variety* opined, "George Burns should sue his writers for breach of promise. There was a lot of promise in the peg 'What will George do now that Gracie's retired?' but it was never adequately fulfilled in the material handed Burns on the opening segment of his new series."[3]

As much as Burns liked playing a producer on this show, he liked even more to sing. In the episode "Tony Martin Visits," singer Martin says he is seeing a doctor who may advise him to rest. George jumps at the chance to take Tony's place at the Coconut Grove nightclub, but it turns out that Tony is fine.

For an episode aired right before Christmas 1958, Burns' writers adopted a familiar plotline (an immigrant having to marry to stay in this country) that had been used in a June 1955 *Burns and Allen* episode. *The George Burns Show*'s take on this situation incorporated George's fondness for singing in the storyline. Burns learns that Collette (Chanlie Noel), one of the nightclub performers from the French Revue he is producing, has to return to France because her visa is about to expire. George tries to hook her up with Von Zell so they can marry, meaning she wouldn't have to return to France. However, she falls for Ronnie, whose girlfriend Judi is away. Neither Ronnie nor Harry wants to marry Collette. She finds out that if she goes to Canada for a few days, she can return to the States with a new visa. Meanwhile, George fills in for her at the nightclub and masquerades as French singer "Georges." When he begins singing "La Vie En Rose," the audience walks out.

In a two-part story in the second half of the season, George books Ronnie and Judi into a nightclub called the Orchid Room. Then he discovers it is a basement restaurant. Thinking that an appearance there could ruin Ronnie's career, George takes over the engagement. In the next episode, "George's Trial," the owner of the Orchid Room sues Burns over his singing since he now has even fewer customers than before. But the owner settles out of court when the publicity about the case increases business.

Burns pursued his singing career by recording an album titled "George Burns Sings?" To promote it, Burns goes on the TV show *Juke Box Jury* thinking that Jerry Lewis, Bob Cummings, Van Heflin, and Danny Kaye will review the album. Ronnie decides to get the offspring of the famous stars for the jury, assuming they will be kinder in evaluating the recording. In "George Invests in a Record Company," George signs a recording contract and gives the company $10,000. The company had signed Cottonseed Clarke (Rod McKuen who in the 1960s became a famous poet, songwriter, and singer) thinking that he would be another Elvis, but his record wasn't a hit. Later, when the company finds that Clarke's record is beginning to sell, they try to give Burns money so he won't record an album for them.

Burns did actually make a record on the Colpix label at the time titled "George Burns Sings?" He wrote letters to radio stations plugging his recording, saying in part, "Tell your disc jockies to STOP spinning whatever platter they're spinning and put this record on. I hate to brag about myself but this is George Burns' greatest album—his first."[4]

On his series, Burns' singing and producing got him in trouble with the building's landlord. Other tenants complained about the noise while

George was rehearsing and about his office being overrun by various vaudeville acts. Mr. Knox (Douglass Dumbrille), the landlord, threatened to boot him in an episode aptly titled "George's Eviction." Ronnie and Judi make up a story about what a fine man George is to get Knox to change his mind. Mr. Knox makes another appearance in "The Landlord's Daughter," a spring episode in which he asks Burns to discourage his daughter Linda (Mary Tyler Moore in a very early TV appearance) from going into show business. Linda dances for Burns, who thinks she is great. Knox is ready to evict George again, but then Linda says that she will finish college before pursuing a career as a professional dancer.

Many of the filmed episodes focused on Burns promoting his son Ronnie's entertainment career with Judi Meredith. In the second episode of the season, George plans on doing a show with Ronnie and Judi. When he rehearses with Judi, Blanche thinks George is trying to revive his act with Gracie using Judi as her replacement. Jack Benny attempts to talk his friend out of doing the act until George explains that the act is really for Ronnie and Judi. In the fourth episode of the season, "A Walk-on for George," Burns' friend, movie producer Bill Goetz, wants Ronnie to star in a film about a teenager and asks George to do a cameo in the film. Burns agrees as long as he is not listed in the credits. When Ronnie overhears the conversation saying his dad will receive no credit for his walk-on, Ronnie quits the picture, not knowing that his dad wanted this arrangement.

In "Ronnie Takes an Apartment," Ronnie does just that, so his dad can get used to him being away from home. He indicates that eventually he wants to settle down and marry Judi. In one late spring episode, Ronnie places an ad for a roommate and singer Jimmie Rodgers moves in. When the two have a housewarming party, Judi sees three attractive chorus girls with the guys, but the girls say that they are not interested in Ronnie—just Jimmie. Burns was never one to miss the chance to cross-promote other TV shows: This episode was intended to publicize *The Jimmie Rodgers Show*, a variety series which premiered in March 1959 preceding Burns' series. In another episode centering on Ronnie, "Breaking Up the Team," Ronnie no longer wants to do the act with Judi because he feels that Judi has all the talent. She makes it clear to Ronnie that they are a team and should stay together.

By December 1958, it had become apparent that *The George Burns Show* was not working. The comedy was up against the hit western *The*

Rifleman on ABC, and so Burns decided to change formats—almost going back to the original live format of *The Burns and Allen Show*. Beginning with the December 16 episode "Eddie Fisher Visits," and continuing with a few exceptions until mid–February, *The George Burns Show* became a thirty-minute live variety series. The cast of the sitcom version appeared in sketches on the live shows. For instance, in the Eddie Fisher episode, Bea Benaderet played a mistress of ceremonies in a sketch about George and Eddie appearing on a local amateur show called *Stairway to Stardom* where Eddie mimed a Burns recording and George did the same with one of Eddie's numbers. Laurie Wilhoute, one of George and Gracie's grand-daughters, also appeared on this episode. Guest Fisher had a one-hour comedy-variety series alternating with *The George Gobel Show*. These variety series preceded *The George Burns Show*. Both were canceled about three weeks before Burns' series was axed.

In talking about the transition of his show from a sitcom to a variety and sketch series, Burns explained:

> What I have been doing so far this season has been too close to what I did with Gracie. The break wasn't clean enough. But I've hit on an idea now that is so good, I've been applauding myself for three days.... After each scene or act, I will step in front of the curtain. When the curtain opens again, you'll see a new set.... Part of the trouble with my first shows this season was that I was cast too much of a heavy. Blanche was the guardian of Gracie's interests. I came up as the villain.... We're changing all that in the writing.[5]

The variety shows were directed by Bob Henry and written by Paul, Fowler, and Willy Burns. In addition to Fisher, guests on the other five variety episodes included western star Dale Robertson from *Tales of Wales Fargo,* Anna Maria Alberghetti, Rosemary Clooney, Xavier Cugat and his wife Abbe Lane, Howard Duff, and Carol Channing. Channing also appeared in "George Signs Carol Channing," one of the sitcom episodes where George, acting in his role as producer, needs a nightclub act and convinces Carol to sign a contract to be the main attraction at the club.

While the pace of the variety shows was faster, moving back and forth between variety acts and sketches, the change in format was not enough to save the series from cancellation. When the last of the live shows was broadcast on February 17, 1958, the filmed sitcom episodes filled out the time slot until the series was canceled after the April 14 episode aired. According to the Trendex ratings at the time, *The Rifleman* scored a 26.8

rating compared with Burns' 15.6. Scoring even lower was another television legend, Arthur Godfrey, in a CBS show that garnered only a 9.7 rating. As mentioned before, TV westerns were extremely popular at the time; *The George Burns Show* was done in by a western, and a western, *The Californians,* replaced it in its timeslot.

In writing about the series in his book *Living It Up or, They Still Like Me in Altoona,* Burns reflected that "[W]e had the same people [from *The Burns and Allen Show*], but any minute you expected Gracie to come through the door. It was like having dinner; we had the soup, the salad and the dessert, but the main course was home playing with her grandkids."[6]

After the demise of *The George Burns Show,* Larry Keating became a regular on another Burns-produced series, *Mister Ed,* where he played Roger Addison, Wilbur Post's next door neighbor, until his death in 1963 from leukemia. Bea Benaderet went on to play the maid on the *Peter Loves Mary* comedy starring Peter Lind Hayes and Mary Healey which aired for a single season. She subsequently became the voice of Betty Rubble on *The Flintstones* and had the lead role on *Petticoat Junction.* Harry Von Zell guest starred on series such as *Bachelor Father, Wagon Train,* and *Perry Mason,* while Ronnie Burns starred on the sitcom *Happy.*

Burns began appearing in nightclubs with a new partner, Carol Channing, filling the role of Gracie. About a year after the premiere of *The George Burns Show,* Burns did a one-hour NBC variety special called "George Burns in the Big Time" with guests Jack Benny, Eddie Cantor, Georgie Jessel, Bobby Darin, and the Kingston Trio. At the end, George tells the audience that it wasn't easy appearing on this special because for years Gracie was always beside him but that he still feels her presence. In a voiceover that George pretends only the audience can hear, Gracie says that he is not alone and that she is home watching him on TV—kind of the reverse from when, during the final seasons of *The Burns and Allen Show,* he watched her on his magic television set. She remarks that George will get the last laugh on the critics who always said he was no comedian; now, working alone, he has a chance to prove it. George declares that he could never retire, and Gracie says now is a good time to get off since her husband always said: "Leave them wanting more." In another reverse of their typical closing on *The Burns and Allen Show,* Gracie tells her husband "Say good night, George" and finally George says "Good night."

George and Mr. Television

In March 1959, Willy Burns and Maurice Morton proposed a comedy anthology series whose working title was *The XYZ Project*. It was to consist of twenty-six episodes with twenty of the stories starring big comedy stars. The other six episodes were to be pilots. In addition to their salaries, the stars of the twenty episodes would each receive an interest in the XYZ Corporation which would own and produce the six pilots. While it appears that this specific proposal never came to fruition, in April 1959, as his own series was canceled, Burns formed a partnership with "Mr. Television," comedian Milton Berle, to produce a half-hour anthology titled *The Milton Berle Comedy Theatre* to start in midsummer 1959. Berle was to host all thirty-nine half-hour episodes and star in thirteen of them, with Burns as executive producer. The company was called B & B Productions. Like Burns, Berle also had an NBC series during the 1958–59 season: He hosted *The Kraft Music Hall*, a half-hour variety show that left the air about a month after *The George Burns Show* was canceled. In commenting to *Variety* about the proposed series, Burns indicated that this comedy project might be bucking the trend of western series on TV. He added, "We just want to do a good show ... We're not trying to start a comedy trend—we just want to book it for 39 weeks."[7] No network picked up *The Milton Berle Comedy Theatre,* and the partnership was dissolved.

That's Edie

In 1961, Burns planned to write and produce a pilot about an airline hostess with Gracie-like tendencies. The writers for the initial script, in addition to himself, were, as usual, his writing staff of Paul, Packard, and Willy Burns. According to *Variety,* George tested Margie Regan and Carole Evern along with Carolyn Kearney for the role of Edie, with Kearney winning out.[8] Fred Beir and Bob Crane, who later starred on *Hogan's Heroes,* tested for the co-starring role of an airline pilot, and Crane was cast.

To save money, instead of filming an entire thirty-minute show, only one scene was shot for advertisers. This pilot effort may have been similar in theme to the *Up on Cloud Nine* pilot McCadden filmed in 1958, but the specific storyline remains unknown. *That's Edie* never became a series.

Family Hymn Sing

One of the more unusual projects, at least different from what Burns normally considered producing, was a proposed 1962 series titled *Family Hymn Sing*. Writer Norman Paul developed a concept of a half-hour program of hymns and spiritual music in which the words would be flashed on the television screen so the home audience could sing along. A master of ceremonies, who was a singer, would introduce the hymns. The emcee as well as a chorus of ten would sing the hymns. To keep costs down in accordance with Burns' management style, all the songs would be in the public domain, and no costumes or special sets would be used.

Singer Jack Smith was under consideration to be the master of ceremonies. This series was pitched probably because of the success of NBC's *Sing Along with Mitch* which had a similar concept but didn't focus on religious songs. No pilot for this proposed series was ever made.

After trying but failing on his own series, Burns, in addition to playing the nightclub circuit and making guest appearances on television, became involved with several projects in conjunction with Filmways Television Productions.

9

George and Filmways

After McCadden Corporation was dissolved with the sale of the *Burns and Allen Show* episodes to Screen Gems for syndication to local TV stations, many of the McCadden executives became part of the Filmways production company and took several pilots developed by Burns' company with them.

Martin Ransohoff started Filmways in 1954 to produce documentaries and commercials. Ransohoff's association with McCadden began in the mid–1950s when both companies engaged in several joint ventures filming TV commercials. As referenced in Chapter 7, because production was at a standstill at McCadden by 1959 with the end of *The Bob Cummings Show*, Al Simon, Vice President in charge of production, left the company in August and joined Filmways where he became President of Filmways Television Productions, a subsidiary of Filmways, Inc. Herb Browar, who had helped produce *The Burns and Allen Show, The Bob Cummings Show, The People's Choice,* and *Panic!,* also joined Filmways and became an associate producer.

21 Beacon Street

One of the first series Filmways produced was *21 Beacon Street,* a summer 1959 replacement for *The Tennessee Ernie Ford Show.* An episode of *Panic!* titled "Fingerprints," described in Chapter 7, served as the pilot for this series. *21 Beacon Street* focused on a team of operatives who devised elaborate schemes for catching criminals. The Paul Chase character from the pilot was renamed Dennis Chase, and the role was taken over by Dennis Morgan. The Karen Adams character became Lola (Joanna Barnes); and the Randy Burke character, still played by Brian Kelly, was simply named Brian, a law school graduate. James Maloney as Jim, dialectician and scientific expert, rounded out the cast. McCadden Productions loaned the 21 Beacon Street Corporation $100,000 to produce the series.

Episodes of *21 Beacon Street* dealt with such schemes as using closed circuit television to help find a crime syndicates payroll list; devising a hoax to swindle a con man out of money that he had taken from a widow; and having Chase pose as a member of an international narcotics ring to track down the killer of an undercover agent.

Leonard Heideman created *21 Beacon Street*. After being story editor for *Flight* and *21 Beacon Street,* Heideman held the same position on the hit western *Bonanza.* Apparently work and family stress caused him to have a psychotic episode and on February 23, 1963, he stabbed his wife Dolores to death. Declared unfit to stand trial, he was committed for an indefinite period to the Atascadero State Hospital in California. Heideman spent fourteen months there. After he pled not guilty by reason of insanity to his wife's murder, and the hospital staff testified that he had fully recovered from his psychosis, he became a free man and changed his name to Laurence Heath. Heath wrote an account of his crime, trial, and treatment titled *By Reason of Insanity,* published in 1966. He subsequently began scripting episodes of *Mission: Impossible.*

Bruce Geller, the creator of *Mission: Impossible,* was sued by Filmways in 1968. Filmways claimed that *Mission: Impossible* bore a striking resemblance to *21 Beacon Street* in its emphasis on gadgetry and a team of experts. Geller said he had never seen *21 Beacon Street,* but he paid Filmways off anyway to settle the suit.

As for Laurence Heath, after *Mission: Impossible,* he wrote scripts for series like Bill Bixby's *The Magician* and *Murder, She Wrote.* He committed suicide by hanging in 2007.[1]

War Birds

Out of the Al Simon–George Burns–produced *Flight* grew the idea for a show about World War I flyers. The original concept for *War Birds,* developed while Simon was still with McCadden, was a romantic adventure series with comedy overtones. The proposed series included French girls and U.S. Army pilots and their comical misadventures. Character actor Joe Maross was cast in the lead. Jean Yarbrough directed the pilot which was written by Leonard Heideman and produced through California National Productions.

When Filmways took over the project in 1961, Simon wanted it to focus on the dramatic elements of the first men to fly airplanes in military combat, particularly the aerial action. The new proposal centered on a squadron commander and his unit of flyers in 1917 France. Tentative storylines for the revamped concept included the squadron finding an enemy observation balloon carrying explosives rather than men, a famous athlete who loses his courage to face the enemy in a dog fight, the squadron commander disobeying orders and attacking enemy railroad yards to break up an attack before it happens, the commander uncovering an enemy plot to outfit a zeppelin to bomb New York, and the squadron capturing a German pilot in order to analyze his parachute to solve the technical problems Allied engineers were having constructing a chute for use by American airmen. General George Kenney, who had hosted the *Flight* series, was to be technical advisor for *War Birds*. The script for the pilot was redone by Elliot Asinof and Sam Neuman. Actor Wayde Preston (*Colt .45*) played the squadron commander with William Wellman, Jr., son of movie director William Wellman, and Don Francks part of his unit. Basil Rathbone had the role of the commandant, and Hoagy Carmichael portrayed the owner of a Paris nightclub where the pilots often hung out. Renamed *Dawn Patrol,* Tay Garnett directed the new effort, and famed stunt pilot Frank Tallman assisted with the aerial scenes. According to Wellman Jr., the pilot did not include much aerial camerawork because CBS, the network for which it was being filmed, was stingy with the budget.[2] Even with all of these changes, the pilot failed to sell.

Mister Ed

The most successful series Filmways produced based on a McCadden pilot was *Mister Ed*. The pilot that McCadden produced did not sell, but when Al Simon became president of Filmways, he saw potential in the concept. According to Simon,

> I looked at the pilot, and I thought there were a lot of very good elements in it, but it had an enormous deficiency. There were a lot of production errors in it ... there was too much in the show that did not involve the

horse, and it took too long to actually introduce the talking horse. The characters were dull. There were a lot of people in the opening who weren't very important.[3]

Simon wanted the focus to be more on the horse as the central character with his owner Wilbur more a supporting character, and he changed the title from *The Wonderful World of Wilbur Pope* to *Mister Ed.*

George Burns along with Alan Young and Connie Hines made a short film to show to Studebaker Motor Company representatives after running a fifteen-minute edited version of the original pilot. They were hoping to get the support of this car company in syndicating the series to local TV stations. Burns began the film by saying,

I'm here to talk about the picture you just saw and how we intend to change it so that next season it could be one of the top comedy shows. First, the locale. It's going to be set in a much higher class neighborhood, which will give us much nicer neighbors ... and many more prob-lems for a man

Alan Young and Connie Hines with Mister Ed. Hines originally auditioned for the Joanna Barnes character in *21 Beacon Street*, but Filmways thought she would be better suited to play Carol Post.

who wants to keep a horse there. Now our leads. This is where I really think we've hit the jackpot.[4]

Burns then gave glowing introductions to Connie Hines and Alan Young, who stepped out of a Studebaker Lark—the company's compact car. The car company gave their support to the project, and a new pilot was made.

Filmways together with Burns and Arthur Lubin formed the Mister Ed Company and made a new pilot with Young and Hines, directed by Rod Amateau (who had directed several pilots for McCadden). Additional changes were made to the pilot besides the nicer neighborhood and the new leads. The last name Pope with its religious connotations was changed to Post, and Wilbur's occupation was changed from lawyer to architect as a way to have the character work in the barn with Mister Ed.[5] Also, Larry Keating as Roger Addison appeared in the revised pilot as the Posts' neighbor, who sold them their new house.

The plot of the revamped pilot was very similar to the one described in Chapter 6, but the ending was changed. Instead of the story about Wilbur having a special rapport with animals to explain why he told everyone Mister Ed could talk, a different explanation was devised. In the new pilot, Ed again advises Wilbur on what to say to have people stop thinking he is crazy. This time Wilbur tells the realtor that he doesn't want the house he just bought and asks for his money back. The realtor informs Addison and assumes that Wilbur made up the story about Mister Ed talking so Addison would think he was crazy, want him out of the neighborhood, and return his money. Addison concludes that Wilbur isn't crazy after all and agrees to cut $2,000 off the purchase price of the house if Wilbur will stay. Roger Addison's wife Kay (Edna Skinner) did not appear in this pilot. Addison said that she was away in New York City.

According to Alan Young, Amateau did not really do a good job directing the new pilot. In his autobiography, Young indicates that the pacing was off, scenes were labored, and the camera angles missed much of the comedy.[6] After the initial screening of the pilot, Burns apologized to the studio and agency executives in attendance, and the episode was re-edited before being broadcast. Arthur Lubin directed most of the subsequent installments of the series.

Studebaker Motor Company sponsored *Mister Ed* for one season in syndication before the show was picked up by CBS beginning in October

1961. Martin Ransohoff, the CEO of Filmways, recalled that Burns "was very involved [with the series]. He was at every final writer's session."[7] Young said that George insisted on staging the first thirteen episodes himself to make sure the comedy got off to a good start.[8] Burns' writers Norman Paul and Willy Burns served as script consultants for the show, which ran for five seasons on CBS.

Mister Ed bore several similarities to other Burns-produced comedies. It pitted the fantasy world of the talking horse against the mundane world of Carol Post and the Posts' neighbors with Wilbur Post caught in between, often appearing to act scatterbrained in his attempts to do something Ed wanted or cover up something Ed did. The Roger Addison character told Carol Post in one episode that whenever Wilbur goes into the barn, "he enters the Twilight Zone." Although certainly not to the extent Burns did on *The Burns and Allen Show* or Cleo, the dog, did on *The People's Choice,* Ed would occasionally speak to the viewers with comments such as "You can fool all the horses part of the time; and part of the horses all the time, but you can't fool this horse any time" and "Time and Ed wait for no man" and, when watching TV, "These westerns; they all look alike," and, when becoming exasperated at Wilbur, "There is only one thing worse than a talking horse—a talking man." Similar to Burns watching his magic television to find out what was happening on an episode, Ed would listen in on the Posts' phone calls and peep through windows to see what was going on.

As he did on his own series with Gracie and on several other projects he helped to produce, George sat in with the writers in coming up with a script. At one point during the show's first thirteen episodes, he got the idea to de-emphasize the Ed character and focus on the Posts and the Addison's. As explained by Ben Starr, one of the *Mister Ed* writers, in Nancy Nalven's book about the series, "When we started the show, we had about seven scripts not shot yet. One day, George said, 'I'm tired of that horse, he keeps talking, I'm sick of it.' So we did a show that focused on the people.... But when the show actually got on, and we saw that people loved the horse, George said, 'Put the horse back in!'"[9]

The episode that centered on the Posts and Addisons more than on the horse, "Missing Statue," was very much like a Burns and Allen "comedy of errors" installment with a back-and-forth situation involving Wilbur, Carol, Roger and Kay. In the episode, Carol purchases a $50 Chinese statue from an antique store, but Wilbur, who is trying to economize on household expenses, returns it. To get back at Wilbur, Carol feeds him fish morning, noon, and night since fish was on sale at the supermarket. Kay decides to buy the statue and keep it at her house until Carol gets Wilbur off his economizing kick. When Roger finds the statue in their closet, he returns it to the store. Carol finally relents and gives Wilbur something other than fish, and Wilbur decides to buy the statue. After Carol sees it in her living room, she thinks Kay brought it over and takes it back to the Addisons. Roger confronts Kay about the statue, and Kay takes it back to the Posts. Carol sees it and returns it to Kay until it finally dawns on her that Wilbur purchased the statue for her. Mister Ed had only a minor role in this episode, worrying about his niece's maiden race at Pimlico race track.

After the initial thirteen episodes of the series, Burns' involvement with *Mister Ed* diminished, and the horse's character changed from that of a wisecracking animal who often advised Wilbur on how to get out of difficult situations to more of a spoiled teenager who manipulates his owner into getting what he wants.

In addition to helping produce the series, George played himself on one episode where, as an entertainer-producer with a fictional company known as George Burns Theatrical Enterprises, he placed a newspaper ad offering $25,000 for a new, never-before-seen novelty act for his Las Vegas show. Wilbur tries to persuade Mister Ed to be the new act, but Ed refuses to talk to anyone other than Wilbur. Wilbur meets with Burns to try to convince him that his horse talks. While George remains unconvinced, Wilbur says he will have a witness verify that Ed talks. He thinks he can have Roger Addison listen to Ed talk in his sleep to persuade Burns that he owns a talking horse. However, before he can produce Roger as a witness, like a fantasy sequence from *The Bob Cummings Show* or *The People's Choice*, Wilbur falls asleep and dreams that Ed reveals to the world that he is able to talk, thereby receiving a diploma from Yale, being elected to Congress, becoming an Army major, and being trapped behind enemy lines, captured, interrogated, and facing a firing squad. When he awakens, Wilbur decides not to force Ed to talk to anyone else.

Besides *Mister Ed*, Burns' Las Palmas Productions also had an interest in three Filmways pilots that originally aired as part of the *Ed* series:

• *The Bill Bendix Show*: This pilot, titled "Pine Lake Lodge," was the next-to-last episode of the first season of *Mister Ed*. Wilbur and Carol are spending a weekend at a lodge owned by Bill Parker (William Bendix from *The Life of Riley*). Parker's niece Ann (Coleen Gray), who has a young daughter named Cindy, helps Bill run the place along with Martha (Nancy Kulp from *The Bob Cummings Show*), the housekeeper and waitress. Bill attends a fund-raising meeting for the Pine Lake Summer Camp for children, and he volunteers to make picnic tables and benches for the camp. When he cannot get a local lumber yard to donate the wood, he decides to cut down a tree on J.F. Thompson's (Will Wright) property without asking permission (Thompson is a notorious skinflint). Bill enlists Wilbur's help in downing the tree, but they both flee the scene after a forest ranger comes by. Without them realizing it, a birdwatcher takes a photo of Bill and Wilbur running away. When Thompson stops by the lodge and informs Bill there was a witness to the incident, Bill admits that he and Wilbur cut down the tree. After Wilbur explains the motive for what they did, Thompson agrees to donate the wood.

Directed by John Rich, the episode was written by Lou Derman and Bill Davenport; Norman Paul and Willy Burns helped to rewrite the script. Filmways had a 50 percent participation in this pilot, while Arthur Lubin had 25 percent and Burns' new corporation, Las Palmas Productions, had the remaining 25 percent. The Bill Parker character was a nice, somewhat befuddled guy who liked to help people, but otherwise was kind of bland.

• *The Trials and Tribulations of Emmy Lou Harper*: The *Mister Ed* episode titled "Ed the Matchmaker" was the second pilot that Las Palmas helped to produce. It aired as the final episode of *Mister Ed's* second season. Filmways owned 75 percent of this project, Lubin 15 percent and Las Palmas had a 10 percent share.

Written by Ben Starr and Robert O'Brien and directed by Lubin, "Ed the Matchmaker" centered on love-crazed teenager Emmy Lou (Noanna Dix) whose family had moved next door to the Posts. Emmy Lou asks Wilbur for a hair from Mister Ed's tail to make a love potion. She wants to win the affections of Arthur (Peter Brooks), a grocery delivery boy who is always eating an apple and so mumbles his lines. Arthur eventually asks Emmy Lou to the movies but has to cancel the date because of a flat tire. Emmy Lou auctions off some of her stuff to raise money for a new tire, but then Arthur's car battery goes dead. Finally, Mister Ed, pretending to be Wilbur, phones Emmy Lou and offers to pull Arthur's car to the drive-in movie. George O'Hanlon and Jeff Donnell played Emmy Lou's parents.

The unsold pilot was based on the United Features syndicated cartoon by Marty Links. Apparently Herb Browar saw the cartoon in the newspaper and brought it to Al Simon's attention. Simon thought, incorrectly as it turned out, that it would make a great series.[10]

• *Moko and Tatti from Outer Space:* Burns helped bring television viewers a dog who verbalized her thoughts and a horse who talked out loud, so it is not surprising that he was also behind a comedy about a talking Martian. Written by Norman Paul and Willy Burns and directed by Arthur Lubin, *Moko and Tatti from Outer Space* combined live action and rudimentary animation. Moko and Tatti were animated characters living on Mars. Unlike Earthlings, Martians had evolved to the point where they have discarded their physical bodies and have become "pure essence of mind." Richard Deacon voiced Tatti, the older, more sensible of the two; Dave Willock was the voice of the prankish Moko. Moko traveled back and forth between Earth and Mars, while Tatti remained on Mars and lectured Moko about his behavior.

Paul and Willy Burns described Moko and Tatti in their script as: "two irregular globs. The glob that is Moko conveys an impish quality. The glob that is Tatti has an intellectual appearance. Both voices should have a slight echo chamber effect, and each voice should be different. Tatti's is serious; Moko's lighter, with a mischievous quality to match his appearance."[11] Moko hasn't been to a party in over 2000 years and, as he explains to Tatti, he is ready to taste some steak, smell a rose, and dance with a woman.[12]

The *Mister Ed* episode, aired May 17, 1964, was simply titled "Moko." At this point in the *Mister Ed* series, the Posts' neighbors were Gordon and Winnie Kirkwood (Leon Ames and Florence MacMichael). Moko travels to Earth to fly into people's ears and make them lose their inhibitions. The Kirkwoods are having a party for a very uptight general to whom Gordon once reported. Wilbur and Carol are invited to the party along with one of Wilbur's clients, sexy blonde actress Gloria Laverne (Joan Tabor). Moko first takes over Gordon Kirkwood's mind to have him invite Miss Laverne and her young friends to the affair. Moko enters Kirkwood's body again at the party to get him to dance the twist with Miss Laverne, and then he takes over Wilbur's mind and body and that of General Lucius Bromley (Robert Barrat). Both dance with the actress, and the next day, all have hangovers from drinking the punch Moko had spiked. During the episode, Moko travels back and forth between Earth and Mars where he is scolded by Tatti about his mischief-making.

Since Burns' writers Norman Paul and Willy Burns created the proposed pilot, Las Palmas owned 50 percent participation in the project; Arthur Lubin had 25 percent; and Filmways 25 percent. If the pilot had become a series, apparently each week Moko would have visited another Earthling and drastically changed his or her personality. For example, Al Simon recalled that Jack Benny might have appeared in an episode with Moko turning the miserly Benny into a spendthrift.[13]

In addition to the above pilots, Simon and Burns were involved in the production of *My Cousin Davey*, a pilot starring a professional dancer turned wrestler, Ricki Starr, who had been featured in two episodes of the *Mister Ed* series: In the January 7, 1962, episode "The Wrestler," Roger Addison takes over the contract for wrestler Tiger Davis (Starr) whose manager could not make the final payment on land he had bought from Addison. Kay and Carol are infatuated with Tiger, and each feed him so much food that he quickly gets out of shape. The girls enroll Tiger in their ballet class so he can lose weight for his next match, which he wins using ballet moves. Starr made his second appearance in "The Bashful Clipper" (October 18, 1962) playing Chuck Miller, a guy who clips Mister Ed's hair. Kay and Carol discover that Chuck is an excellent hair stylist, but Chuck says that women make him nervous and that animals are easier to deal with. However, Chuck eventually decides to accept Carol and Kay's suggestion to open a hair salon, and the two wives convince their husbands to invest in the shop. When Chuck learns that his first customer is a fashion editor for the newspaper, he becomes nervous, says he can't do her hair, and leaves the shop. Wilbur tries to cut and style the woman's hair but makes a mess of it. When Chuck hears Mister Ed's voice telling him to go back to the beauty salon, he thinks it is his subconscious talking. He returns to the salon and undoes the damage done by Wilbur.

My Cousin Davey was made as a pilot for the 1963 TV season. It was directed by Arthur Lubin and written by Danny Simon, playwright Neil Simon's brother. The storyline of the pilot is not known. However, given the type of character Starr portrayed on *Mister Ed,* it is probably safe to assume that he played a similar character in the pilot—a macho man with, at least for the 1960s, certain feminine qualities. *My Cousin Davey* was never picked up as a series.

Four Obscure Burns-Filmways Projects

At least four other projects with which George Burns had been involved were subsequently pursued by Filmways in 1959; not much is known about them:

- *The Life and Hard Times of Barney Benedict*: This private eye comedy, created and written by Harold Swanton and produced by Al Simon, was said to have a premise similar to the James Whitmore series *The Law and Mr. Jones,* which concerned a compassionate lawyer always on the side of the underdog.
- *Mr. Cellini*: This situation comedy was to be a co-production between Ralph Levy, the original producer-director of *The Burns and Allen Show,* and Filmways. The subject of the Arthur Alsberg-Mel Diamond script is unknown. It appears the pilot was never made.
- *Double Take*: Devised by Jay Sommers who later created the Paul Henning–produced comedy *Green Acres, Double Take* was a comedy-adventure farce starring Tom Poston.
- *Joe Domino*: This proposed mystery series dealt with Joe Domino, a rather shadowy character who magically appeared at odd moments and, for money, would accomplish things not easily achieved through normal methods. It was produced by Al Simon and written by Leonard Heideman; actor Nick Conte was rumored to be interested in starring in the series.

George Burns would have somewhat better luck in getting series on the air while working with Warner Brothers and with United Artists.

10

George and Warner Brothers

Wendy and Me

In 1963, Jack Webb, the *Dragnet* star who was then head of Warner Brothers' TV division, announced a deal with George Burns to be creative supervisor of a comedy starring Dorothy Provine; Burns would also be the narrator. Norman Paul, Elon Packard, Robert O'Brien, and Willy Burns would be the writers. Originally *Mind Over Marriage,* the series title was changed to *Wendy and Me.* Provine, star of Warner Brothers' television series *The Roaring 20's* and *The Alaskans,* had joined Burns as his partner in his nightclub act after the departure of Carol Channing. When Provine's movie career began to take off, she dropped out of the nightclub act as well as the proposed sitcom. Connie Stevens took over the lead role. Stevens had previously been featured on Warner Brothers' *Hawaiian Eye* detective series.

In *Wendy and Me,* Burns' second attempt after Gracie's retirement for a successful comedy series on his own, Burns went back to his first TV success, *The Burns and Allen Show.* He also continued to use his singing talent (or lack thereof) as an ongoing gag: The premise of *Wendy and Me* was that George had purchased a building, the Sunset de Ville apartments, to use one of the units to rehearse his singing. He had written into every tenant's lease a provision that they could not evict the landlord presumably for singing. Wendy Conway (Stevens) and her husband Jeff (Ron Harper), a pilot for Trans-Global Airlines, occupied one of the apartments. Jeff's boss was Willard Norton (Bartlett Robinson). Jeff's co-pilot and friend, charming bachelor Danny Adams (James Callahan), lived across the hall from the couple.

On *Wendy and Me,* Burns continued to combine familiar characters and plots with new settings and actors. Callahan's character reminded one of Bob Collins on *The Bob Cummings Show.* Although Stevens' character was similar to the one Gracie Allen had played, Stevens didn't have all that many scenes with George. Also, her fast, clipped delivery of lines was not as effective in portraying a "dumb Dora" as Gracie had been. Sensible husband Ron Harper would usually clear up confusing situations at the end of an episode like Burns had done on his show with Gracie. Missing from *Wendy and Me* were any of the more fanciful elements found in the comedies Burns had produced (*The People's Choice, Mister Ed, Moko and Tatti from Outer Space*).

George interacted mostly with Mr. Bundy (J. Pat O'Malley), the building's superintendent—a character like Harry Von Zell on *The Burns and Allen Show*, often help-

Burns, Connie Stevens and J. Pat O'Malley from *Wendy and Me*.

ing Wendy with her schemes. Burns would interrupt an episode with his monologues, comment on events, tell viewers about the next scene, and sometimes move the storyline along. Generally, this happened before a commercial break with George using the catchphrase "Do it" to go to commercial. He would sometimes even use the same lines from *Burns and Allen*. For example, in explaining to viewers a particular situation in which Wendy found herself, he said that if they saw something like it on television, they would think someone made it up but here it is happening

158

in real life. Or he would note, as he had remarked about Gracie, that in order to cut down on their light bill, Wendy shortened all the cords to save electricity.

While Burns had implicitly played the role of producer in his original series and explicitly played this role in his own series, on *Wendy and Me* he would tell viewers (but not the characters) that he was the show's producer. He would say, for example, "Everyone in this show had more lines than me, and I'm the producer" or inform the audience that he was the producer when instructing the crew to turn the lights on for a scene taking place at night. Many times, George would be in the lobby of his apartment building and direct characters to the Conways' apartment. He would also advise the viewing audience of the passage of time, letting them know if, for instance, a scene was taking place twenty minutes or three hours after the previous scene.

Warner Brothers and Natwill Productions jointly produced the comedy. "Natwill" stood for Nathan, George's original first name, and for Willy, George's brother. George owned 75 percent of the company and Willy had the remaining 25 percent. Except for the pilot episode directed by Richard Crenna, all the other *Wendy and Me* episodes were directed by Gene Reynolds. Norman Paul, Elon Packard, and Willy Burns penned all of the scripts with Robert O'Brien helping the three write the premiere.

Before the comedy began airing, Gracie Allen visited the set for lunch in August 1964. According to George, "When she walked on the set, everything stopped. She looked so lovely, so full of life. People just started applauding. We stopped shortly and went across the street to a small restaurant for lunch. For a minute, for a second, Gracie was back where she belonged, in the middle of show business. But it only lasted a minute, then she was gone."[1]

Shortly after this visit, Gracie, who had a history of heart problems, passed away. The date was August 27, 1964, two and a half weeks before the debut of *Wendy and Me*.

Like the Gracie character, Wendy would jump to conclusions about situations and devise plans to help others—plans that were not all that well thought out. "Molehills and Mountains," the first episode, ran on September 14, 1964. Danny Adams has to pass his physical for the airlines and Wendy wants to help by keeping him from dating for twenty-four hours. She switches apartment numbers so Linda, a woman who wants to see Danny, will visit Wendy instead. Wendy then pretends she is Danny's

Swedish housemaid. Jeff ends up taking Linda to a nightclub. George tells Danny where Jeff and Linda went, and Wendy and Danny go to the same club. In the final scene, Jeff, much like George did at the end of a *Burns and Allen* episode, has to clarify the situation for everyone.

In "Wendy, the Waitress," a waitress at a restaurant where Wendy is having lunch with George says that she would like to attend her sister's wedding that evening but will lose her job if she leaves work. Wendy volunteers to do her job but learns that Jeff's boss wants to take her and Jeff out to dinner that evening. Wendy makes up a story that she has to go to night school that evening and, as only happens on a situation comedy, Jeff and his boss end up at the restaurant where Wendy is the waitress. She joins them at their booth but keeps making excuses to leave so she can handle her waitress duties.

This episode was based on a November 1955 episode of *The Burns and Allen Show*. In that installment, Gracie wanted to help Lola, a waitress who had had an argument with her boyfriend. She instructed Lola to buy new clothes, while Gracie took over her waitressing duties.

In "Wendy Is Stranger Than Fiction," Wendy meets famous writer William Norman Packard (note the inside reference to *Wendy and Me*'s writers) who has moved into the apartment building. He wants to know how to handle a situation he is writing about and asks Wendy how a husband would react if he discovered that his wife was previously married and her first husband, who had been lost at sea, has turned up alive. Since Wendy wants to get Jeff's honest reaction, she announces that she was married before and her first husband is alive. George gets Danny to dress as Wendy's fictitious first husband and visit her.

Also, like Gracie, Wendy would make wrong-headed assumptions, and an entire episode would be devoted to getting things straightened out. In "Wendy's Private Eye," Wendy finds lipstick in the pocket of one of Jeff's coats and thinks that Jeff is having an affair (actually, the lipstick is hers). Similar to a Burns and Allen episode when a private investigator spied on Harry Morton having lunch with Blanche at a restaurant not knowing she was his wife, Wendy hires a private eye to follow Jeff. The investigator thinks that Danny is Jeff, sees him with a girl, and informs Wendy. Later, when Jeff says he has to go to a meeting, Wendy thinks he is seeing the girl. Wendy leaves Jeff, but then George explains that the detective confused Danny with Jeff and that it was Wendy's lipstick in Jeff's pocket.

When Mr. Bundy catches the bouquet at a wedding in "A Bouquet for Mr. Bundy," Wendy concludes that he will be getting married and so goes to a matrimonial agency to find him a wife. The head of the agency thinks that Wendy is the one who wants to get married and suggests a Texas millionaire. Wendy thinks the millionaire is a woman and not a man that the agency is recommending. While at the agency, Wendy meets Theresa, a girl from Italy. In a familiar plot line, Theresa needs to marry within a week or go back to her home country. Predictably, the Texas millionaire, Mr. Beaumont, ends up marrying her.

Also, like Gracie Allen's character, Wendy Conway took as gospel anything a fortune teller predicted. In "Tea Leaves for Two," a fortune teller informs Wendy that a man, other than Jeff, is in love with her. Meanwhile, Jeff buys his wife a mink jacket as a surprise gift and temporarily leaves it with Danny. Bundy sees the jacket which Danny says is for Wendy and concludes that Danny is in love with her. Bundy informs Wendy that Danny bought her a mink jacket because he loves her. Wendy tells Jeff who then watches Wendy play a Mae West–type character to discourage Danny's supposed love. Finally, Jeff explains to Wendy that he bought the mink for her.

Many episodes of *Wendy and Me* were similar to *Burns and Allen* shows, and some were actual remakes of scripts from that series. The April 5, 1965, episode "You Can Fight City Hall" was based on an April 1955 *Burns and Allen* in which Gracie receives a parking ticket and does not want to pay it. Wendy receives a ticket for overtime parking even though she insists she stuffed a dollar bill in the meter. She refuses to pay the ticket, and Danny says he will get the ticket fixed. Jeff and Danny go to the courthouse where Jeff pays the ticket but fibs to Wendy that he got it fixed by a judge. When Mr. Bundy receives a ticket, Wendy goes to the same judge to get it fixed, saying that Danny recommended him for fixing tickets. The judge comes to see Danny, and he and Jeff have to explain everything.

"Wendy's Instant Intellect," the April 19 episode, was adapted from a *Burns and Allen* episode titled "Questions and Answers," in which Gracie wants to join the Ladies of Oyster Bay Literary Club where Blanche is a member. However, to become a member, she needs to answer certain questions about literature. To please Blanche, Mrs. Sohmers, the president of the club, gives Gracie the answers to the questions before the meeting. Gracie memorizes the questions, but not the answers. Mrs. Sohmers decides to hide the answers to the questions around Gracie's apartment so she can find them when asked the questions.

In the *Wendy* episode, Wendy wants to join Mrs. Norton's (Jane Morgan) literary club. She first needs to be screened by the club president, Mrs. Cartwright (Doris Packer, who played Mrs. Sohmers on *The Burns and Allen Show* episode). Wendy tries to bone up on literary giants but becomes frustrated and asks George for help. He suggests pasting notes all through her apartment and having Mr. Bundy pose as a professor to ask her literary questions. When Mrs. Cartwright and Mrs. Norton arrive for the interview, Mrs. Cartwright discovers one of the notes in her sandwich but nevertheless lets Wendy join the club.

The following week's *Wendy* came from a *Burns and Allen* episode in which Ronnie rents an apartment for his friend Frank Brody and his wife. When Gracie receives a phone call for Ronnie about the date on the rent check, Gracie thinks that Ronnie is moving out. She goes to the apartment after Frank, his wife, and his new baby have moved in. The Brodys' neighbor is taking care of the baby while Frank and his wife are out. Gracie tells the neighbor that she didn't know her son was married and had a baby. The neighbor leaves Gracie with the baby, and she decides to take the baby home so George can see his "grandson." The baby's mother comes to the Burns home after reading the note that Gracie left, and George has to make clear to his wife that the baby is not Ronnie's.

In the *Wendy and Me* episode, Danny has rented an apartment in another building for friend Gene Simpson, his wife, and baby. Wendy receives a message that Danny's check for the new apartment has bounced and concludes that he is moving out. Wendy goes to the new apartment where the landlady says it was rented for a pilot and his family. Both Wendy and the landlady assume that Danny is living a double life. After Wendy takes the baby to confront Danny, Gene's wife comes looking for her child and clarifies the situation.

"Wendy's Five Thousand Dollar Chair," the May 10 episode, was a remake of an episode that Burns and Allen had done twice, once in August 1955 and again in December 1957. The episode involved Gracie falling in a department store, and the store offering funds to cover any liability. At a restaurant, Wendy sits in a chair, it breaks, and she falls. Later the restaurant phones Wendy saying it will settle for $100 which she interprets *a la* Gracie as meaning she has to pay the restaurant $100 for the broken chair.

Representatives of the restaurant subsequently raise the settlement offer to $500 and then $1,000 with Wendy trying to obtain the money. Finally representatives from the establishment visit Wendy, and say they will settle for $5,000. Wendy accepts the $5,000 and gives them the money back for the broken chair.

While Gracie would pretend, as part of her schemes, to be someone else, Wendy took the pretense one step further and dressed as someone else. Usually Wendy did this to get on a flight with Jeff. In "George Burns While Rome Fiddles," Wendy wants to fly with Jeff to Rome, and dons a black wig to pose as a stewardess. The disguise doesn't fool anyone, and Danny and Jeff decide to play a trick on her. Danny mentions that Joanne, the stewardess she is pretending to be, is really Jeff's girl, and Jeff tells "Joanne" to meet him at their special place. When Wendy, dressed as Joanne, shows up, Jeff says that his only love is Wendy.

Like Gracie, Wendy's naiveté often helped her in potentially perilous situations. In "How Not to Succeed in Stealing," an airline attendant brings her friend Wendy a set of pearls from Hong Kong. Unbeknownst to the friend is that a pair of thieves switched her imitation pearls with real pearls thinking that she could easily get them through customs. After one of the thieves fails to switch briefcases holding the pearls at the airport, Wendy invites him to stay with Danny, not knowing he is a thief. After Wendy gives the real pearls to Mr. Bundy to fix a broken clasp, George calls the customs agency to arrest the thief.

Since George Burns and Connie Stevens were known for their singing talent (well, at least Connie was), there were opportunities for both to sing on the series. In "Five Minutes to Show Time," Jeff is in charge of the airline's annual variety show, and Wendy and George sing "If I Could Be with You."

Two soon-to-be-major stars made early appearances on *Wendy and Me*. Marlo Thomas played Danny's girlfriend Carol, who accompanied Danny and the Conways to a restaurant to celebrate the first anniversary of Jeff and Wendy's engagement. In another episode, Raquel Welch played Lila, another of Danny's girlfriends; along with many others, she sailed on Mr. Norton's boat where George entertained and Wendy sang.

Burns told *Variety*, "If ABC doesn't renew *Wendy*, they're idiots.... If *Wendy* is renewed for another season, it will be here for ten."[2] Slotted against *The Lucy Show* on CBS and *The Andy Williams Show* on NBC,

Wendy and Me came in third in its time slot and was cancelled by ABC after one season.

Wendy and Me was Burns' last appearance as a regular character on a TV sitcom. He did later host (but not act on or produce) a CBS comedy anthology series titled *George Burns' Comedy Week* that lasted half a season in 1985. Connie Stevens subsequently made guest appearances on several television shows such as *The Love Boat, Murder, She Wrote,* and *8 Simple Rules.* Her husband on *Wendy and Me,* Ron Harper, starred on several, mostly short-lived series in the sixties and seventies including *The Jean Arthur Show, Garrison's Gorillas, Planet of the Apes,* and *Land of the Lost.* James Callahan had regular roles on two comedies, *The Governor & JJ* and the Scott Baio series *Charles in Charge* where he is probably best remembered as Mr. Powell. J. Pat O'Malley guest starred on many TV shows after *Wendy and Me* and became a regular on Shirley Booth's series *A Touch of Grace* and Bea Arthur's sitcom *Maude.*

No Time for Sergeants

This television comedy was based on the novel by Mac Hyman about his experiences in the Air Force. The novel was turned into a TV play, then a Broadway play, and finally a Warner Brothers movie before becoming a television series. Burns' *No Time for Sergeants* centered on Georgia farm boy Will Stockdale (Sammy Jackson) who always seemed to be getting in trouble as an airman at Oliver Air Force Base due to his naiveté about military rules and regulations. From a rural background, Will did not quite understand that the military was not one big happy family. Will was like Gracie in her naiveté about aspects of life in general.

Sgt. King (Harry Hickox) was Will's NCO; Airman Ben Whitledge (Kevin O'Neal, Ryan O'Neal's brother) was Will's best friend; and Millie Anderson (Laurie Sibbald), the waitress at the PX and Will's girlfriend. Her grandfather was Jim Anderson (Andy Clyde). Other characters included Capt. Martin (Paul Smith), Col. Farnsworth (Hayden Rorke), and Capt. Krupnick (George Murdock). The series preceded Burns' *Wendy and Me* at 8:30 p.m. on Mondays and ironically was pitted against *The Andy Griffith Show*—"ironically" because Griffith had starred in the play and the film version of *No Time for Sergeants.* Norman Paul and Willy

Burns acted as script consultants for the comedy. PenCam
Productions, which according
to Burns stood for "from pen to
camera," produced the comedy
with Warner Brothers. Reportedly, the day after Gracie's
funeral, George went to his
office at the usual time, to be
with the writers of *No Time for
Sergeants* and make suggestions
for changes to the scripts.[3]

Originally, CBS had exp-
ressed interested in the comedy, and Richard Crenna was
considered for the lead. Crenna
did end up directing the pilot.
After Crenna, Bobby Bare and
Will Hutchins were tested for
the lead role. Sammy Jackson
finally won the role of Will
Stockdale, and ABC decided to
pick up the series. Jackson, from

Sammy Jackson as Will Stockdale with his
dog Blue. After *No Time for Sergeants*, Jackson appeared on shows such as *The Virginian*, *Adam-12*, and *The Fall Guy*.

Henderson, North Carolina, had read in *Daily Variety* about Warner Brothers
turning the *No Time for Sergeants* movie into a television series and decided
that he was right for it.[4] After being advised by his agent that the film studio
was not interested in him, Jackson sent a letter to studio head Jack Warner
asking him to look at an episode of *Maverick* in which Jackson had appeared.
Ten days later, the studio called and said they were sending him a plane ticket
to fly from North Carolina to Hollywood to make the pilot.

The first episode of *No Time for Sergeants*, "The Permanent Recruit"
(September 14, 1964), was written by Packard, Paul, Willy Burns, and John
L. Greene. In the episode, Will is inducted into the Air Force and drives
his commanding officer to near apoplexy by talking out of turn and playing
the mouth organ in the middle of the night. He is assigned to KP but
becomes popular by serving excellent food. The colonel finds that Will is
brewing moonshine and trading it to local farmers for good food.

Many *No Time for Sergeants* episodes were written by Ed James and Seaman Jacobs. James had created the characters on which the *Father Knows Best* series was based. He and Jacobs also wrote the pilots for *F Troop* and *The Addams Family*. Jacobs later wrote monologues for Bob Hope and George Burns. Leslie Martinson and Charles Rondeau directed most of the sitcom's episodes.

Like other naïve newcomers in Burns-produced series, Will would attempt to do good deeds but with unintended consequences. For example, when Capt. Martin wanted a dress uniform cleaned and pressed for the officers' ball in "Have No Uniform—Will Travel," Will is handed the task by an airman, but the uniform ends up being shredded in a wood chipper. With the help of Sgt. King, Will obtains Capt. Martin's measurements while he (the captain) is sleeping and finds that he has to fly to Hong Kong to have a new uniform made in time for the ball. After he and Ben return with the new uniform, they discover that the outfit was really for the general and not for Capt. Martin. Of course, the new uniform doesn't fit the general, who tells Martin that he truly didn't want to attend the ball after all. Capt. Martin puts on the uniform and takes Millie to the affair but, as they leave, Will tries to remove a loose thread and the entire outfit becomes undone.

In "How Now, Brown Cow," Grandpa Anderson's prize cow Elizabeth is upset by the jets overhead and won't produce milk. Will decides to take the cow to the base so she can get accustomed to the jets. He wants to introduce her to Sgt. King, but Ben says he needs to hide the cow from the sergeant. When Sgt. King discovers the cow in the shower and informs Capt. Martin, the captain doesn't believe him. Will takes the cow around the base so she can see the jets in order to cure her nerves and then puts the animal in a truck to take her back to the farm. However, someone else drives the truck away. Will subsequently discovers the cow in Capt. Martin's quarters. Grandpa Anderson, who has come to the base for Elizabeth, finds that she is producing milk again. Grandpa later says his chickens are not laying eggs because of the jets so Will decides the cure for them is the same as it was for Elizabeth.

What most would see as punishment, Will thought of as a reward and was always volunteering for assignments that no one else wanted. In "Stockdale's Island," he volunteers to take a survival test on a tropical island and enjoys himself so much that a psychologist is called in to find out what is wrong with him. When his superiors think that he will screw up a task, Will would exceed expectations. Will and Ben participate in a physical fitness test in "A Hatful of Muscles," so that the Air Force can find out if it needs to make its standards more stringent; Will impresses the doctor in charge with his stamina. Since his family didn't have a mule on their farm, Will used to pull the plough which made him so strong. As a result, a new physical fitness manual is created with more strenuous exercises which no one except Will can perform. The doctor agrees to retest Will. Sgt. King tries to exhaust him before the new tests with plenty of work, but Stockdale is not fazed. The sergeant then adds weights to Will so he can't do as many exercises, and the old fitness program is reinstated. In "Whortleberry Roots for Everybody," Will volunteers to be inoculated with a tropical disease serum and proves to be immune. He reveals that his remarkable good health is due to his daily dose of whortleberry root juice from home. In "Target: Stockdale," Will takes an IQ test, and no one can believe the amazing results.

Like an episode from *The Burns and Allen Show,* "Will's Misfortune Cookie" has Will jumping to conclusions and thinking his friends are in danger after reading his fortune cookie which says, "Take supreme care or good friends of yours will have accidents before two suns have set." Stockdale makes everyone in his unit so nervous that they begin having mishaps. When his unit has to demonstrate free-fall parachute jumping for a visiting general, all the men pretend they are injured and can't jump. After Will tells the general what his fortune said, the general attempts to convince him that fortune cookies can't predict the future. However, the general postpones the parachute jump after he injures himself.

As with *Wendy and Me, No Time for Sergeants* lasted for only a single season. Sammy Jackson appeared sporadically on various television series following its cancellation. He eventually became a country and western disc jockey and passed away in 1995 at age fifty-seven from heart failure.

After the demise of the two comedies he had produced for them, Burns terminated his agreement with Warner Brothers and went to work on shows for United Artists.

11

George and United Artists

Mona McCluskey

In April 1965, United Artists TV announced a deal with Burns to produce and develop new series. For *Mona McCluskey,* originally titled *Meet Mona McCluskey,* the first show he produced under this new deal, Burns resurrected his old company name—McCadden—specifically McCadden Enterprises. His usual writing team of Norman Paul, Elon Packard, and Willy Burns were *Mona McCluskey* script consultants. Don McGuire, who had created *Mona McCluskey* based on characters conceived by Sumner Arthur Long, had previously created, written, and directed Jackie Cooper's second television comedy *Hennessy* and had also written the screenplay for the Spencer Tracy movie *Bad Day at Black Rock.*

Mona McCluskey centered on Mona Carroll (Juliet Prowse), a movie star married to Mike McCluskey (Denny Miller), a sergeant in the Air Force. (Initially the character of Mike McCluskey was to be a Navy chief petty officer, but it appears that when Burns came on board, the character was changed to an Air Force sergeant.) Mona really believed in love, honor, and obey, particularly the latter, when it came to marriage. While she had fame and fortune, she subordinated all of this to her husband's desire to prove he could support her. She made $5,000 a week; he made $500 per month. Mona promised not to use her money to augment his income.

Mona, unlike Gracie and Wendy, was not a dumb Dora character unless one considers a woman who agrees to live on $500 a month when she makes ten times that amount in a week as not the smartest person around. In many respects, Mona was the female antithesis of the Bob Collins character on *The Bob Cummings Show.* Whereas Bob would never commit to marriage, Mona was just the opposite. She was overly committed to her marriage even if it meant letting her husband support her entirely. Trying to obey Mike and keep the promises she made to him was not always easy and led to many of the comedic situations. Mona charmed Mike and other people for (what she generally perceived was) their own good. But unlike manipulative charmer Bob Collins who went to great lengths to maintain his sophisticated playboy world for his own good, Mona didn't really want to be part of the fanciful world of celebrity; she wanted to be an ordinary wife and homemaker living on an Air Force base. In this respect, the character of Mona McCluskey was just the opposite of Lucy Ricardo in *I Love Lucy* who sought a show business career and didn't want to be an ordinary homemaker.

Juliet Prowse and Denny Miller from *Mona McCluskey*. As pictured, movie star Mona was still mastering the skills of a homemaker.

Robert Strauss as Sgt. Gruzewsky; Elena Verdugo as his girlfriend Alice; Bartlett Robinson as Frank Caldwell, the head of Caldwell Studios; and Herb Rudley as General Crone rounded out the cast. According to Denny Miller, Burns was always at rehearsals making jokes and singing his unique songs.[1]

In the first episode, "Presenting Mona McCluskey" (September 16, 1965), written and directed by Don McGuire, Mona sends a letter to the secretary of the Air Force demanding that he increase Mike's salary so that they can afford to move into a better house. After Mike and Mona argue over the letter, he leaves her. John J. Johnson, Mona's boss at the studio, puts pressure on General Crone to talk to Mike about getting him back with Mona. Mike goes to see her at the studio, and the couple makes up.

The pilot was originally offered to ABC for a Friday 9:00 p.m. slot, but the network passed on the series, preferring to green light a show in which it had an ownership interest. ABC scheduled the detective series *Honey West* in that time slot.

George Burns got involved with *Mona McCluskey* when the pilot was picked up for a series. United Artists received a firm commitment from NBC for twenty-six episodes.

In the original pilot, Mona's boss at the studio, John Johnson, was played by Olan Soule. The Johnson character was dropped and Bartlett Robinson, whom Burns knew from *Wendy and Me,* became Mona's boss. Joanie Lawson played Maxine, Mona's hairdresser on the pilot, but this character was then deleted altogether. Creator McGuire got angry when Burns was named producer. He didn't like the fact that he would not produce the series and so left the project.

Mona McCluskey's premiere episode received mainly poor reviews. *Variety* stated, "It is short on characterization, weak of plot, and in the main, dependent upon a paled premise."[2] All of this plus grueling competition on the other networks made the show, according to the paper, an early candidate for cancellation. The comedy's competition on Thursday nights was the hit *Peyton Place* on ABC and the Thursday night movie on CBS.

Most of the remaining twenty-five episodes were directed by Richard Whorf and written by Fred S. Fox and Irving "Iz" Elinson. Whorf would later produce the very short-lived *Tammy Grimes Show.* Fox and Elinson had written several scripts for Lucille Ball, Andy Griffith, and Danny Thomas. In addition, Elinson had co-scripted the original pilot for *Mister Ed.*

Fred Fox later co-wrote the screenplay for the Burns movie *Oh God! Book II.* In *Living It Up or, They Still Love Me in Altoona,* George writes that Fox stuttered. Fox would often joke about his problem, and Burns relates the time, as Fox was leaving the office, that he said, "G-G-G-George, if you have a p-p-p-problem with the script, just c-c-c-call my house. If nobody answers, th-th-th-that's me."[3]

As might be expected, many *Mona McCluskey* episodes found Mona surreptitiously trying to supplement Mike's income and otherwise attempting to keep the promises she made to him. In the second episode, "All That Dough and No Place to Go," Mona and General Crone conspire for Mike to win at poker so he has enough money for a Mexican vacation. In "All in a Night's Work," when Mona's movie is behind schedule, her boss demands that she work nights, but Mona doesn't want to break her promise to Mike that she would never do this. Mona buys a $1,500 sculpture in "Michelangelo's Rival" and then pretends she created it herself to keep Mike from learning how much she paid for it. In "Mail Against Female," Mona fails in her promise to never open Mike's mail. When Mike is broke and refuses to let Mona buy a color television set, she decides to plant a coin worth hundreds of dollars in his pocket in "Mona, the Soft Air Force Recruit." In still another episode focusing on promises not kept, "How to Turn Off a Laser Beam," Mike makes Mona pledge she will not invest in an electronics company that he thinks is a fraud, but Mona ignores his instructions.

Mona meddled in various aspects of Mike's life. In "Down from the Blue Yonder," Mike says he isn't re-enlisting and will get a higher paying civilian job, but Mona wants him to stay in the Air Force. She works to get him fired from the different civilian jobs he tries so he will return to the military. In "Operation—Chicken Soup," Mike doesn't tell Mona he is going on a rugged Air Force survival test despite having a bad cold. When she learns of this, Mona rents a plane and parachutes into Mike's bivouac area to deliver a home remedy for his cold.

Mona's acting career impacted her life with Mike in various ways. In "Mona Carroll versus Mona McCluskey," she wants to give up acting and become a full-time homemaker after General Crone informs her that he has recommended Mike for officers' training school. In "My Husband, the Wife-Beater," Mona's two spinster aunts from Muncie, Indiana, Margaret (Madge Blake) and Agatha Kindcade (Dorothy Neumann), come for a visit and expect to find Mona living the Hollywood life in a luxurious mansion. They think that Mike is a gigolo who spends all of Mona's money, and thus is responsible for Mona not living in the lap of luxury. The aunts snub Mike much to his bewilderment. At night, when they hear Mona and Mike having a pillow fight downstairs, they think he is beating her. The aunts have Mona's former high school boyfriend from Muncie fly out to teach Mike a lesson. After Mona arrives home and sees Mike and her former beau ready to fight, she demands an explanation and tells her aunts that she and Mike have a beautiful life together.

In "Love, Chimp Style," a chimpanzee that worked with Mona on a jungle movie has grown fond of her and complicates her home life. And in "Snow Valley Snow Job," Mike enters Mona in a downhill ski race after seeing her ski in a movie, not knowing that Mona's double did the ski scenes.

Other episodes concerned Mike and Mona becoming jealous when either one was with a member of the opposite sex. In "In Every Life a Little Wife Must Fall," Mike is mistrustful when Mona reluctantly agrees to dine with a visiting maharajah-playboy at the request of the State Department. Mike also is jealous when he sees Mona rehearsing a love scene with an Italian movie star in "Good for the Goose, Bad for the Gander." Mike thinks he will make Mona jealous when he kisses an attractive woman in an Air Force training film, but when Mona sees the scene, she coaches Mike on how to be more romantic with the actress. The tables are turned in "How to Put Out an Old Flame," when Mona goes to a restaurant where Mike is supposedly attending a reunion of his old squadron to see him with his beautiful ex-girlfriend.

About a month after the series premiere, Juliet Prowse, realizing the ratings for the comedy were poor, told Dave Kaufman of *Variety* in an article subtitled "I Can't Carry the Show Alone" that her sitcom placed "too much emphasis on the fact that I can't use my money because my husband won't let me. We must loosen up the husband; his character is tied up by this. They can make him not so stubborn."[4]

In order to broaden the show, Prowse was persuaded to use her dancing talents from her nightclub act more. In "Dance, Kookerina, Dance," to keep secret an award the general is planning to give Mona for entertaining the troops with her dance act, he informs her that another dancer will do the act this year. Her reaction to the news is not positive, to say the least.

Other episodes also attempted to deal with more than the income disparity and the impact of celebrity on Mona's home life. Several had Mona and occasionally Mike interfering in the lives of others, especially Sgt. Gruzewsky and his girl Alice. In "Let's Play Cupid," Mona and Mike try to patch things up between Stan and Alice by making Alice think that Stan is interested in another woman. Mona takes the sergeant dancing, and Mike accompanies Alice to the same place. But the plan hits a snag when Alice has eyes only for Mike and ignores Stan. When Stan postpones his marriage to Alice after seeing a fortune teller, "Mona, the Mystic" resorts to her own crystal ball to put the ceremony back on track. (Burns' writers loved to develop stories around a character accepting anything a fortune teller reveals.) Mona and Mike finally persuade Stan to marry Alice only to have General Crone tell Stan how miserable marriage is in "Will He, or Won't He?"

Mona also liked to assist others, with things not always working out as expected. In "How to Cure an Old Ham," she attempts to help an old actor who can't get any work, and when she does, he becomes a permanent houseguest with her and Mike. General Crone's nephew (Sal Mineo) visits, and the general doesn't like the fact that he has become a hippie, defined in this episode as playing a guitar, having hair covering the ears, and wearing vests. In "The General Swings at Dawn," Mona encourages the nephew to change his appearance to conform to his uncle's wishes. He gets a haircut, dresses in a regular suit, and announces he is going to join the Air Force.

In the last episode of the series, Mona is planning a big surprise for Mike's birthday. Mike thinks the surprise is that Mona is going to have a baby. But she says the real surprise is a visit from Mike's five-year-old nephew. The next day, Mona finds out that she *is* pregnant. If the comedy hadn't been cancelled because of low ratings, the audience would no doubt have seen an addition to the McCluskey household.

After the cancellation of *Mona McCluskey,* Prowse resumed her nightclub act, performing mainly in Las Vegas and in touring companies of Broadway musicals. She died of pancreatic cancer at age fifty-nine in 1996. Denny Miller guest starred on several popular shows such as *Dallas* and *Magnum PI,* but is probably best known for playing the fisherman in the Gorton's seafood commercials.

McNab's Lab and Other Comedy Projects

Part of Burns' deal with United Artists was to develop comedy pilots. One such effort was *McNab's Lab* starring Cliff Arquette, best known for his Charlie Weaver character with the squashed hat, round glasses, and suspenders over his wrinkled shirt. The pilot, directed by John Rich and written by Paul, Packard, and Willy Burns, was broadcast in July 1966 as part of ABC's summer burn-off of pilots called *Summer Fun.* Andrew (Michael in the original script) McNab, a widower, was a small-town druggist and

Cliff Arquette as Andrew McNab working in his laboratory. Arquette was the grandfather of actors Patricia, Rosanna, Alexis, Richmond and David Arquette.

amateur inventor who had a daughter, Ellen (Sherry Alberoni), and a son, Timmy (David Bailey).

According to Alberoni, the pilot was shot in the fall of 1965 over a two-day period. Director John Rich asked her to play the part of Ellen. She remembers "George Burns always being on the set (he was good friends with John Rich) and I vividly remember him sitting in his director's chair with a cigar in his mouth. He was very friendly and kind and very funny

174

(as was Cliff Arquette), always cracking jokes and making the cast and crew laugh a lot. It was a very professional set but also very relaxed and happy."[5]

McNab's Lab was in many respects another fantasy comedy but, instead of talking animals or aliens from outer space, it focused on a "mad" inventor of implausible gadgets. McNab's inventions were like George's magic television from *The Burns and Allen Show* if Gracie had invented it. In the introduction to the script for the pilot, Burns offered the following description:

> McNab's inventions are so complicated and ridiculous that for the most part they are entirely useless, except to him. When they are useful, they inevitably break down and cause more confusion than the useless ones.
>
> Against these wild inventions we play McNab as a perfectly normal, likable and intelligent person, and a good father. Also, to enhance the comic value of these inventions, the stories will be warm, home-spun and simple. A normal background played against these screwball inventions will give you the ingredients for a great comedy series.
>
> Music and sound effects are very important in this show. All inventions will be accompanied by appropriate comic sound effects.[6]

The pilot shows McNab's drug store equipped with a computer that makes sodas and other counter fare and a lie detector that causes a person to sneeze after telling a fib. Underneath the store is McNab's laboratory where he develops inventions and uses an elevator, which often gets stuck, to go from his lab to the store. Ellen informs her dad that Timmy is worried about his little league championship game because he's in a hitting slump. Timmy is receiving batting advice from Steve (Jan Crawford), an older player who wants to date Ellen. Even though Timmy assures Steve that Ellen doesn't like him, Steve phones Ellen anyway, and she agrees to date him.

When Steve comes by for his date with Ellen, McNab has him stand on the lie detector machine. Steve denies taking girls to a lover's lane lookout, then starts sneezing. Thinking he has a cold, he leaves. Ellen, all dressed up, explains to her father that she agreed to date Steve so that he would convince Timmy's coach to let him play in the championship game.

McNab goes down to his lab wanting to invent something to help build Timmy's confidence in hitting a baseball. He constructs a bat that works as a magnet for baseballs, but it isn't perfected yet. At the game, Timmy is benched. After his dad successfully tests the bat, he rushes to the game and talks the coach (Elisha Cook) into letting Timmy hit. McNab gives his son the bat he invented. Timmy's first and second balls are both foul. When McNab's bat breaks, the coach gives Timmy a new bat. Timmy hits a home run, and his team wins the game. Back at the lab, a Mr. Nichols (Jonathan Hole) stops by to purchase McNab's baseball bat invention, but McNab turns the offer down so that Timmy will never learn that he had some help.

In addition to producing the *McNab's Lab* pilot while associated with United Artists, Burns had several other ideas for comedy series for the 1966–67 TV season, but none ever made it to the pilot stage.[7] He proposed a fantasy series titled *It Shouldn't Happen to a Planet* that seemed like an outer space version of *Gilligan's Island*. The premise was about five people going to Mars: Professor Muhler, a female professor, a doctor, an astronaut, and a twenty-two-year-old woman. The night before they are due to blast off, Professor Muhler gets cold feet. A bellboy takes his place, and everyone tries to make sure the Russians don't find out. Most of the series was to take place on Mars because the only one who could get the crew back to Earth, Professor Muhler, was home in Minneapolis.

In line with his attempts at producing a teen comedy (Burns having passed on *Dobie Gillis* and having failed at turning *Maggie* into a series), he wanted to make a sitcom titled *The Impossibles*, about a group of tough juvenile delinquents who have been assigned to a social worker to straighten them out. They grow fond of the social worker, and instead of him taking care of them, they take care of him.

Burns had three other ideas for sitcoms that never came to fruition: *Coward for Hire, The Indian Givers,* and *A Lady Named Kelly.* The first concerned a cowardly private eye with two secretaries. Burns wanted Robert Stack for the private eye role, perhaps thinking he would play the character straight as Stack did for the character he portrayed in the film *Airplane!* To play the two secretaries, George wanted the Kessler twins, very popular in Europe as singers, dancers, and actresses during the fifties and sixties. *The Indian Givers* was about the Seminole Indians who long ago had declared war on the United States. Still in a state of war, they refused to pay taxes. They drove around in convertibles living the good life. *A Lady Named Kelly,* created for actress-dancer Cyd Charisse, was about a high-end fashion designer. It appears that, like the others, no pilot was ever made.

When none of these projects became a series, Burns' McCadden Enterprises was dissolved on March 27, 1967.

12

George and the Final Pilot

I Love Her Anyway

In 1981, George Burns' career as a producer came full circle with his participation in a remake of *The George Burns and Gracie Allen Show*. Titled *I Love Her Anyway,* the pilot was filmed before a live audience on March 25, 1981, and aired in August as part of an *ABC Comedy Special*. Diane Stilwell played a Gracie-like character, Laurie Martin, married for five years to sensible, understanding Jerry (Dean Jones). Living with them were Jerry's medical student brother Fred (Charles Levin) and Fred's wife Mona (Jane Daly), Laurie's best friend. While Fred attended medical school, Mona earned a living selling real estate like what the original version of the Harry Morton character did on *Burns and Allen*. Peter Boyden played Willie Winslow, the Harry Von Zell character, who was Jerry's friend. Written and produced by Elliot Shoenman, the pilot was directed by John Tracy.

While filming *I Love Her Anyway,* Dean Jones met Burns for the first time. Jones said that he never felt more of an unlikely character in portraying Burns, but that he would give it his best try, to which George responded with his dry wit, "Just think how I feel."[1]

According to Diane Stilwell, George mentored her in playing a quirky character like Gracie: "Gracie doesn't think she's dumb. She thinks she's smart," Burns told her.[2]

Like the Burns TV character, Jerry is aware of the viewing audience and speaks directly to the camera to recap the story and straighten out the situations caused by Laurie's meddling. The basic plot of the pilot, similar to when Gracie kept a doctor's appointment for Blanche, concerned Laurie pretending to be Mona and keeping a doctor's appointment for the real Mona.

The pilot opens with Fred and Mona arguing about money, and Laurie finding a stray cat which she coincidentally names Mona. She hides the

(From left to right) Dean Jones, Diane Stilwell, Jane Daly, and Charles Levin of *I Love Her Anyway*, Burns' final production effort. Photo courtesy of Diane Stilwell.

stray from her husband because he doesn't like animals. However, Jerry knows about the cat and sends it to the vet to have it examined. In true Gracie fashion, Laurie explains to her sister-in-law that she leaves her car's headlights on all the time to remind her that the key is in the ignition. She figures the battery won't go dead because it is guaranteed for the life of the vehicle.

Dr. Peterson's office calls to remind Mona of her appointment with him but, since she has already left for work, Laurie goes in her place to save Mona money for not keeping the appointment. Dr. Peterson (Howard Witt) thinks Laurie is Mona and believes, as they converse, that she has some mental problems. The doctor's nurse calls Fred to inform him that Mona is very ill and on the verge of a nervous breakdown, and advises him to treat his wife with tender loving care. Meanwhile, Willie Winslow takes

KTLA & VIA COM PRODUCTIONS
KTLA TELEVISION — STAGE 5
5800 Sunset Blvd., Hollywood, CA 90028
Entrance on Van Ness Avenue

"I LOVE HER ANYWAY"

Starring

DEAN JONES & DIANE STILWELL

No one under 16 admitted

WEDNESDAY
MARCH
25
1981

SHOW TIME
7:30 p.m.

DOORS CLOSE
7:00 p.m.

Studio audience ticket to a taping of *I Love Her Anyway*.

a phone message for Jerry from Dr. Stone, the veterinarian, informing him that Mona is pregnant, and he advises Jerry of this. When Laurie returns home from Dr. Peterson's office, she reads the message that Mona is pregnant. Thinking the message is from Dr. Peterson regarding her appointment with him, she believes she is pregnant, not realizing the message refers to the cat.

After a man brings the cat back from the vets, Mona, Fred's wife, comes home from work. She asks Laurie to pop a frozen dinner in the oven for Fred's dinner. When Laurie hears Jerry calling for her, she puts the cat in the oven to hide it from him. Fred starts acting uncommonly nice toward Mona, and, when he checks the oven for a frozen dinner, he discovers the cat, affirming in his mind that Mona is crazy.

Jerry has come to realize that his wife thinks she is pregnant. Laurie goes to give Fred and Mona the news. However, Fred sees the note about Mona's pregnancy and thinks that his wife had the doctor say she was on the verge of a nervous breakdown because she was reluctant to tell him that she is pregnant. To the audience, Jerry says that if the writer can resolve all the confusion, he will give him a sports coat. After Laurie informs Fred that he and Mona will have to find a new place to live because she is expecting a baby, Fred responds that Mona is pregnant as well. Finally, as George Burns would often do at the end of a *Burns and Allen* episode, Jerry clears everything up, indicating that the only one pregnant is the cat, which he lets

Laurie keep for their anniversary. Then the Martins' doorbell rings and a character named Ed Rutledge (Milt Jamin) enters with a sports coat for the show's writer, Elliot Shoenman. After Jerry confers with all the characters, they agree that they are happy with the episode's events and the show ends.

Although Burns was not listed in the credits of *I Love Her Anyway*, according to *Variety* he was one of the executive producers. Based on Burns' renewed popularity appearing in the movies, particularly in the *Oh, God!* films, Jerry Zeitman, a producer who had been George's agent, sold the idea of a remake of *The Burns and Allen Show* to ABC.

According to Elliot Shoenman, he met with George and his manager, Irving Fein, and they said he could use anything he wanted from George's series with Gracie. George provided him with notes on each draft of his script. When ABC tried to make script changes, he and Burns met with network representatives at George's house in Beverly Hills—the same home shown on the *Burns and Allen* TV series. Burns came to the meeting in his bathrobe and without his toupee. His first comment to the network guys was, "So what didn't you like? Personally, I loved it."[3] The network then backed off on making any major changes to the storyline.

Variety reviewed *I Love Her Anyway* favorably, stating, "Performances were appealing and the whole idea stylish enough in its own way to suggest that ABC could do worse than ordering a few more episodes to determine if *I Love Her Anyway* could sustain its initial impact as a regular series."[4]

ABC did initially decide to turn the pilot into a series for their fall 1981 line-up on Thursdays at 8:00 p.m. (the original time slot for *The Burns and Allen Show* on CBS). However, the network later made the decision to renew *Mork and Mindy* for one final season instead, and so *I Love Her Anyway* never went beyond the pilot stage.

I Love Her Anyway was the final time George Burns, then eighty-five years old, acted as a producer.

Reflecting on his career in television in a 1984 *TV Guide* article, Burns remarked:

> Of all the media, I've worked in, television is the hardest. In vaudeville, you never changed anything. If you had 17 minutes of vaudeville, you could work for 50 years. When we switched to radio, we thought that was hard, but we really stole the money. What was radio? You read off a piece of paper. Television was different. You had to have exits, you had to have entrances. It was like doing a one-act play every week.[5]

He went on to say that he and Gracie made such a good team because she had a very big talent on stage and he had a talent off stage relating to his ability to determine what would be funny. As Mr. Burns pointed out, "I was able to think of things and Gracie was able to do them. That's what made us work."[6]

George and Gracie—Together Again

George Burns passed away in 1996, about six weeks after his 100th birthday.

As his manager and friend Irving Fein eulogized:

> One of the many things I admired about George was his absolute determination to keep doing what he loved best in the world: working in show business. Always on time (or early), always prepared, he never missed a single performance and was the consummate professional. And as the years advanced, I would discuss his possible retirement, [and] he would say "Retire? What am I supposed to do, stay home and play with my cuticles?" Or he'd say, "Quit? I can't quit. Who would support my mother and father?"

George Burns was interred next to Gracie in the Freedom Mausoleum at Forest Lawn Memorial Park. Their epitaph read: "Gracie Allen. George Burns. Together Again."

Chapter Notes

Chapter 1

1. George Burns with Cynthia Hobart Lindsay, *I Love Her, That's Why! An Autobiography* (New York: Simon & Schuster, 1955), 246.
2. George Eells, "George Burns: The Improbable Tycoon," *Look,* March 18, 1958, 36.
3. George Burns, *I Love Her, That's Why!,* 13–15.
4. George Burns, *Living It Up: Or, They Still Love Me in Altoona!* (New York: G.P. Putnam's Sons, 1976), 153.
5. Charles Isaacs, "Comedies Can Be Funny," *Variety,* November 2, 1953, 132.
6. Quoted in Herb Fagen, *George Burns in His Own Words* (New York: Carroll & Graf, 1996), 68.
7. Susan O'Leary, "*The George Burns and Gracie Allen Show:* Life in a Domestic Comedy," *Emmy,* January–February 1984, 49.
8. George Burns, *Gracie: A Love Story* (New York: G.P. Putnam's Sons, 1988), 293–94.
9. Ibid., 243.
10. Fred De Cordova, *Johnny Came Lately* (New York: Pocket Books, 1988), 89.
11. The correct spelling of William Burns' nickname is something of a mystery. In some works, his nickname is spelled "Willy," while in others it is spelled "Willie." Since "Willy" appears on memoranda in the Burns and Allen Collection, that spelling will be used here.
12. George Burns, *Living It Up,* 178.
13. Jordan R. Young, *The Laugh Crafters: Comedy Writing in Radio and TV's Golden Age* (Beverly Hills: Past Times, 1999), 40.
14. Lawrence J. Epstein, *George Burns:*

An American Life (Jefferson, NC: McFarland, 2011), 152.
15. Cheryl Blythe and Susan Sackett, *Say Goodnight, Gracie! The Story of George Burns and Gracie Allen* (Rocklin, CA: Prima, 1989), 85.
16. Ibid., 141.
17. Ibid., 86.
18. Carol Channing, *Just Lucky, I Guess: A Memoir of Sorts* (New York: Simon & Schuster, 2002), 159.
19. Elaine Woo, "Al Simon: Producer Who Paved Way for TV Reruns," *Los Angeles Times,* May 24, 2000.
20. "Burns and Allen Build Vast Vidpix Business by Not Playing for Casualties," *Variety,* February 9, 1957.

Chapter 2

1. George Burns, *I Love Her, That's Why!,* 106–07.
2. Ibid., 195.
3. George Burns, *Gracie: A Love Story,* 243.
4. George Burns, *I Love, Her That's Why!,* 106.
5. David Grote, *The End of Comedy: The Sit-com and the Comedic Tradition* (Hamden, CT: Archon Books, 1983), 158.
6. George Burns, *Living It Up,* 176.
7. George Burns, *Gracie: A Love Story,* 245.

Chapter 3

1. Susan O'Leary, "*The George Burns and Gracie Allen Show,*" 49.
2. George Burns, *I Love Her, That's Why!,* 199.

3. George Burns, *Gracie: A Love Story*, 257.

4. George Burns, *I Love Her, That's Why!*, 196–197.

5. Ibid., 196.

6. Cheryl Blythe and Susan Sackett, *Say Goodnight, Gracie!*, 138.

7. Ibid., 140

8. *Variety*, June 29, 1953.

9. George Burns as told to Kenneth Turan, "Lessons I Learned from TV," *TV Guide*, September 15, 1984, 36.

10. Cheryl Blythe and Susan Sackett, *Say Goodnight, Gracie!*, 148.

11. Dave Kaufman, "On All Channels," *Variety*, June 28, 1955.

12. George Burns, *Gracie: A Love Story*, 142.

13. George Burns, *Living It Up*, 172.

14. Bob Graten, "Never Too Late to Change," *TV Views*, November 16, 1956.

15. Martin Gottfried, *George Burns and the Hundred Year Dash* (New York: Simon & Schuster, 1996), 173–74.

16. "Burns (& Allen) Refuses to Get Stampeded," *Variety*, May 17, 1957.

17. Yvonne Lime Fedderson, private communication with author, March 4, 2013.

18. Letter dated October 10, 1957, from George Burns to Bill Paley, Burns and Allen Collection, USC.

19. George Burns, "George Burns on Westerns," *TV Guide*, September 28, 1957, 19.

20. Louella Parsons, "Gracie Allen Retires," *The Desert News*, February 19, 1958.

21. George Burns, *Gracie: A Love Story*, 279–280.

Chapter 4

1. Robert Pegg, *Comical Co-Stars of Television: From Ed Norton to Kramer* (Jefferson, NC: McFarland, 2002), 85.

2. Ibid.

3. "Up-And-Coming Cummings," *TV Guide*, April 9, 1955, 15.

4. Charles Mercer, "Neither Schultzy Nor Any of Cute Models Near Matrimony on Bob Cummings Show Script," *Austin Daily Herald*, May 24, 1958.

5. Martin Gottfried, *George Burns*, 165.

6. *Variety*, January 27, 1955.

7. Rosemary DeCamp, *Tigers in My Lap* (Baltimore: Midnight Marquee Press, 2000), 190.

8. Dwayne Hickman and Joan Roberts Hickman, *Forever Dobie: The Many Lives of Dwayne Hickman* (New York: Birch Lane Press, 1994), 62.

9. Martin Gottfried, *George Burns*, 169.

10. Ann B. Davis, Archive of American TV interview, March 13, 2004.

11. Ibid.

12. Bob Cummings, *Stay Young and Vital* (Englewood Cliffs, NJ: Prentice Hall, 1960), 32.

13. Rosemary DeCamp, *Tigers in My Lap*, 193.

14. Ibid., 188.

15. Olive Sturgess Anderson, private communication with author, March 2, 2012.

16. David Marc and Robert J. Thompson, *Prime Time, Prime Movers: From I Love Lucy to L.A. Law—America's Greatest TV Shows and the People Who Created Them* (Syracuse: Syracuse University Press, 1995), 32.

17. Ann B. Davis, private communication with author, July 19, 2012.

18. *Variety*, December 17, 1958.

Chapter 5

1. Jackie Cooper with Dick Kleiner, *Please Don't Shoot My Dog: The Autobiography of Jackie Cooper* (New York: William Morrow, 1981), 217.

2. Ibid., 219.

3. George Eells, "George Burns: The Improbable Tycoon," 34.

4. Irving Brecher as told to Hank Rosenfeld, *The Wicked Wit of the West* (Teaneck, NJ: Ben Yehuda Press, 2009), 214. In the George Eells 1958 *Look* magazine article about Burns, this same story is described with one variation. Instead of George supposedly asking his brother Willy to give Brecher the money, the magazine article states that Burns asked Maurice Morton, his vice-president for business affairs, for the money.

5. Ibid., 216–17.

6. *TV Guide,* August 3, 1957.

7. Private letter from Brecher to Burns dated May 20, 1955, Burns and Allen Collection, USC.

8. Martin Gottfried, *George Burns,* 168.

9. George Eells, "George Burns: The Improbable Tycoon," 38.

10. Jackie Cooper with Dick Kleiner, *Please Don't Shoot My Dog: The Autobiography of Jackie Cooper* (New York: William Morrow, 1981), 218.

11. Yvonne Lime Fedderson, private communication with author.

Chapter 6

1. George Eells, "George Burns: The Improbable Tycoon," 36.

2. Max Shulman, letter to Ray Stark of Famous Artists, February 15, 1956, Max Shulman Collection, Howard Gotlieb Archival Research Center, Boston University.

3. Max Shulman, letter to Ben Benjamin of Famous Artists, November 15, 1956, Max Shulman Collection, Howard Gotlieb Archival Research Center, Boston University.

4. Louella Parsons, "Buddy Ebsen Will Star in New Series with McCadden Productions Starting in December," *Waterloo Daily Courier,* November 20, 1956.

5. Jay Dratler, "The Fabulous Oliver Chantry," *Esquire,* September 1955, 91.

6. Dave Kaufman, "On All Channels," *Variety,* April 19, 1957.

7. Claudia Scenes Introduction, date unknown, Burns and Allen Collection, USC.

8. Walter Brooks, "The Talking Horse," *Liberty,* September 18, 1937, 38.

9. Ibid.

10. Army Archerd, "Just for Variety," *Variety,* June 2, 1959.

Chapter 7

1. *Variety,* January 7, 1955.

2. "McCadden Huddles for Grey Yarns," *Billboard,* September 3, 1955.

3. John Lester, "Patti Page to Go Dramatic," *The Milwaukee Journal,* April 21, 1957.

4. "TViewers Now Smart; Producers No Longer Can 'Cheat'—Al Simon," *Variety,* April 25, 1957.

5. Lee Goldberg, *Unsold Television Pilots Volume 1: 1955–76* (Lincoln, NE: iUniverse, 2001), 50.

6. Ibid.

Chapter 8

1. Letter dated September 3, 1958, from George Burns to Walter Annenberg, Burns and Allen Collection, USC.

2. George Burns, *100 Years, 100 Stories* (New York: G.P. Putnam's Sons, 1996), 27.

3. *George Burns Show* Review, *Variety,* October 29, 1958.

4. Undated form letter from George Burns to radio stations, Burns and Allen Collection, USC.

5. Hal Humphrey, "Jackie Gleason Give Up, But George Burns Will Try Again," *The Evening Independent,* January 15, 1959.

6. George Burns, *Living It Up,* 76.

7. Bob Chandler, "Sound and Picture," *Variety,* April 10, 1959.

8. *Variety,* November 30, 1961.

Chapter 9

1. Stephen Bowie, "Murder, He Wrote," classictvhistory.com, retrieved June 10, 2012.

2. William Wellman, Jr., private communication with author, June 21, 2013.

3. Nancy Nalven, *The Famous Mister Ed: The Unbridled Truth about America's Favorite Talking Horse* (New York: Warner Books, 1991), 13.

4. Undated introduction to *Mister Ed* pilot presentation, Burns and Allen Collection, USC.

5. Alan Young, Archive of American TV interview, February 6, 2001.

6. Alan Young, *Mister Ed and Me and More!* (N.p.: Geordie Press, 2007), 12.

7. Nalven, *The Famous Mister Ed,* 103.

8. Young, *Mister Ed,* 36.

9. Nalven, *The Famous Mister Ed,* 103.

10. Ibid., 221.

11. Norman Paul and William Burns, "Moko the Martian," draft script, October 28, 1963.

12. Ibid.
13. Nalven, *The Famous Mister Ed,* 222.

Chapter 10

1. George Burns, *Gracie, A Love Story,* 317–318.
2. Dave Kaufman, "On All Channels," *Variety,* February 16, 1965.
3. Martin Gottfried, *George Burns,* 198.
4. Dave Kaufman, "On All Channels," *Variety,* July 22, 1964.

Chapter 11

1. Denny Miller, private communication with author, October 13, 2012.
2. "Television Review," *Variety,* September 22, 1965.
3. George Burns, *Living It Up,* 169.
4. Dave Kaufman, "On All Channels," *Variety,* October 27, 1965.

5. Sherry Alberoni, private communication with author, November 5, 2012.
6. George Burns, "A Brief Note of Explanation," *McNab's Lab* final revised script, undated.
7. Dave Kaufman, "On All Channels," *Variety,* August 10, 1965.

Chapter 12

1. Dean Jones, private communication with author, February 21, 2013.
2. Diane Stilwell, private communication with author, March 14, 2013.
3. Elliot Shoenman, private communication with author, January 9, 2013.
4. "Television Review," *Variety,* August 12, 1981.
5. George Burns, "Lesson's I Learned from TV," *TV Guide,* September 15, 1984, 36.
6. Ibid.

Bibliography

Blythe, Cheryl, and Susan Sackett. *Say Goodnight, Gracie! The Story of George Burns and Gracie Allen*. Rocklin, CA: Prima, 1989.

Brecher, Irving, as told to Hank Rosenfeld. *The Wicked Wit of the West*. Teaneck, NJ: Ben Yehuda Press, 2009.

Burns, George. *Gracie: A Love Story*. New York: G.P. Putnam's Sons, 1988.

_____. *Living It Up: Or, They Still Love Me in Altoona!* New York: G.P. Putnam's Sons, 1976.

_____. *100 Years, 100 Stories*. New York: G.P. Putnam's Sons, 1996.

Burns, George, with Cynthia Hobart Lindsay. *I Love Her, That's Why! An Autobiography*. New York: Simon & Schuster, 1955.

Burns and Allen Collection, Cinematic Arts Library, University of Southern California.

Channing, Carol. *Just Lucky, I Guess: A Memoir of Sorts*. New York: Simon & Schuster, 2002.

Cooper, Jackie, with Dick Kleiner. *Please Don't Shoot My Dog: The Autobiography of Jackie Cooper*. New York: William Morrow, 1981.

DeCamp, Rosemary. *Tigers in My Lap*. Baltimore: Midnight Marquee Press, 2000.

De Cordova, Fred. *Johnny Came Lately*. New York: Pocket Books, 1988.

Epstein, Lawrence J. *George Burns: An American Life*. Jefferson, NC: McFarland, 2011.

Goldberg, Lee. *Unsold Television Pilots Volume 1: 1955–76*. Lincoln, NE: iUniverse, 2001.

Gottfried, Martin. *George Burns and the Hundred Year Dash*. New York: Simon & Schuster, 1996.

Hickman, Dwayne, and Joan Roberts Hickman. *Forever Dobie: The Many Lives of Dwayne Hickman*. New York: Birch Lane Press, 1994.

Marc, David, and Robert J. Thompson. *Prime Time, Prime Movers: From I Love Lucy to L.A. Law—America's Greatest TV Shows and the People who Created Them*. Syracuse: Syracuse University Press, 1995.

Nalven, Nancy. *The Famous Mister Ed: The Unbridled Truth about America's Favorite Talking Horse*. New York: Warner Books, 1991.

Pegg, Robert. *Comical Co-Stars of Television: From Ed Norton to Kramer*. Jefferson, NC: McFarland, 2002.

Young, Alan. *Mister Ed and Me and More!* N.p.: Geordie Press, 2007.

Young, Jordan R. *The Laugh Crafters: Comedy Writing in Radio and TV's Golden Age*. Beverly Hills: Past Times, 1999.

Index